Services Marketing

Services Marketing

Text and Cases

Second Edition

Steve Baron
and
Kim Harris

First edition 1995
Reprinted five times
Second edition 2003

Published by
PALGRAVE MACMILLAN
Houndmills, Basingstoke, Hampshire RG21 6XS and
175 Fifth Avenue, New York, N.Y. 10010
Companies and representatives throughout the world

PALGRAVE MACMILLAN is the new global academic imprint of
St. Martin's Press LLC Scholarly and Reference Division and
Palgrave Publishers Ltd (formerly Macmillan Press Ltd).

ISBN 0–333–77792–1 hardback
ISBN 0–333–77793–X paperback

This book is printed on paper suitable for recycling and
made from fully managed and sustained forest sources.

A catalogue record for this book is available
from the British Library.

10   9   8   7   6   5   4   3   2
12   11 10 09 08 07 06 05 04 03

Printed in China

Contents

List of figures

Case-studies figures

List of tables and exhibits

Tables

Exhibits

Preface to the second edition

The first edition of this book was published in 1995. It is staggering how much the opportunities for different forms of learning have changed over seven years, through technology, and the internet in particular. Nevertheless, an appropriate textbook, in hard copy, is still a fundamental learning aid for course units.

New features of the second edition

In preparing the second edition, we have responded to feedback from full-time and part-time students and fellow lecturers. As a result, we have maintained the strengths of the first edition, especially the style of writing, the use of illustrative examples, and the inclusion of case studies of small service businesses. In addition, we have added more theoretical content, extra sections on technology-based services and consumer experiences, an expanded list of references, chapter objectives, outcomes and discussion questions and two case studies with a business-to-business focus. Therefore, this edition provides a comprehensive treatment of the sub-discipline of services marketing in an accessible and reader-friendly way. After reading it, you should have gained a good understanding of services marketing – sufficient for you to pass your examinations and appreciate the practical value of the various theories and frameworks.

However, if you rely only and totally on this book, we feel that we have partially failed in our aims as educators. We really hope that the book is a catalyst for you to pursue some of your own ideas and interests, and, most of all, for you to apply your own thinking to the range of service issues that are raised in the chapters. This is because we believe that the study of services marketing is an active rather than passive pursuit, and that real enjoyment and achievement is achieved through 'doing' to complement the reading. Researchers have shown that higher levels of customer participation in services can lead to greater customer satisfaction. This, we believe, is also true in the study of services marketing, and is probably the way to get the best out of the book.

Getting the best out of the book

Below are some of the things you can do to increase your active participation in the learning and stimulate your thinking on the issues raised in the book.

First, use your computer literacy skills. It is now relatively easy to 'search' for journal and other articles that give original sources and up-to-date material on the topics covered in the book. Most university and college libraries have electronic databases, such as *Emerald*, *ABI Inform* or *Infotrac*, that will give you (almost) immediate access to additional material. If you are interested in knowing more about, say, service branding, service advertising or service pricing, just type in these terms as keywords, and sift out the more relevant articles. The academic articles are not the only further sources of insights. You can use the more generic search engines (www.google.com is the best at the time of writing) to identify companies that are actively using, say, customer relationship management, by entering the term in the search box. In this second edition, the notes and references for the chapters give website addresses that we have found to provide helpful insights. Try the ones that you are interested in, but also follow your own instincts.

Second, remember that there is a lot 'out there'. You are consuming services, and engaging in experiences, day in and day out. While we would not want you to become a social bore through your analysis of every single service encounter, we do feel that you can take a healthy, informed interest in the way service organisations behave in practice. Why do you feel that your chosen restaurant or bar is inviting? What is the cause of your anxiety in the hospital outpatients' department? How did the flight booking on the internet compare with the one at the travel agent? However much we try to link theory to practice in the book, it is not going to be as effective as the links that you make for yourself through your own real-life examples.

Third, find out more about actual service organisations, large and small. The case studies featured at the end of the book examine *small* service businesses to explore fundamental principles and practices of services marketing. Our own teaching experience, and that of other lecturers, has reinforced our view that students can identify with the issues facing the small businesses. They can then concentrate on linking theory with practice in a meaningful way, rather than spending a lot of time simply trying to understand what the case company does. However, you should also be interested in finding out about the activities of other service organisations. The first chapter of this second edition looks at the case of airline/airport services, and demonstrates the complexities of managing service organisations. You will also find plenty of information on larger service organisations, such as hotel chains, financial institutions, holiday companies or leisure organisations, in other services marketing textbooks and in journal articles. In order to find out even more, you can (to paraphrase the words of a former MBA student of services marketing) 'follow up the leads' given, in particular, in Chapters 10 and 11. You can find out as much detail as you wish about, say, global service providers such as IBM, or the largest hotel in the world (The Venetian in Las Vegas).

Finally, study a service company in detail. We hope that you get the opportunity to study a small service organisation yourself in some depth. A template of preliminary questions for such a study is provided at the end of Chapter 1 (Table 1.1), but you may wish to delay the study until you have read the whole book and can adapt the template for yourself.

We hope that you enjoy reading this edition, and become as enthusiastic about services marketing as we are ourselves, and that the enthusiasm encourages an active approach to your learning.

STEVE BARON
KIM HARRIS

Acknowledgements

Once again we have received tremendous support during the preparation of this second edition of this book. Most notably we would like to thank the students and companies who have developed the material for the additional cases in this edition. First, Anne Templeman from Durham High School for Girls, and the MBA students, Tom Reay, Franke Burke, Colin McDougall and Edith Newrick. Second, Mike and Sally Waterston from Waterstons and the MBA students, Norman Gordan, Yves Hausammann, John Robinson and Chris Storey. Third, Martin Rocke from North West Design Associates and students, Neha Gudka, Charlotte Fairhurst, Lindsay Rocke and Sara Simmonds. To all these people we express our sincere thanks. Finally, we would like to thank our families for their encouragement and support throughout this endeavour.

STEVE BARON
KIM HARRIS

The authors and publishers are grateful to the following for kindly allowing the use of copyright material: *American Marketing Association*, publishers of the Journal of Marketing, for Figures 2.1, 6.9, 6.10, 6.11; MCB Publishers for Figure 6.7; *Harvard Business Review* for Figure 10.3. Every effort has been made to contact all the copyright-holders, but if any have been inadvertently overlooked the publishers will be pleased to make the necessary arrangement at the earliest opportunity.

Introduction

Why study services marketing? Why pick up a textbook on services marketing?

There may be a variety of reasons – you are working in a service business, you are representing consumers, you have 'got to' because you are a student, and it is part of your course. Whichever direction you start from, however, we believe that, like us, you will find services marketing a fascinating field of academic study, firmly embedded in the real world.

It is real, because we all *consume* services as part of our everyday life. A day in our life may involve, for example, listening to a favourite radio programme, travelling on a train or bus, visiting the shops and buying a snack at lunchtime, arranging a dental appointment, attending lectures and tutorials, buying a book via the internet and calling into the pub for a drink in the evening. At work, we may rely on administrative, technical and clerical support services, and come to expect that offices, toilets and other rooms are regularly cleaned. Furthermore, we probably have an opinion on the level of service offered in all these areas, and are quite prepared to share our feelings of satisfaction/dissatisfaction (with the services) with others. When we consume certain types of services on a less frequent basis – for example, going on a package holiday, eating in an expensive restaurant, making a claim on an insurance policy – we are usually highly attuned to the service provided, and perhaps even more likely to express our opinions of the quality of service.

But for many of us, we are not simply service consumers (or customers); we also *provide* service. We are both consumers and providers of services. If you are reading this book, it is likely that you work full-time in a service industry, or that you have had some part-time jobs in the service industry. This is a wonderful position from which to appreciate the issues involved with the marketing and management of services. In addition, you may well find that you have played several different service roles. In our own case, for example, although our service job may described as 'teaching' or 'lecturing', we have played other roles, such as researching, student counselling, consulting and editing, with varying degrees of success.

In the course of your study of services marketing, you can, and should, make use of your experiences of consuming and providing services. The experiences can enable you to be constructively critical of the theory, and to add creatively to theory. We believe that in building an understanding of services, and hence of services marketing and management, you should wherever possible draw on experiences and intuitions. In so doing, this ensures a more interactive and lively vehicle for learning.

So our answer to the question 'why study services marketing?' is that it is an invigorating exercise in combining theory and practical knowledge to further an understanding of something which is an important part of life.

If we look at the historical development of services marketing, it has been acknowledged that 'services marketing developed academically because it filled a need in marketing practice'.[1] Service executives persuaded academics that a different approach was required to understand the marketing of services from that used for the marketing of goods. It may not be obvious immediately, but it will soon become apparent that many services are incredibly complex, and provide different challenges for marketing practitioners and academics alike. The complexity is illustrated by a story of a particular service experience and the analysis that follows.

A 'service' experience

To introduce many of the features of service provision, and identify the exchange relationships between the service provider organisation and its customers, we start with a story of a service experience. The story is fictional. It is an amalgam of several personal and reported experiences. However, the incidents described in the story should strike a chord with you, and hence provide an understandable scenario for a more general discussion.

To encourage a more purposeful reading of the story, we suggest that you consider the following questions about the nature of the service itself and the service experiences of the main characters.

- What is the service the passengers (the Townsends) are paying for? How might the service be defined? When does the service start and finish?
- Is the service *provision* different for the two passengers (John and Jack Townsend)? Is the service *experience* different for them? To what extent might the service experience be affected by employees of the service providers? By the physical settings in which the service takes place? By other customers (passengers)?

The story

John Townsend and his son Jack (aged 14) were travelling to Singapore to join John's wife Jane who was completing a spell as a visiting lecturer at the National University of Singapore. They had chosen to fly with Singapore Airlines. John had booked the flights through the internet. He was also very pleased with himself that his websearch had unearthed lots of information about Singapore. In particular, he had been able to book a Sunday 'brunch' at the Raffles Hotel in Singapore for the three of them – an experience a friend had told him not to miss. John had never flown on 'long haul' before. His only experience of a scheduled flight was a British Airways flight to Geneva. Jack had flown on package holidays to Menorca and Crete with the family and definitely did not like flying. The 13-hour flight from Manchester to Singapore was viewed with mixed feelings. John regarded it as part of a wonderful, never likely to be repeated, experience (with the bonus of seeing Jane after three months apart). Jack just wanted to get it over.

They arrived at Manchester Airport's Terminal 1 three hours before the flight time (as instructed on their tickets). The reception hall was very crowded and noisy, but it was clear from the information on the handily placed, multiple monitors that they should check in at Desk 21. The next problem was actually finding Desk 21. They could see plenty of desks with destination indicators above them, but they could not spot that particular number. An armed security guard was the only airport official around so they asked him for assistance. He directed them politely to Desk 21. After passing several long queues of passengers with trolleys full of baggage, they were pleasantly surprised to see a small queue of only two passenger groups. The surprise turned to frustration when they were informed that they had mistakenly joined the 'Raffles Class' (that is, first class) passenger queue – the red carpet should have been the giveaway – and had to join, instead, the much longer economy class queue at Desk 22.

In the queue, John spent the time talking to a couple of Manchester University female students who were flying home to Singapore. He learnt a lot about types of food and places to eat, and about which tourist attractions were good value for money (and which were not). Whilst checking in the baggage, John and Jack were asked a number of security-related questions. Although they were standard practice, the questions added a hijacker dimension to Jack's fear of flying. Finally, they were able to secure plane seats in a non-smoking area, which was very important to both of them in view of the length of the flight. Despite his economy class status, John felt quite pleased that he was travelling with an airline that to him was a symbol of exotic travel. Jack couldn't have cared less.

Baggage successfully despatched, and with over two hours still to wait, they made their way to the main concourse. It was brightly lit with a variety of shops (including, John was surprised to see, a branch of Harrods), located around a central seated area. The seats were arranged so that only about 20 per cent of the passengers could see flight information monitors clearly. Yet passengers needed this information to know when to proceed to passport control. This situation seemed to increase congestion, with passengers frequently vacating their seats to look at the monitors, leaving their partners to spread out luggage to hold on to seats. This clearly irritated many passengers, and John shared a mutual moan about the lack of information with a family travelling to Dubai. John found the hour's wait before proceeding to passport control interminable. Jack, with heavy metal music blasting through his 'Discman', and many friends to chat to on his mobile phone, was unperturbed.

After an uneventful passage through Customs, they entered the departure lounge. There were some tables covered with uncollected crockery and glasses, an expensive coffee bar, a self-service snack bar and several shops, including duty-free outlets. It was very crowded. Passenger information was provided on monitors at various locations in the lounge, hypnotically flashing messages about the departure times and instructions to proceed to 'gates'. Occasional flurries of passenger activity meant that instructions to proceed to appropriate gates had flashed up. Jack, with the common sense of youth, had spotted the two Singaporean students sitting in front of one of the monitors. 'Relax dad,' he said, 'just follow them when they move.'

It turned out to be Gate 2 which was a good ten minutes away, even on the moveable walkway. Through the windows they could see several planes waiting to depart. John was pleased and reassured to see that their plane was one of the biggest. However, when they got on board, although the interior was bigger that any they had seen before – eight seats to each row, and two corridors – the individual space per seat was disappointingly small, particularly for John's 6ft 3in. frame. They were both very impressed with the in-flight entertainment system. Each passenger had individual controls and his/her own monitor on the seat in front. Not only were up-to-date films available for viewing, but the system was interactive! Jack immediately sought out the flight magazine to find out the range of video games available. John soon stopped worrying about where to put his feet as he started to look around at the fellow passengers. There was a mix of families, couples, ages and ethnic groupings, but quite a few empty seats as well. The children of the family in front appeared to be very worldly wise, and were already talking about Changi airport and making plans to 'get one of the free toothbrushes from the toilet before they are all taken'. John mused to himself that he had already experienced so much and yet they had not even started on the flight.

Jack stiffened during the cabin crew's demonstration of emergency procedures, but relaxed visibly when the pilot calmly described the flight route. John began to relax after the complimentary drink and Jack worked out his personalised programme of movie watching. The cabin crew, one man and three women, all very elegantly dressed, were extremely polite and helpful. Nothing was apparently too much trouble. At one stage, they searched the complete economy section looking for a 'smoker' who would be prepared to swap seats with a non-smoker seated in the smoking area. This, however, was not possible. They even found out the English football results at the request of a passenger. Jack decided that he needed to go to the toilet at the very time when the cabin crew had started to serve dinner, but there was no way past the meal trolley for the next 30 minutes. He had to sit and suffer. John and Jack tucked into the 'Shrimp Newburg', and listened to the co-pilot explain how they could follow the route on their video system. As the pins and needles in his legs increased, John thought enviously of the business class passengers, not to mention 'Raffles' class passengers, in their spacious seats. When the plane was over Calcutta, he even wished he had paid twice as much for the extra comfort.

Analysing the experience

Almost all the incidents described in the story could happen to air travellers irrespective of their point of departure or of airline used. Therefore, this is not a story specifically about Manchester Airport or about Singapore Airlines, but describes the feelings and apprehensions of the service customers as well as the facilities offered by the service providers. It contains elements and issues that are common to most types of services (not just air travel). These elements and issues form the content of much of the services marketing academic and practical literature. We start with an examination of three fundamental aspects of services – process, people and physical evidence, the management of which contributes to the success, or otherwise, of the marketing of the services. We then take a different perspective by focusing on the visible and invisible (to the passenger) elements of air transport service provision to highlight issues of relevance to the marketing of all services.

The process

Shostack, in the early 1980s, affirmed that service is not a thing but a process – 'the process is the product'.[2] Services are processes that occur over time. The very way that the story of John and Jack's flight to Singapore is told emphasises the process elements. 'They entered the concourse, *then* they looked at the information screen, *then* they asked the way to Desk 21, *then* ...' The complexity of the service experience can be appreciated very clearly when it is broken down into the many process components. Even what may appear, at first glance, to be a relatively simple service, for example, a gent's barber, can be seen to be quite complex when viewed as a complete process (see Chapter 6). It is always surprising to discover how many distinct process elements there are for a service – try counting the number of clicks on the mouse for a straightforward service by the internet, such as checking your current account balance using your bank's website.

The fact that a process has many elements can have several implications for service managers.

First, while there may be a 'core' service that the customers are paying for, there are also many 'peripheral' elements to the service. The core service offering is the 'necessary outputs of the organisation which are intended to provide the intangible benefits customers are looking for'. Peripheral services are those which are either 'indispensable for the execution of the core service or available only to improve quality of the service bundle'.[3] In the airport scenario, the flight itself is obviously a major component; that is, the means of travelling quickly and safely from Manchester to Singapore. This could be described as the core element in this context. There are, however, a range of extra components of the service which are still highly valued, such as meals and drinks on the plane, in-flight entertainment, and pillows, blankets and toothbrushes for passenger comfort (the peripheral elements). Of course, passengers may not think this way, and may give more weight to some of the peripheral elements than to the core service. How often have you heard people voicing complaints about the food served on a plane or the (lack of) drinks, even though the flight was on time with smooth take-off and landing? Furthermore, *each separate element* in the process, whether it is core or peripheral, can be a cause of customer (dis)satisfaction.

Second, when does the service begin and end for the customer? For the Townsends, the first contact with the service provider (Singapore Airlines) was via their website. The last contact (for this journey at least) would probably be at Changi airport in Singapore, where a whole new set of services would have been provided. As will be discussed in Chapter 4, certain encounters with the service organisation may be more important than others from the customers' perspective, especially the first encounter! The website has to be easy to use.

Third, the Townsends had a relatively stress-free service experience. It is not unknown, however, for various elements in the flight process to result in service 'failures' – for example, the flight is delayed, the baggage goes missing, the available food on the flight does not correspond with the menu. Passengers, in the main, will understand the reasons for service failures, but will also expect the service providers to 'recover' the situation to their satisfaction. Service organisations study the service process in great detail to ensure that they have sound 'service recovery' strategies in place. Service recovery is a very important aspect of services marketing and is dealt with in both Chapter 6 and Chapter 9.

Fourth, unlike physical goods, 'time' cannot be stored and used later. The empty seats on the Manchester to Singapore flight cannot be resold. With processes, appropriate management of supply and demand is crucial to business success.

Finally, the process is not exactly the same for all passengers. The Raffles first-class passengers, for instance, were given different treatment both before and during the flight. They would have faster check-in, a wider choice of food and drinks, more leg room, greater speed of service, and so on. The design of a higher level of customisation of service for Raffles passengers relates to the design of the process.

The people

The story highlights the importance of people involved in the service, in terms of their individual behaviour and attitudes, and their interactions with each other. The people in this context are the customers (passengers) and the contact personnel (the people providing the service for John and Jack). There were several different contact personnel involved in the story. John and Jack came into contact with the pilot and co-pilot, the cabin crew, the baggage checkout personnel, and the security guard. The latter, although not employed by the airline, is still a contributor to passengers' service experiences. The appearance and manner of contact personnel, as well as the words they actually speak, their 'scripts' (to use a drama analogy), can significantly affect the passengers' overall perception of the service. Their status will also influence the extent to which they can vary the nature of the interaction with the passengers, or are constrained by a predetermined script. For example, the baggage checkout employees must go through their set security script even if it is distressing to Jack, whereas the senior cabin crew steward may be allowed to use initiative and improvisation to calm a nervous passenger.

It is a major challenge for many service organisations to train all employees to promote their ideals of customer service, especially if some contact personnel are employed by other companies (for example, security guards, restaurant staff or cleaners). The issues are covered in more detail in Chapters 7 and 9. The important role played by the contact personnel is emphasised by Bateson[4] who notes that 'the contact personnel can be a source of differentiation'. This is particularly appropriate with a service such as an airline where, because 'many airlines offer similar bundles of benefits and fly the same planes from the same airports, their only hope of a competitive advantage is from the service level'.

Just as the different personal characteristics of the contact personnel will influence the nature of the service, so too will the different personalities of the customers. The customers typically experiencing a particular service may differ according to characteristics such as age, gender and socio-economic group. The Townsends' fellow passengers tended to be well-off families from many ethnic groups – quite a different mix from those on the package holiday to Crete. Fellow customers in the service setting can clearly influence a service experience. They may be acquainted (e.g. John and Jack) or strangers, so-called 'unacquainted influencers'.[5]

The story of John and Jack Townsend illustrates that *customer perceptions* of a service encounter differ, even if the customers receive the same core and peripheral services. Personal and situational factors govern the service perceptions. John was looking forward to the flight and had planned to make the most of the whole experience. Jack, on the other hand, was nervous about flying and just wanted the flight to be over as soon as possible. Various cognitive, emotional and physiological responses affect their service experience. John believed that a long-haul scheduled flight would be better than a charter flight, had categorised Singapore Airlines as exotic, and both he and Jack had been reassured by the size of the plane. John felt frustrated by the lack of available information (and thus the lack of control) in the departure lounge. Jack, although becoming increasingly anxious by virtue of security checks and guards, was happy to sit and listen to personal music in the lounges. Both were affected by the lack of space on the plane. In John's case, it was proving very uncomfortable. On a related issue, customer *expectations* of service can vary. The Townsends' expectations stemmed from previous flight experiences, Singapore Airlines advertisements and website and Jane's account of her flight. In contrast, the Singapore student seasoned travellers had far more experience with the airline on which to form their expectations. Customer expectations and perceptions of services are key components of the measures of customer satisfaction and service quality; covered in detail in Chapter 8.

From the above, it can be seen that, unlike physical goods that can often be mass-produced and standardised, services will always vary because of the people element. No two coffees will be served exactly the same, even by the same cabin crew member. No two customers will interpret the crew member's manner or demeanour in exactly the same way. No two cabin crew members will have responded to their training in exactly the same way. Of course, part of the variation in services is due to the customer's participation in the service, either physically (lifting baggage on to the scales, walking to the correct gate) or verbally (stating the requirement to sit in a non-smoking area, ordering the flight meal). Customers help *produce* the service as well as *consume* it.

The physical evidence

By physical evidence, we mean the exterior and interior environment to the service setting and the equipment and technology that customers may encounter in their dealings with the service provider. Although the core service for the Townsends – quick, safe transport from Manchester to Singapore – is essentially intangible, the story clearly shows that there are many tangible aspects that may affect their perceptions of the total service experience.

The exterior and interior environmental dimensions of the service would include the ambient conditions of the airport and aeroplane (temperature, air quality, music, noise, and so on), the utilisation of space (equipment, layout, furnishings) as well as signs, symbols and artifacts. These elements make up what has been labelled the 'servicescape'.[6] In our story, the Townsends noticed noise and heat at the airport and the lack of signage and seating arrangements at the terminal. The lack of space inside the plane itself affected both the passengers and the cabin crew. The service provider has a great deal of control over this part of the service package. For example, designing individual, interactive entertainment systems for passengers with monitors on the seat in front gives the passengers more control, and improves their flight experience. Airlines also recognise the importance of tangible mementoes for the passengers to take away with them to remind them of the occasion, for example in-flight magazines, toothbrushes and printed meal menus. These are often determinants of repeat purchase. In Chapter 6, we look at the design of the physical evidence of services as well as the design of the service process.

The equipment and technology which the Townsends encountered include the internet, an in-flight entertainment system, and moving walkways, each of which have been designed to operate independently of any contact persons. They are examples of technology-based services[7] that were unavailable until the 1990s. These forms of self-service are of great interest to all service providers, as they increase hours of business (for example, ATMs, 'pay at the pump' petrol/gas stations, flight ticket machines), and may reduce the inherent (human) variability of the service provider. John and Jack are more likely to take notice of other equipment in the servicescape if it does not work as it should. Broken baggage return conveyor belt systems cause delays and a lot of ill feeling.

Visible and invisible elements of services

The extended service experience of the Townsends is determined by elements that are visible to them (for example, the behaviour of a contact person, or the layout of the aeroplane) and those which are invisible to them (for example, the staff training programmes, the computerisation of the baggage handling system, the catering preparation). Using the analogy of a service being like a drama performance,[8] the visible elements are 'front-stage' whereas the invisible elements are 'backstage'.

The elements that are visible to John and Jack are essentially people and physical evidence as demonstrated above. However, it is their *interactions* with people and the physical evidence that determine the service experience. They engage in interpersonal interactions with each other, and with other customers (for example, students in the queue, family from Dubai in the destination lounge). These are known collectively as *customer-to-customer interactions*. They engage in interpersonal interactions with the many contact personnel – *customer–employee* interactions. They engage in interactions with the physical environment, equipment and technology.

The visible elements (people and physical evidence) are common to most services (hospitals, education, restaurants, hotels, sporting occasions, retail outlets, banks, package holidays, hairdressers, and so on), and, likewise, the resulting interactions are determinants of the customer experience in these services, albeit with varying degrees of relative importance. Chapter 4 is devoted to an understanding of interactions within service encounters. It also highlights the importance of efforts made by service providers to control the interactions. With customer-to-customer interactions, for example, most managerial emphasis has been on reducing the possibility of negative exchanges between one customer and another. This can be achieved by, for example, arranging the seating so that John, a non-smoker, does not have to sit next to a smoker. Some strategies have been put forward, however, to encourage positive interactions by 'rewarding' customers who give useful advice to other customers.[9] A resulting, pleasant conversation with a fellow traveller is both satisfying and makes the time pass more quickly.

The invisible elements largely support the service process as described above. Although the invisible components are not valued directly by customers, they are recognised by writers and managers alike as being important components of the service package.[10] Airport and airline services spend huge sums of money on improving and enhancing computerised systems and other technology in order to move passengers more efficiently through the process. Jack, who wanted to get the 'ordeal' over with as quickly as possible, would no doubt appreciate the management concentration on the backstage.

The language used in understanding and writing about services, and services marketing, employs two metaphors – the factory metaphor and the drama/theatre metaphor, each of which relates to different goals of a service organisation. If the goal is efficiency (probably with a concentration on the invisible elements of a service operation) then service is likened to a factory, with an emphasis on inputs and outputs to the process. If, however, the goal is the customer 'experience' (probably with a concentration on the visible elements – the people and the setting), then service is likened to a theatrical production, with an emphasis on the performance. What may be particularly exasperating to the people charged with the marketing and management of services is that a goal of efficiency may suit one customer (for example, Jack), but not another. John, for example, may prefer more of an experience to remember, savouring every moment. Service goals and the use of metaphors are considered in Chapter 3.

The structure of the book

The story has provided specific examples of many of the issues and key areas of services marketing. Clearly, a single scenario will not address all the issues. However, the story, and our brief discussion of the elements that make up the service experience, provide a useful starting point for explaining the structure of the remainder of the book.

In Chapter 2, we set the context by examining the ways in which services can be defined and the potential range of application of services marketing theory. As will be seen, it is not just businesses that refer to themselves as 'services businesses' that can make use of the theory. Some fundamental building blocks of the theory – characteristics of services, perceived risk of services, the services marketing mix, and classification of services – are introduced. All can be related back to the story above, but clearly have widespread applications, which will be illustrated with examples from a range of services. The importance of services in many economies is increasing rapidly and some national and global statistics are provided to emphasise the scope of development of the service economy. The chapter also charts the evolution of services marketing as an academic sub-discipline, and outlines the 'hot issues' of the twenty-first century. Finally, theory and practice are brought together through the discussion of the elements of a research instrument, SER*VOR, which companies can use to measure service orientation: are they really structured to provide good, or even excellent service?

The use of metaphors in services marketing is well recognised by academics and practitioners alike. The two most common metaphors for services are 'factory' and 'drama/theatre'. With the former, we happily use expressions such as 'service delivery', 'service productivity', 'efficiency', and 'process'. With the latter, we talk of 'service performance', 'roles and scripts' (for employees and customers), 'front- and backstage', and 'service setting'. Both metaphors are helpful in understanding services, and providing a language of communication. In Chapter 3, we explore the use of the metaphors in some detail, especially relating to the service goals (to mix metaphors!). We firmly believe that the metaphor usage is important in constructing how service is perceived by customers and service organisations (is the service goal efficiency or performance?), but equally, we are aware of its limitations.

Our airline passengers interacted with contact personnel, the built environment (represented by the airport and the aeroplane) and with other passengers. They benefited from efficient, but invisible, service elements such as flight meal preparation and computerised reservation systems. Their encounter with the service was for a finite period. These features are common to many services. In Chapter 4, we concentrate on the 'service encounter' and its central role in the marketing of services. The personal, situational, cognitive, emotional and physiological factors peculiar to particular customers, are relevant here, and affect the *content* of the service encounter. Interpersonal service encounters are extremely important, but the internet in particular has rapidly increased the need to learn more about technology-based service encounters.

In the late 1990s and early 2000s, there has been a great interest, by practitioners and academics, in providing holistic service *experiences* for consumers. In the story, we see, for example, that John was expecting more than a routine flight between two destinations, and also that the flight was perhaps only a component of a never-to-be-repeated overall travel experience. In other contexts, such as shopping mall[11] and store[12] design, the intended consumer experience is paramount in planning the setting and activities. There are even claims that the service economy is being replaced by an experience economy.[13] Chapter 5, which is new for this edition, builds on the drama/theatre metaphor to explore the consumer experience.

The factory metaphor emphasises service as a process. The design of service processes is covered in Chapter 6, with a special focus on service blueprinting. This approach ensures that the invisible elements supporting service delivery are understood and fully integrated. We have found that the service blueprint is not only integral to service design and positioning, but it also provides a useful visual tool for creative service ideas.

In Chapter 7, we explicitly acknowledge the *people* aspects of services, particularly the roles of the contact personnel. Attention is given to internal marketing (marketing to employees as internal customers) and human resource service management issues. As the story demonstrates, customers (passengers) may make contact with several people who are providing the service, some of whom are more empowered than others to improvise, but all of whom should, as far as the company is concerned, be offering passengers the service which is promised. This represents a great challenge to most service organisations, large or small.

John and Jack Townsend each had their own prior expectations of air travel service. On meeting Jane in Singapore, each could recount his actual perceptions of that same service. What did they think about the quality of service? Were they satisfied with the service? Or even delighted? Did their views differ? If their expectations were exceeded, it is likely that they would be satisfied and would give a high quality verdict. Service quality and customer satisfaction are recognised as important service output measures. To increase service quality and/or customer satisfaction, within an appropriate budget, is normally part of the mission of a service organisation. Chapter 8 examines the current work and debates on service quality and customer satisfaction, and looks at the models that are based on 'gaps' between customers' expectations and subsequent perceptions of a service.

Given Jane's working relationship in Singapore, there is a possibility that the Townsends may visit Singapore again in the future. Both Manchester Airport and Singapore Airlines would wish them to travel with them again. In other words, they wish to retain them as customers. A concentration on customer retention, through a marketing policy which merges marketing, customer service and quality elements, is termed 'relationship marketing'.

This is covered in Chapter 9, and builds on the material in earlier chapters, particularly Chapters 7 and 8.

Implicit in the management and marketing of services is the desire for the organisation to make a profit (or break even, in the case of not-for-profit services) and to achieve certain levels of productivity. Perhaps surprisingly though, there is still little explicit reference in the services marketing literature to the issues of service profitability and productivity. Chapter 10 looks at work in this area.

Finally, in Chapter 11, we look forward and outline some potential futures and associated research issues. We are made aware regularly of the interest in services marketing by the number of students at undergraduate and post-graduate level who undertake dissertations in the field. This chapter contains ideas for such work.

Characteristics of case studies in the book

The book has 10 case studies. The case studies enable practice and theory to be integrated. They are different from, but complement the case studies that are in many of the other textbooks on services marketing. The cases in this book generally share the characteristics outlined below.

Small-scale operators

First, the majority of the case studies describe the issues and concerns that affect *small-scale* service operators that are generally neglected in the wider services marketing literature. Although these businesses may not make such a significant financial contribution to the service economy as the large-scale operators frequently cited in the literature (for example, banks, building societies, insurance agencies, telecommunications organisations, hotel chains), they often make a significant social contribution to the welfare of the communities in which they operate.[14]

The social role performed by the services covered in this book is an important theme running through the cases. As Czepiel *et al.* point out: 'Service encounters are a form of human interaction important not only to their direct participants (clients and providers) and the service organizations that sponsor them, but also to society as a whole.'[15]

Human involvement in the service experience

The services selected involve a high level of human interaction. Most commonly this consists of interaction between contact personnel and customers, but it may also be between fellow customers during the service experience. This perspective enables us to focus on the whole range of problems faced by service managers struggling to control human involvement in the service delivery process. Solomon in Czepiel *et al.* uses quotations from service managers to illustrate the unpredictability and importance of human exchanges in the service experience in their article on service encounters.[16]

In a service business, you're dealing with something that is primarily delivered by people to people. Your people are as much of your product in the consumer's mind as any other attribute of the service. People's performance day in and day out fluctuates up and down. Therefore, the level of consistency that you can count on and try to communicate to the consumer is not a certain thing.

The cases illustrate the importance of the development of long-term personal relationships to the continued success of many service operations.

Easily replicated format

Although reading, studying and analysing written case studies provides an effective means for matching theory and practice, it is not the same as actively studying a real service organisation. We have found that under-graduate and postgraduate students can gain enormous benefits from *writing their own case study* of a small service business. Indeed, three of the case studies in this book were written by student groups we have supervised in the past three years.

An in-depth study of a real (small) service organisation can often be achieved over a period of two months or so, and any interviews with the service owners/managers can be guided by the checklist of questions below (Table 1.1). We highly recommend it.

Table 1.1   Checklist for gathering suitable information from owners/managers of small service businesses

History of the business
  When was the business founded?
  By whom?
  How has it developed/changed?
  Location(s)?

Staffing
  How many?
  Who?
  Personal details; age, qualifications, experience, attitudes/beliefs?

Nature of the business
  What sort of business are you in?
  How do you define the service you offer?
  Who are your competitors?

Location
  If important, collect maps, diagrams.

Physical environment
  Ask to look around 'outlet' of interest (front- and backstage).

Method of payment
  How do customers pay for the services?
  What variety of methods are offered?

Making contact with customers
  How do you make contact with new customers; advertising, promotion, PR?
  How do you retain contact with existing customers?

Table 1.1 *contd.*

Relationships (other than with customers)

What other parties do you deal with; suppliers, accountants, agencies, societies?
What was in your diary over the last month? Refer to key telephone/fax numbers, addresses, email, etc.

Invisible elements

Typical transactions with business associates?
What equipment has to be purchased? Why?
How are records kept?
Try to obtain flow diagram from first customer contact to final purchase.

Peripheral services

What else is offered on-site to improve overall service?
Any examples of special services offered to particular customers?

Customers (1)

Who are the typical customer variations?
If I wished to become a customer, how would I go about it? (*repeats, but important*).
How do you build up good relationships with customers?
Which customers are most likely to repeat buy?
Can you give examples of where your service exceeded/did not meet customer expectations?

Customers (2)

Describe some examples of staff interactions with customers

(a) incidents that went well
(b) incidents that went badly for whatever reason.

Customers (3)

Describe some positive/negative incidents of customers interacting with other customers

(a) conversations
(b) altercations
(c) cooperations

How do they affect the business?

Contact personnel

How are they trained/prepared for the job?
How much initiative can/should they use? Give examples.
What are the attributes of a very good member of your staff?
What are the minimum requirements of a member of staff?

Recovery

Give examples of an incident which was going wrong, but which was recovered to the customer's satisfaction (more than one if possible).

General

How do you define service quality in the context of your business?
Do you have a mission statement and/or company objectives?

OVERALL LEARNING OUTCOMES

Having read the chapters and undertaken the case studies, you will be able to

1. *Identify the theoretical aspects of services marketing*. In particular, you will be able to

- critically evaluate the theoretical contributions to services marketing

- interrelate consumer, customer and provider perceptions of services.

2. *Understand how theory translates into service practice.* In particular, you will be able to

- choose appropriate services marketing frameworks to analyse a service business

- apply flexibility in your study of new and developing service practices.

DISCUSSION QUESTIONS AND EXERCISES

1. Think of three services you have used in the last seven days. What are the *processes* involved with these services from your (customer) perspective?

2. Name two services where companies have attempted to replace contact personnel with machines. To what extent has the change-over been successful?

3. Why is physical evidence important in services?

4. In what type of services might it be an option to make the invisible elements of the service more visible?

5. What small service businesses are run by members of your family or by friends?

Notes and references

1. Berry, L. L. and Parasuraman, A., 'Building a New Academic Field: The Case of Services Marketing', *Journal of Retailing*, vol. 69, no. 1, Spring 1993, pp. 13–60.
2. Shostack, G. L., 'Breaking Free from Product Marketing', *Journal of Marketing*, vol. 41, April 1977, pp. 73–80.
3. Carman, J. M. and Langeard, E., 'Growth Strategies for Service Firms', *Strategic Management Journal*, vol. 1, 1980, pp. 7–22.
4. Bateson, J. E. G., *Managing Services Marketing: Text and Readings*, 2nd edn, Dryden Press, London, 1992.
5. McGrath, M. A. and Otnes, C., 'Unacquainted Influencers: When Strangers Interact in the Retail Setting', *Journal of Business Research*, vol. 32, 1995, pp. 261–72.
6. Bitner, M. J., 'Servicescapes: The Impact of Physical Surroundings on Customers and Employees', *Journal of Marketing*, vol. 56, April 1992, pp. 57–71.
7. Meuter, M. L., Ostrom, A. L., Roundtree, R. I. and Bitner, M. J., 'Self-Service Technologies: Understanding Customer Satisfaction with Technology-Based Service Encounters', *Journal of Marketing*, vol. 64, July 2000, pp. 50–64.

8. Grove, S. J. and Fisk, R. P., 'The Dramaturgy of Services Exchange: An Analytical Framework for Services Marketing', in L. L. Berry, G. L. Shostack and G. D. Upah (eds), *Emerging Perspectives on Services Marketing*, American Marketing Association, Chicago, 1983.

9. Pranter, C. A. and Martin, C. L., 'Compatibility Management: Roles in Service Performances', *Journal of Services Marketing*, vol. 5, Spring 1991, pp. 43–53.

10. The 'servuction' model of service delivery systems explicitly recognises 'invisible' components: see Langeard, E., Bateson, J., Lovelock, C. and Eiglier, P., *Marketing of Services: New Insights from Consumers and Managers*, report no. 81–104, Marketing Science Institute, Cambridge, Mass., 1981.

11. The Mills Corporation, for example, wishes to draw consumers into its malls 'who are not only ready to shop, but are also ready to have an experience'. http://www.millscorp.com/

12. See, for example, ImagiCorps, and its offer of 'Retail Theater'. http://www.imagicorps.com/retail.html

13. Pine, B. J. II and Gilmore, J. H., *The Experience Economy: Work is Theater and Every Business a Stage*, HBS Press, Boston, Mass., 1999.

14. Baron, S., Leaver, D., Oldfield, B. M. and Cassidy, K., *Independent Food and Grocery Retailers: Attitudes and Opinions in the Year 2000*, Manchester Metropolitan University, Manchester, June 2000.

15. Czepiel, J. A., Solomon, M. R. and Surprenant, C. F. (eds), *The Service Encounter: Managing Employee/Customer Interaction in Service Businesses*, Lexington Books, Lexington, Mass., 1985.

16. Ibid.

Setting the context

LEARNING OBJECTIVES

Overall aim of the chapter:
To provide an overview of, and background to services in modern economies, and the basic building blocks of services marketing research.
In particular, the *chapter objectives* are

- to emphasise the scope and characteristics of services in a range of business formats

- to demonstrate the economic importance and growth of services in advanced economies

- to provide a summary of historical advances in services marketing, and the importance of the services marketing mix

- to illustrate various service classification systems and their applications in sharing successful practice and clarifying managerial issues

- to introduce the concept of service-oriented businesses, and the elements that contribute to (a measurement of) service orientation.

In the previous chapter, through use of the story, we identified a number of important components of a service experience. Interest in these components has resulted in research, and an established body of knowledge of services marketing. A key feature of much of the research has been the clear link between theory and practice. We now set the context for the more detailed study of theory and practice in services marketing.

This chapter is divided into four sections. First, we look at the *scope of service provision* and at *the importance of services* in many of today's economies. Second, we examine the *evolution of the sub-discipline of services marketing* over time and reflect on its current status. Third, we summarise some of the *systems that have been used to classify services*. Finally, we explore the concept of *service orientation* of a business and the management toolkit for its measurement – a specific example of linking theory to practice.

Scope and importance of services

Scope of service provision

It is difficult to think of organisations that are not involved with service in some form or other.

- Some organisations declare the *whole* business to be a service business.

  There are many examples. In the *private sector*, this would include consultancy business (for example, IT, public relations, accounting), airlines, estate agents, hairdressers, dry-cleaners and travel agents. In the *public sector*, for many countries, it would include, for example, health or education. In the *not-for-profit sector*, it would include charities, and many local government services. In the *business-to-business sector*, it would include delivery services, technical services, maintenance services and recruitment services.

- Some organisations declare services to be *part* of their business.

  Many organisations have service providers within their business. Multiple retailers, for example, rely on administrative services and technical services from within their own organisation. There is always a decision to be made as to whether these services are better provided within an organisation, or whether they should be 'out-sourced'. The use of information technology by business, for example, is being transformed by the growth of 'pay-as-you-go' services; that is, application service providers who hold software at data centres and allow customers to use it over the internet or a private network.[1]

- Some organisations declare services as an *augmentation* of manufactured goods.

  This is seen extensively with sales of traditional manufactured goods. For example, a new car comes with warranties, free delivery, and so on, or the purchase of a new carpet includes a fitting service.

The categorisation above is probably familiar to most readers. It demonstrates the wide and varied number of services that are carried out, typically, each and every day by organisations of all sizes. The body of knowledge built up in services marketing will apply whether service is the whole business, part of a business or an augmentation of manufactured goods. In particular, there are certain common characteristics of services that apply in all these cases. These characteristics – intangibility, heterogeneity, inseparability and perishability – which distinguish services from physical goods, have 'become the fundamental building blocks of most services marketing research, and are as fundamental to the study of services marketing as the 4Ps (Product, Price, Promotion and Place) are to the field of marketing in general'.[2]

Given their importance, we consider each characteristic in turn.

Intangibility

Pure services, such as a consultancy session with a psychiatrist, cannot be touched. Nor can travel on a train or aeroplane, although the train and aeroplane are themselves tangible. Nor can you touch the 'atmosphere' on a train or aeroplane, nor can you touch the conversations with fellow passengers. You cannot touch an aerobics class and can only make a full assessment of the quality of the service offered after having attended the class. A service is 'something which can be bought and sold, but which you cannot drop on your foot'.[3] This clearly differs from the purchase of a nectarine, for example, where the customer can touch the product beforehand and decide whether or not to buy it based on its colour and/or texture. Different aspects of marketing become more important in the service context. For example, a customer may rely heavily on the advice of a friend when considering whether to take part in the aerobics class, whereas a special price promotion that could more easily influence the decision to buy a nectarine.

The intangibility characteristic of services often increases risk for the purchaser. Some services are perceived to be riskier than others depending on whether they are high in

● search factors

● experience factors, or

● credence factors.

A service that is high in search factors is one about which customers can get some (prior) information as to what they will receive. For example, the sun-tanning shop may promise that after five sessions you will look as brown as the person on the photograph, or the breakdown service may claim to provide assistance within two hours for any part of the country. In each case, your search has provided some information that affects your perception of the risk involved with the purchase.

A service that is high in experience factors is one that customers must try out (experience) before they can decide whether or not it is a good deal. Paying for a holiday package, for example, is high in experience factors as it involves so much more than can be conveyed by the holiday brochure. Paying for the experience of a bungee jump is a more extreme example. Purchase of these services is perceived to be more risky than of those that are high in search factors.

A service that is high in credence factors is one that is difficult to evaluate even after experiencing it. These are services that are often offered by professionals or experts in their field. For many of us, it would be difficult to evaluate whether services offered by doctors, vets, car mechanics, plumbers or surveyors are value for money, simply because we do not have the knowledge to question them. Services such as these are perceived to be very risky, and require high degrees of reassurance from the service providers.

Heterogeneity

Organisations providing services to customers know that no two service provisions are exactly the same, whatever the attempts to standardise them. In the story in the previous chapter, it was recognised that serving meals on an aeroplane to different passengers would differ not only in the delivery but also in the evaluations by different passengers. Similarly, train operators recognise the great differences both in the service provided, and in passengers' perceptions of the service provided, between trains running off-peak and those running in the rush hours. The quality of any service will vary when offered by different employees, probably at different times of the day. Customers who cannot distinguish between physical goods (say, television sets off the same production line) will normally be able to distinguish between services (say, that provided by receptionists in the same hotel).

Inseparability

Inseparability refers to the notion that, in many service operations, production and consumption cannot be separated; that is, a service is to a great extent consumed at the same time as it is produced. For example, although the hairdresser may prepare in advance to carry out the service (that is, gather the necessary equipment, undergo specialised training, and so on), most of the hairdressing service is produced simultaneously as the customer consumes the service (that is, sits in the chair).

This characteristic raises various marketing problems primarily related to the fact that customers (who cannot be controlled totally by the service provider) are *involved and participate in the production process*. This is completely different from physical goods, where production and consumption are separated, and the customer has no involvement with the production process. The inseparability of production and consumption in services means that quality is more difficult to measure and ultimately control. Unlike the car factory, where production is out-of-bounds to consumers, and where potential quality failures can often be dealt with out of their sight, the production of many services is in the full spotlight of the consumer.

Perishability

This refers to the fact that, unlike physical goods, services cannot be stored. Even nectarines, which have a relatively short life, can be stored by the retailer for several days and sold at any point during that time to the consumer. An appointment with a dentist, in contrast, at a given time on a given day, cannot be stored and offered again to customers. If a customer cancels an appointment at the last minute, that particular service opportunity is lost and the dentist will have lost valuable revenue.

The problem of perishability is frequently compounded by the fact that the demand for many services is characterised by distinct peaks and troughs. Although trains are overloaded with customers between 7.30 am and 9.00 am most weekdays, expensive rolling stock will lay idle at midday and weekends. To overcome problems associated with perishability and uneven demand for services, careful attention is paid to production scheduling and demand forecasting. Pricing and promotion are used extensively to encourage customers to utilise services at a time convenient to the service operator. Some management implications and potential actions resulting from the four characteristics of services are outlined first here. They will be reinforced in the theory and case studies later.

First, the intangibility of services is recognised often by firms *stressing the tangible elements* of the service. So the conference organisers will ensure that delegates receive a clear programme of events with copies of important papers presented. The airline company will aim to provide good quality food during the journey. Service firms will also try to *facilitate positive word-of-mouth*. The car mechanic will encourage the satisfied customer to tell friends of his location, or the travel company will include stories of satisfied customers in the newsletter or brochures.

The heterogeneity of services is often addressed by companies through *service design* methods which reduce variability. In particular, they will try to standardise parts of the service that are invisible. For example, in hospital out-patients departments, a carefully designed and fully understood (by the nurses) system for ensuring patients are seen in the appropriate order will reduce patient feelings of unfairness due to variability in waiting room management. Also, it is argued that *empowerment of front-line staff* can improve the demeanour of customers who suffer the consequences of unseen variation in service provision. Passengers on a delayed train, for example, may feel better if the rail staff can provide information and even offer free drinks without needing management approval.

The implication of the inseparability characteristic of services is that customers take part in the production of services. This has been embraced by some service companies who *view their customers as partial employees*. They will pay as much attention to letting customers know what to do in order to participate in the service production as they do to employees. Students, for example, are informed as to their expected levels of participation in different formats: lectures, tutorials, seminars. Many services take place in the presence of other customers, who may also be partly responsible for the production of your service. The *management of customer-to-customer interactions* then becomes important. For example, the swimming pool staff can institute separate 'lane swimming' and 'fun swimming' areas so that the 'production' needs of both groups of swimmers can be met. Similarly, the design of restaurants to include appropriate smoking and non-smoking areas reduces the likely incompatibilities of different customer groups.

Service issues brought about by the perishability characteristic require management to have contingencies that allow them to *stimulate/reduce demand or increase/reduce supply*. In the travel business, when supply exceeds demand, there are empty seats on trains/aeroplanes that cannot be stored and resold. Likewise, gaps in the appointments books of hairdressers/dentists are lost business. Conversely, when demand exceeds supply, customers invariably have to wait for services. Here, *impression management* methods may be used to reduce customer irritations with queueing/waiting. In Disney theme parks, for example, where visitors can spend half the day waiting in lines, there are many devices for reducing irritation. The queueing areas are designed so that people are nearly always moving (which is better that standing for some time in the same place), monitors at regular intervals show films/videos which are related to Disney or the particular attraction, signs showing likely waiting times are prominently displayed (and which routinely overestimate the time, so that visitors feel good that they have queued for less time than expected), and there is a clear 'first in first out' system to reduce anxiety.

Finally, in discussing management implications and actions associated with the four characteristics of services, it is easy to overlook how *complex* the management of service provision may be. Often there is a range of influences on decision-making in services, making it difficult for some businesses to focus on service delivery issues. Consider train travel service. There are many stakeholders – the Shadow Strategic Rail Authority, the individual rail operators, Railtrack (who manage the infrastructure) and the groups representing rail passengers – each of whom have their own views as to what the service for passengers should be, and what the pricing structure should be.

Importance of services

In many advanced economies, consumers spend more on services than on tangible goods. Depending on definitions, service industries account for around 75 per cent of gross domestic product, and the labour force, in the USA, Western Europe, Australasia and Japan. In Hong Kong, the figure is nearer to 85 per cent.

Here are some statistics that present a perspective on just how important services are:

● One of the biggest employers in the UK – the Post Office – employs over 200,000 people;

● The tourism industry in the UK employs 1.75 million people; more than agriculture, coal mining, steel, car manufacturers, aircraft, food production and textiles together;

- The 'take-away' sandwich industry contributes more to UK net gross domestic product than farming;
- On a global level, PriceWaterhouseCoopers employs 30,000 consultants who bring in almost £3.7 billion in fee income.[4]

There has been a substantial growth in services in the last two decades. Healthcare services, business services, personal services, legal services, amusement and recreation services, accounting, engineering and architectural services, automotive services and hospitality services have grown at approximately double the rate of other industries since the mid-1980s.[5] Some of the reasons for the growth in many countries are:

- Deregulation: Major service industries, such as financial services and transport services have been deregulated, resulting in increases in the numbers and types of service providers in these sectors.
- Increased affluence: In general, people with more disposable income consider purchasing services previously undertaken in the home, such as ironing, cooking, cleaning, children's parties. This has resulted in increases in service businesses offering dry-cleaning, takeaway meals, domestic cleaning, and the generation of novel ways to provide birthday party experiences out of the home.[6]
- Increased free time: People fill their time with leisure pursuits, travel, 'surfing the net', and so on. David Lloyd Leisure, for example, opened up 32 clubs across the UK between 1995 and 2000 claiming that the 'unique club environment has been specifically designed to offer a wide range of sporting and social activities to ensure that members enjoy their most valuable leisure time'.
- Changing demographics: The increase in both the number of working women and the number of people aged over 55 years in the UK, has resulted in the increase of specific services which recognise the changes; for example, nanny/baby-minding services and pre-school nurseries, off-peak holiday packages and social activities such as 'bingo'.
- Information and digital technology in the home: Service companies have set up, or have attained a presence on the internet in recognition of the potential for online service purchases made at home. Retailers, in particular, are keen to seek opportunities of shopping from home. For example, in April 2000, Tesco, the UK Grocery retailer, planned to treble the number of stores from which it runs its internet shopping (Tesco Direct) to cover 90 per cent of the population. It announced that it had set up Tesco.com as a separate wholly-owned company in which it will invest £35 million in the year.[7]

The service economy can be seen to be very important, but even so, Pine and Gilmore[8] see it being replaced by an 'experience economy'. They say that consumers of the twenty-first century are looking to purchase experiences, and that businesses should be geared up to selling experiences. Their argument is that, over time, economies have moved from primarily trading commodities, to primarily selling manufactured goods, to primarily selling services, to a position where businesses selling experiences will be the profitable ones.

They use the commodity, the coffee bean, to illustrate their point. People who harvest and sell coffee beans on the futures market receive the equivalent of 2 cents a cup. Once the beans are ground and packaged by the manufacturers, the customer pays the equivalent of 5 to 25 cents per cup at the grocery store. If the ground beans are brewed in the most basic of cafes and served to customers, the cost per cup moves up to, say, 50 cents per cup. If the coffee is served in a 5-star restaurant or an idyllic location, the price per cup may be $5, or even as much as $15, in, for example, one of the cafes in St Mark's Square in Venice. They argue that customers will gladly pay the $15, because an hour-long stay in an open-air café in Venice represents an 'experience' well worth the extra money.

Whether you accept their argument or not, more and more retail and service businesses are claiming that they provide experiences for consumers. Belinda Earl, on being appointed Chief Executive of Debenhams, a UK Department Store chain, claimed that she wanted to boost 'interactive services with customers ... by creating different experiences for customers in the store, such as offering makeovers'. As a result of creating the experiences, she expects to 'persuade women to purchase six times more products, stay with us longer, and spend more'.[9] In the USA, the Mills Corporation, which develops shopping malls, claims on its web-site that their typical mall 'draws consumers who are not only ready to shop, but are also ready to have an experience. By offering the best in retail, coupled with the hottest entertainment and recreational venues, we consistently capture the imaginations of our shoppers from all over the world.' We will return to this theme in Chapter 6.

The evolution of the sub-discipline of services marketing

In an article entitled 'Tracking the Evolution of the Services Marketing Literature', written in 1993, Fisk, Brown and Bitner[10] identified three distinct stages in the evolution of services marketing that are reflected in the literature:

1. the 'Crawling Out' stage which took place prior to 1980;
2. the 'Scurrying About' stage between 1980 and 1986;
3. the 'Walking Erect' stage from 1986 to 1993 and beyond.

Each of the stages will be explained, so that you can evaluate the research work and practice in services marketing in the context of its evolutionary stage. We also provide two alternatives for a possible Stage 4 in the evolution, based on the services marketing literature of 1993 to 2000.

'Crawling out'

In the 'crawling out' stage, discussion centred around the need for a separate body of literature to deal with the specific problems of the service sector.

Papers considered whether there was anything significantly different about operating a service business that would necessitate a distinct body of marketing theory. To address this issue, writers clearly had to take into consideration the full range of marketing theories that existed and reflect on their usefulness in a service context. Specific areas of marketing theory were examined and found to be insufficient or inappropriate when it came to handling service sector problems and concerns. Donnelly,[11] for example, highlighted the differences between the marketing 'channels' used for services and those used for physical goods and implications for marketing strategy.

Criticisms were aimed at the existing discipline of marketing with its 'product' orientation. 'Can corporate banking services really be marketed according to the same basic blueprint that made TIDE a success?' asked Shostack in her provocative article in 1977.[12] She criticised traditional marketing for being 'myopic' in having failed to create relevant paradigms for the service sector. In response to these criticisms, marketing tradition-alists argued that service organisations did not need a separate body of theory, and that existing marketing theories could, and should, be applied to service organisations. They argued that services could not be defined tightly enough to deserve special treatment and, in many instances, were so closely linked to the physical product that they needed to be considered as part of the 'offer' when developing marketing strategy. For example, the after sales service guarantee supplied with a motor car could be valued as highly as the interior design features of the car itself.

'Scurrying about'

In the 'scurrying about' stage between 1980 and 1985 the quantity of academic literature produced about services marketing increased consider-ably. Efforts were made to classify services more clearly[13] and attention focused heavily on the crucial issue of managing quality in service opera-tions. Zeithaml, Berry and Parasuraman developed their pioneering 'gaps model' of service quality,[14] which highlighted the importance of efforts made to assess quality in services. Other topics emerged as being particularly important to the management of service organisations, including a better understanding of the components of the 'service encounter' (that is, the interpersonal aspects of the service), 'relationship marketing' and 'internal marketing'. For the first time textbooks on services marketing began to be produced, establishing it more firmly as a legitimate field of academic study.

Booms and Bitner[15] developed their expanded 'marketing mix' for services that took into account the distinctive characteristics of services: intangibil-ity, inseparability, heterogeneity and perishability. The 'marketing mix' is the term traditionally used to describe a specific set of tools available to managers to help them shape the offer they present to consumers. McCarthy[16] presented one of the most commonly used 'mixes' in 1960; the 'four Ps', highlighting Product, Price, Promotion and Place decisions as being the most critical areas for consideration. Booms and Bitner added three more Ps to this original mix to make it more appropriate to services:

People, Process and Physical Evidence. This became the *services marketing mix*:

- Product
- Price
- Promotion
- Place
- People
- Process
- Physical evidence

The relevance and importance of people, process and physical evidence is re-emphasised every time consumers are asked to relate critical incidents of services (memorably good incidents, or memorably bad incidents) in their own words. Table 2.1 provides examples of critical incidents, related by mature students. They are typical of all the stories provided by the student group. For consumers, good/bad experiences with people, processes, and physical evidence often dominate their evaluations of the experience.

Table 2.1 Critical service incidents described by consumers

Memorably good incidents:

'Last year, we booked a discount holiday – an all-inclusive trip to Kenya – 10 days before we were due to go, via teletext. I booked over the telephone, and within 24 hours had tickets, luggage labels, books on Kenya and safaris, complimentary passes to local places, a travel bag, and all the information we could possibly have wanted. The travel company phoned four days before we went, to check everything was OK. The holiday service was absolutely excellent. The travel company sent us a questionnaire when we returned, and a "welcome home" pack. We have raved about it ever since.'

'On arriving at the restaurant, we were offered seats at the bar to wait for a table. Within 10 minutes we were shown to one by an exceptionally good waitress, who went through the menu with us before getting more drinks and taking orders. Both the starter and main course arrived within five minutes, and were of superb quality. The waitress regularly checked that we were OK, fetching drinks, etc., as and when required. The overall experience was a pleasurable one, from entering the restaurant to taking the mints on the way out.'

Memorably bad incidents:

'Prior to going on holiday, I had my purse stolen, with all the usual cards inside. I went to my bank branch with my cheque book (which had not been stolen) and thought that they would allow me to draw out some money from my account. In order to save myself some embarrassment, I first checked at the enquiry desk whether it would be OK to draw money from my account with only my cheque book. The gentleman said it would be OK. I then queued to speak to a cashier. I explained my situation, and told her what the man at "Enquiries" had said. She asked me for further identification, and I explained that it had been stolen. She said "Sorry, no money can be drawn from your account, without further proof of identity." I suggested that she phoned a helpline as we do in retail stores under such circumstances, to check information such as mother's maiden name. She said the helpline was not available as it was a Saturday. By this time, I was very annoyed … it seemed ludicrous that the bank has no such facilities. She said that she could not help me and that I would have to wait until Monday …'

'I took my car to XYZ on a Saturday, as the exhaust was blowing. They said they would check on the computer if the part was in stock, but they couldn't replace it for an hour. They confirmed that the part was in stock, so I left the car with them. I returned in 90 minutes, and the car was still outside, not repaired. I asked when it would be ready, and they said "Oh, about another hour, mate." I returned after an hour. The car had been moved, so my hopes were raised. However, on asking, it became apparent that the part wasn't in stock, and my original exhaust had been removed, and cut in two. I asked what they were going to do, and they said they were expecting a delivery on Tuesday morning, "would that be OK?" I explained that I worked Sunday and Monday, and needed my car. They said they would try and get a part locally, and promised to ring at 5.30 pm with an outcome. No phone call …'

'Walking erect'

In the 'walking erect' stage, Fisk, Brown and Bitner note that there has been 'almost no discussion of whether services are different from goods, but rather the literature has focused on specific marketing problems of service organisations'. The issues that they identify are covered in the chapters that make up the remainder of this book. They include consideration of service encounters, service design, perceived service quality and customer satisfaction, internal marketing and relationship marketing. In keeping with the development of academic material in the field, the theoretical chapters adopt a multidisciplinary perspective, drawing on material from consumer behaviour, human resource management and more obviously from traditional marketing. The Fisk, Brown and Bitner article was published in 1993. What may be the consequences of the 'walking erect' stage, at the start of the twenty-first century? We discuss two possible scenarios. The developments in other subject disciplines over history suggest the following possibilities:

● 'Erecting fences'

Now that that the sub-discipline of services marketing is well established, there could be a move (by existing services marketing academics and practitioners) to protect its status by placing more rigid boundaries around it. This would involve an agreement of what is 'allowed' to be called services marketing in terms of content and methodology, and what is not. There would be a 'club' mentality, and you can only be a service marketer if you abide by the rules, and stick within the boundaries. The erection of fences around the sub-discipline clearly signifies the rules and membership credentials.

If 'walking erect' involves 'erecting fences', then there is a security of knowing that ideas can be shared and communicated unambiguously between people working within the agreed rules. The downsides of 'erecting fences', however, include a slowdown in the growth of new ideas and perspectives, a narrow cultural focus (largely on the western world), and a loosening of the link between theory and practice which was so important in Stages 1, 2 and 3.

● 'Exploring'

The confidence in having a well-established services marketing sub-discipline could result, however, in the academic and practitioner community being even more ready to go 'exploring'. They may look outside the existing perimeters for new ideas (often based on studies of services in practice), engage in further interdisciplinary research, and adopt a mix of research methodologies.

If 'walking erect' involves 'exploring', it should ensure new perspectives and continued dynamism. It could, however, lead to the field being less well defined and therefore more difficult to teach and learn.

The two scenarios represent extremes, and the consequences of 'walking erect' may well be a mix of them.

It is worth noting that in the 'crawling out' and 'scurrying about' stages, much of the development of services marketing theory was based on service organisations engaging with customers on a face-to-face basis – people delivering services to people. In the 'walking erect' stage, some attention has been given to technology-based services – machines providing services to people. There are predictions[17] of a future where 'private embedded devices' will allow *things to provide services to things*. For example, electrical items such as fridges will be able to purchase their own electricity and insurance and share data on their owner's activities, cars will renew their road tax, and so on. Maybe services marketing will need to 'crawl out' again to cope with inanimate customers!

Classifying services

Starting in the early 1980s, there have been a number of very useful suggestions for classifying services. The two main reasons for service classifications are:

● *to provide a checklist of service dimensions possessed by a particular service provider*, for example, does your service have a people focus or an equipment focus? Is it carried out in the consumer's home or in the provider's premises? By using an appropriate checklist, a service organisation can identify other services which operate in a similar way, and compare marketing activities.

● *to provide a basis for determining strategic roles in the marketing and management of their service*. Service classification schemes enable current and future market positioning to be identified and justified.

Five classification methods, which have been proposed in the literature, are briefly described. They are classifications based on:

● service operations dimensions
● level of tangibility
● customer–employee presence during the service
● level of customisation/empowerment
● service delivery and processing focus.

Classification based on service operations dimensions

Silvestro *et al.*[18] provide a summary of six service dimensions against which any particular service should be viewed. The list emanates from service operations management literature.

1. Does the service have a people focus (e.g. an accountant) or an equipment focus (e.g. an automatic teller machine)?
2. What is the length of customer contact time in a typical service encounter?
3. What is the extent of customisation of the service, i.e. is it tailored to the specific needs of individual clients?

4. To what extent are the customer contact personnel empowered to exercise judgement in meeting customer needs?

5. Is the source of value added mainly 'front office' (e.g. a hairdresser) or 'back office' (e.g. in a bank)?

6. Does the service have a product focus (e.g. a car mechanic) or a process focus (e.g. a higher education course)?

By comparing the six dimensions above with a ranking of services according to volume of customers (that is, the number of customers per day processed by a typical unit), they classified services in three broad categories; professional, service shop and mass services, as seen in Table 2.2.

Table 2.2 Classification of service categories

Class of service process	Volume customers	Characteristics
Professional eg. accountant	Low	People focus High contact time High customisation High level of empowerment Front office value added Process focus
Service shop e.g. bank, hotel	Medium	People and equipment focus Medium contact time Medium customisation Medium level of empowerment Front and back office value added Process and product focus
Mass service e.g. transport	High	Equipment focus Low contact time Low customisation Low level of empowerment Back office value added Product focus

Source: Adapted from Silvestro *et al.* (see note 18).

The authors argue that the 'service strategy, control and performance measurements will differ significantly between the three (classes of service process)'. As such, the classification is of value. However, as with other classification systems, there are services which do not fit well into any of the classes – for example, spectator sports occasions, which, by virtue of volume of customers should be 'mass services', share only one (that is, low customisation) of the six typical characteristics of a mass service shown in the third column of Table 2.2.

Classification based on level of tangibility

Shostack[19] has used the level of tangibility as a way of classifying services on a goods–services spectrum. From the consumer perspective, the more

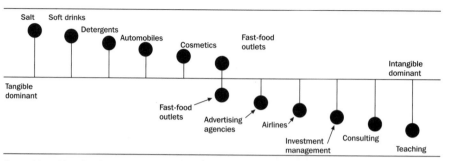

Source: Adapted from G. L. Shostack, 'Breaking Free from Product Marketing', *Journal of Marketing*, April 1977.

Figure 2.1 Scale of marketing entities.

tangible a product (that is, a good), the easier it is to evaluate (in terms of quality, suitability, and so on), whereas for the more intangible product the opposite is true. Figure 2.1 allocates products (both goods and services) on a product tangibility scale. For those products that are predominantly services, the provider may need to give more attention to the consumer's concerns about the product.

Classification based on customer–employee presence during the service

Bitner,[20] whilst researching the importance of the physical surroundings (the so-called 'servicescape') on customers and employees involved with service provision, has classified service organisations as

- self-service (customer only), e.g. ATM, golf course
- interpersonal services (both customer and employee), e.g. school, dry-cleaner
- remote service (employee only), e.g. insurance company.

Clearly, in the context of designing servicescapes, (marketing) management need to be clear as to which of the three classes their organisation fits best. Should the emphasis be on front office or back office design? In addition to a consideration of physical surroundings, the simple three-way classification can aid the focus of management activity on either operations efficiency or marketing effectiveness.[21]

Classification based on customisation/empowerment

The most comprehensive treatment of classification of services is contained in the pioneering article by Lovelock.[22] He suggests five different two-dimensional classifications of services. As an illustration, one of them is reproduced here, as it combines the dimensions (3) and (4) identified by Silvestro *et al*.[23] above. (The interested reader should refer to Lovelock's article for the four remaining classifications.)

Comparison of the extent of customisation of services with the extent of the empowerment of the customer contact personnel can be seen in Table 2.3. Such a table may provide insights into the positioning, and hence operations of a service organisation.

Table 2.3 Services classified according to customisation of service and empowerment of employees

Empowerment of employees	Level of customisation of service	
	Low	High
Low	Food retailing superstore	Telephone banking
High	National Health dental care	Accountant

Adapted from Lovelock (see note 13).

For example, a restaurant chain may wish to distance itself from a fast-food image by offering a higher level of customisation (or vice versa).

Classification based on service delivery and processing focus

This classification[24] uses a similar breakdown of service delivery systems as Silvestro *et al.* p. 29, but uses the labels 'job shop', 'assembly line' and 'batch processing' instead of professional, service shop and mass service, respectively. The other dimension of services is the processing focus, that is, whether the service focuses on the body, the mind, the tangible or the intangible assets of customers. Table 2.4 provides some examples of services with different service delivery/processing focus combinations.

Table 2.4 Services classified according to delivery system and processing focus

Processing Focus	Delivery system		
	Job shop (one-to-one) sequential)	Assembly line (one-to-one)	Batch processing (one-to-many)
Body	Doctor's appointment	Immunisation clinic	Aerobics class
Mind	Counselling	Video games in arcade	Classroom lecture
Tangible assets	Surveyor	Car wash	Retail (self-service)
Intangible assets	Financial advice	Bank teller	Financial seminar

Any process of classifying services can help in determining differences and similarities between services offered in a range of contexts, and therefore provide a basis for the sharing of successful practice.

Additionally, service classifications can clarify appropriate managerial issues. Two illustrations are given below.

1. *Using the classification based on service operations dimensions to identify common services marketing problems.*

Clemes et al.,[25] using information collected from 145 marketing managers, identified common problems facing professional services, service shops and mass services as follows:

- *Professional services:* have problems with displaying and communicating their services, calculating costs accurately, setting prices, promoting their services and controlling service quality
- *Service shops:* have problems with consumers being involved in the production of services, levels of customisation and the level of discretion to be given to employees
- *Mass services:* have problems with customers feeling no tangible ownership of the service, sense of crowding and loss of control.

Having identified common problems, businesses in the three classes can concentrate on devising methods to address them.

2. *Using the classification based on delivery system and processing focus to assess the value of 'programmed employee behaviours' such as friendliness.* Parker et al.[26] argue that the development of programmed behaviours of friendliness in employees may be more appropriate and effective in some classes of service than others. They suggest that opportunities for employees to exhibit friendliness may vary.

- *By mode of service delivery:* in 'job shop' services (for example, doctor's surgery), the opportunity for employees to show friendliness is normally limited to when the core service is being delivered (whereas customers may interact with other customers during waiting times). In 'assembly line' services (for example, a car wash business), there are opportunities for employees to offer programmed personalisation and 'good cheer'. In batch processing (for example, an aerobics class), employee friendliness can be directed towards creating a sense of shared purpose amongst customers.
- *By the nature of what is being processed*: for encounters involving people and possession processing, employee friendliness may lead to loyalty and positive customer response. Care needs to be taken over levels of friendship or friendliness shown by, or expected of service employees where intangible assets or mental stimuli are the processing focus. The question 'where are you going for your holidays?' may be acceptably friendly, and showing personal interest if asked by the hairdresser or vet, but may convey different meanings if asked by a divorce lawyer or therapist.

The classification of services by delivery system and processing focus allows service businesses to determine the appropriateness and hence the economics of training staff to behave in certain scripted ways.

Service orientation of organisations

The examples of critical service incidents, shown in Table 2.1, demonstrate that, from the customer's perspective, some service organisations are more able to deliver outstanding service quality than others. Those that deliver outstanding service quality embrace practices and procedures that demonstrate a *service orientation*.

But what are the practices and procedures that contribute to service orientation?

Lytle *et al.*[27] devised a diagnostic tool labelled SERV*OR, which provides a measure of service orientation that companies can use to devise benchmarks and explore variations. It was tested originally in building supplies and banking services, and is being further tested for its generalisability and cultural bias.[28] But, nevertheless, the dimensions (scale items) of SERV*OR are helpful in their own right as a checklist for service companies. The ten dimensions of SERV*OR are:

- customer treatment
- employee empowerment
- service technology
- service failure prevention
- service failure recovery
- service standards communication
- service vision
- servant leadership
- service rewards
- service training.

Each dimension is briefly discussed.

Customer treatment

This dimension is concerned with how well the organisation is set up to treat customers in the service encounters which form the basis of customers' evaluations of service quality. Managers and employees give their levels of agreement with statements such as 'Employees go the "extra mile" for customers' and 'We are noticeably more friendly and courteous than our competitors.'

Employee empowerment

This dimension is concerned with the responsibility and authority that employees are given in order to meet customer needs in a quick and effective way. Managers and employees give their levels of agreement with statements such as 'Employees often make important decisions without seeking management approval'.

Service technology

This dimension is concerned with the utilisation of modern technology in creating a system for excellent service delivery. Managers and employees give their levels of agreement with statements such as 'We enhance our service capabilities through the use of "state-of-the-art" technology' and 'Technology is used to build and develop higher levels of service quality.'

Service failure prevention

This dimension is concerned with the capability of the organisation to pro-actively prevent service failures. Managers and employees give their levels of agreement with statements such as 'We go out of our way to prevent customer problems' and 'We actively listen to our customers.'

Service failure recovery

This dimension is concerned with the capability of the organisation to respond effectively to service failures or customer complaints. Managers and employees give their levels of agreement with statements such as 'We provide follow-up service calls to confirm that our services are being provided properly' and 'We have an excellent customer complaint handling system for service follow-up.'

Service standards communication

This dimension is concerned with the extent to which service standards or benchmarks are understood by all employees. Managers and employees give their levels of agreement with statements such as 'Every employee under-stands all of the service standards that have been instituted by all depart-ments' and 'We use internal standards to pinpoint failures before we receive customer complaints.'

Service vision

This dimension is concerned with the clarity of pronouncement of an organisation's service goals and objectives. Managers and employees give their levels of agreement with statements such as 'There is a true commit-ment to service, not just lip service' and 'It is believed that the organisation exists to serve the needs of its customers.'

Servant leadership

This dimension is concerned with the extent to which leaders of the organisation set service standards by their own behaviour and style of management. Managers and employees give their levels of agreement with statements such as 'Management is constantly measuring service quality' and 'Managers regularly spend time "on the floor" with customers and front-line employees.'

Service rewards

This dimension is concerned with the link between employee service per-formance and compensation/reward. Managers and employees give their levels of agreement with statements such as 'This organisation noticeably celebrates excellent service.'

Service training

This dimension is concerned with the extent to which the organisation strives to improve employee skills beyond the simple but important courtesies. Managers and employees give their levels of agreement with statements such as 'Every employee receives personal skills training' and 'During training sessions, we work through exercises to identify and improve attitudes towards customers.'

It is useful for managers of service businesses to address the issues in each of the dimensions. If the SERV*OR instrument is applied subsequently, it will provide a *measure* of the business's service orientation according to its responses to the ten dimensions of service orientation.

SUMMARY

In this chapter, we have provided a contemporary and historical context for the study of services marketing. Given the scope and importance of services in many economies, few people will question the attempts by academics and practitioners to improve the understanding and practice of the marketing and management of services. Although knowledge and understanding of services marketing is increasing, and technology is changing the service offer in many cases, there are ideas from the 'crawling out' and 'scurrying about' stages which are still very influential.

In particular, the four characteristics of services – intangibility, heterogeneity, inseparability and perishability – are as fundamental today as in the 1970s and 1980s. Equally, the services marketing mix (and especially the people, process and physical evidence elements) provides a tremendously useful focus for important consumer service concerns in the twenty-first century. The various classifications of services, some of which are shown above, are used to share, practice and identify strategic directions.

In the 'walking erect' stage, there are continual efforts by companies to offer services that satisfy, or even delight customers. These efforts depend on the company's service orientation. The SERV*OR dimensions (and measures) provide a valuable contribution to understanding service orientation.

LEARNING OUTCOMES

Having read this chapter, you should be able to

● appreciate that the application of services marketing ideas can be useful in many businesses – those that were originally manufacturing businesses, as well as purer service businesses

- understand, and appreciate the managerial implications of the 'four characteristics of services' – intangibility, inseparability, heterogeneity and perishability

- have a keen awareness of the development of services marketing research and of the value and relevance of the expanded marketing mix for services

- critically evaluate and compare different service classification systems, and understand their value for practitioners

- appreciate what is meant by a service orientation and the factors that contribute to the orientation.

DISCUSSION QUESTIONS AND EXERCISES

1. Provide further examples of services that are high in search, experience and credence factors.

2. Take the story in Chapter 1 and identify instances that reflect the four characteristics of services.

3. How might the increase in Information and Digital Technology in the home affect services traditionally taking place 'on-site'?

4. Identify the people, process and physical evidence elements that occur in the critical incident stories in Table 2.1.

5. Provide further examples of services that fit in the 12 cells of Table 2.4.

Notes and references

1. Sumner-Smith, D., 'Pay-as-you-go software slashes bill for information technology', *Sunday Times: Business*, 12 November 2000.
2. Martin, C. L., 'The History, Evolution and Principles of Services Marketing: Poised for the New Millennium', *Marketing Intelligence and Planning*, 17(7), 1999, pp. 324–8.
3. Gummesson, Evert, as quoted in 'Services Marketing: A European Perspective', Christopher Lovelock, Sandra Vandermerwe, Barbara Lewis, Prentice Hall, Englewood Cliffs, NJ, 1996, p. 7.
4. Kemeny, L., 'Computer giants expand into consultancy', *Sunday Times: Business*, 17 September 2000.
5. Rodie, A. R. and Martin, C. L., 'Competing in the Service Sector: the Entrepreneurial Challenge', *International Journal of Entrepreneurial Behaviour and Research*, 7(1), 2001, pp. 5–21.
6. Freely, M., 'Party Politics', *Sunday Times*, 5 November 2000.
7. Nelson, F., 'Tesco widens Net for direct sales', *The Times*, 12 April 2000.
8. Pine II, J. B. and Gilmore, J. H., *The Experience Economy: Work is Theater and Every Business a Stage*, Harvard Business School Press, Boston, Mass., 1999.

9. Steiner, R., 'Debenham's girl who bagged the top job', *Sunday Times*, 17 September 2000.

10. Fisk, R. P., Brown, S. W. and Bitner, M. J., 'Tracking the Evolution of the Services Marketing Literature', *Journal of Retailing*, 69(1), 1993, pp. 61–91.

11. Donnelly J. H. Jr, 'Marketing Intermediaries in Channels of Distribution for Services', *Journal of Marketing*, 40 (January), 1976, pp. 57–70.

12. Shostack, G. L., 'Breaking Free from Product Marketing', *Journal of Marketing*, 41 (April), 1977, pp. 73–80.

13. Lovelock, C. H., 'Classifying Services to Gain Strategic Marketing Insights', *Journal of Marketing*, 47 (Summer), 1983, pp. 9–20.

14. Zeithaml, V. A, Berry, L. L. and Parasuraman, A., 'A Conceptual Model of Service Quality and its Implications for Future Research', *Journal of Marketing*, 49 (Fall), 1985, pp. 41–50.

15. Booms, B. H. and Bitner, M. J., 'Marketing Strategies and Organisation Structures for Service Firms', in J. Donnelly and W. R. George (eds), *Marketing of Services*, American Marketing Association, Chicago, 1981, pp. 51–67.

16. McCarthy, J. E., *Basic Marketing: A Management Approach*, Irwin, Homewood, Ill., 1960.

17. Barnatt, C., 'Customer Organisation Interfaces', Cyber Business Centre Briefing Paper, 2000. http://www.nottingham.ac.uk/cyber/Cbp-cim1.html

18. Silvestro, R., Fitzgerald, L., Johnston, R. and Voss, C., 'Towards a Classification of Service Processes', *International Journal of Service Industry Management*, 3, 1992, pp. 62–75.

19. Shostack, 'Breaking Free from Product Marketing'.

20. Bitner, M. J., 'Servicescapes: The Impact of Physical Surroundings on Customers and Employees', *Journal of Marketing*, 56, 1992, pp. 57–71.

21. Bateson, J. E. G., *Managing Services Marketing*, Dryden Press, London, 1992.

22. Lovelock, 'Classifying Services to Gain Strategic Marketing Insights'.

23. Silvestro *et al.*, 'Towards a Classification of Service Processes'.

24. Parker, C., Goodwin, C., Harris, K., and Baron, S., 'Delivering Service, Delivering Friendship: How Social Dimensions Vary Among Types of Service', *University of Nottingham Business School Discussion Paper*, Current Issues in Services Marketing (vol. II), 1999.

25. Clemes, M., Mollenkopf, D. and Burn, D., 'An Investigation of Marketing Problems across Service Typologies', *Journal of Services Marketing*, 14 (6/7), 2000, pp. 573–94.

26. Parker *et al.*, 'Delivering Service, Delivering Friendship: How Social Dimensions Vary Among Types of Service'.

27. Lytle, R. S., Hom, P. W. and Mokwa, M. P., 'SERV*OR: A managerial measure of organisational service-orientation', *Journal of Retailing*, 74(4), 1998, pp. 455–89.

28. Lynn, M. L., Lytle, R. S. and Bobek, S., 'Service Orientation in Transitional Markets: Does It Matter?', *European Journal of Marketing*, 34 (3/4), 2000, pp. 279–98.

Service goals: the use of metaphors

隐喻

LEARNING OBJECTIVES

Overall aim of the chapter:
To provide an understanding of the importance of the factory and drama/theatre metaphors in the study of service processes and content.
  In particular, the *chapter objectives* are

- to outline the uses (and limitations) of metaphors in services marketing/management theory development

- to explore the structural 'services marketing system' model which adopts the service factory concept, and to examine a range of practical service issues arising from the application of the model

- to explore the notions of customer roles and 'intended effects' on customers arising from the transposition of the drama/theatre metaphor into retail and service management.

- to provide a summary of the potential uses and range of applications of the factory and drama/theatre metaphors.

We have emphasised the importance of linking theory with practice in the study of services marketing. In this chapter some theoretical frameworks are introduced which guide practical thinking. The theory results from the creative use of metaphors in services, especially the factory and drama theatre metaphors. We start with a brief discussion of the uses and limitations of metaphors in marketing and management. A *structural* framework – the services marketing system – that is based primarily on the factory metaphor is then presented. This is followed by a demonstration, based on the theatre metaphor, of how the intended effect (of the service performance) on the consumer can be varied by the staging of the *content*. In each case, the implications for service management are given.

The uses and limitations of metaphors in marketing and management

Metaphors have been adopted widely by management academics and practitioners to achieve a variety of outcomes, most notably to:

● develop new perspectives on situations through evocative imagery

● clarify areas of uncertainty

● direct employees' behaviour in particular ways.[1]

Aristotle's dictum was that the greatest thing by far is to be the master of the metaphor.[2] In the field of services marketing, the contribution of the factory and drama metaphors to help researchers explicate service encounters and service delivery, and the contribution of the marriage metaphor to help clarify relationship marketing, have been highlighted.[3,4] There is little doubt, as we shall see, that metaphor usage has helped academics and practitioners increase their understanding of services marketing.

However, concerns have been expressed about the (over)use of metaphors in business and other contexts,[5] leading to inappropriate decision-making. For example, one of the most frequently used metaphors is the war metaphor. While this metaphor may provide evocative language – 'strategy', 'tactics', 'battles', 'outflanking' – it assumes the business has a particular goal; that is, winning. It does not have as its main goal, 'building and sustaining relationships', which is a goal more appropriate to the marriage metaphor. It has even been argued that far from us being masters of the metaphor, powerful metaphors can be masters of us. A chilling account of the use of the war metaphor in sport (rugby union) provides a reminder of the care that needs to be exercised in metaphor usage.[6]

We concentrate here on the factory and drama/theatre metaphor usage in services marketing and management.

What are the goals of the factory and drama/theatre metaphors? What insights about services, and service customers will the metaphors yield?

Using the factory metaphor: the service as a system

The use of the factory metaphor leads to some very helpful structural models of service systems that apply to a range of different services.

The 'servuction system' model

According to the 'servuction system' model (presented by Bateson, but originally developed by Eric Langeard and Pierre Eiglier[7]), customers receive a bundle of 'benefits' from each service experience as a result of their interaction with visible elements of the service system. Visible elements would include:

- all contact personnel employed by the service provider
- aspects of the inanimate environment and
- other customers within the service system.

When receiving a haircut, for example, customers come into contact with receptionists and stylists, the physical dimensions of the salon itself, heating, seating, and so on, and other customers within the salon. The model draws the distinction between visible elements and invisible components of the system. The latter would include all the other organisational activities taking place out of sight of the customers, for instance, staff training and administration. According to the model, in order to receive the benefits from the service experience the customer must be part of the system thus explicitly acknowledging the inseparability characteristic of services.

The services marketing system

Building on the original components of the 'servuction system', Lovelock[8] presents the 'services marketing system', in which service businesses are conceptualised as comprising three overlapping systems:

1. the service operations system;
2. the service delivery system; and
3. the service marketing system.

The model illustrates how the three functional areas – marketing, operations and human resources of the service business – are integrated together.

Figure 3.1 identifies the various components of the services marketing system as related to a hairdressing service. While this particular service is used for illustration, it should become obvious that the structure can be applied to services ranging from theme parks to rail travel, hospitals, retail stores and higher education courses, to name a few.

The service operations system

The service operations system comprises activities which are invisible to the customer, such as staff training, stock replenishment, and so on, as well as the visible aspects of the operation experienced directly by the customer, such as how they are treated by employees as soon as they enter the salon, or how quickly they are moved around from the washbasins to the cutting chair (if they are receiving a cut and blow-dry for example). Although there is generally no need for the customer to see most aspects of service operations (therefore they are kept invisible), some service providers deliberately expose

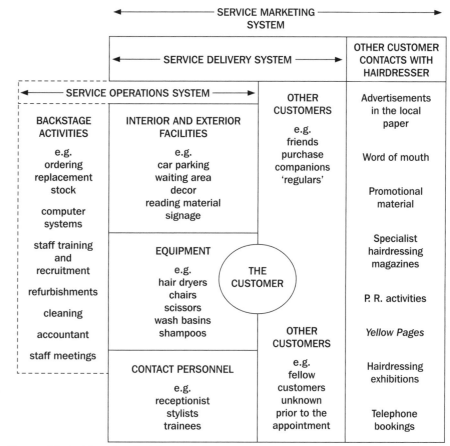

Source: Adapted from Lovelock (see note 8).

Figure 3.1 The unisex hairdresser as a services marketing system.

customers to 'backstage' activities in an attempt to influence positively their perceptions of the quality of the service provided. Restaurants frequently invite customers to visit kitchens where the food is being prepared either before or after they have eaten. This is designed to reinforce an image of fresh food prepared in a hygienic cooking environment that may influence their perception of the overall quality of their experience.

The service delivery system

The service delivery system encompasses not only the visible elements of the service operating system, employees and the physical facilities, but also includes exposure to other customers. In many service businesses, positive on-site interaction can have a significant impact on customers' overall perception of their experience. In the hairdressing salon, customers may find themselves waiting for a period of time for their particular stylist in a communal reception area. Conversations frequently take place at this point between customers who have never met prior to entering the delivery system.

善意地　取笑

Although the discussions may consist largely of banter and pleasantries not directly connected with the hairdressing service (for example, conversations about the weather, traffic in town, and so on), the exchanges can for many customers improve their overall experience by making the time pass more quickly. Occasionally, when conversations turn to the service itself, the provider can benefit positively from the exchange. For instance, one customer who has visited the salon several times may comment on the skill and expertise of a certain stylist, and the generally professional attitude of all employees. To new customers attending for the first time the comments might have a positive influence on their opinion of the salon.

The service marketing system

The service marketing system incorporates elements of the service experience that may contribute to the customer's overall view of the organisation but are not specifically part of the delivery system. Clearly, many of these are the elements which the organisation may not be able to control, such as conversations customers may have about the salon with friends or relatives at home, or exposure to the service they may get from reading a hairdressing editorial in the local paper.

Lovelock feels that by conceptualising the service experience as three overlapping systems, services managers are forced to consider their business from a customer perspective rather than a purely operations perspective. It highlights the importance of managing all elements of the business that are visible to customers.

Using the structural models to understand services

A number of issues for service managers arise directly from a consideration of the structures above.

- How can/should we control customer involvement in the service?
- What attention should we give to contact personnel?
- How do we deal with customers' multiple points of contact in the service delivery system?
- How do we maintain a balance between marketing effectiveness and operational efficiency?
- Given that a service is provided at a specific time and over time, how do we manage the timing of consumption?
- What limitations to growth may be implied by the structural elements of services?

We deal with each of these questions in turn.

Controlling customer involvement in the service

The models highlight the involvement of the customer in the service experience. As Bateson[9] points out, consumers are always involved in the factory, and although their participation may be active or passive, they are always there. In an aerobics class, for example, to get maximum benefit from the experience, customers are expected to exert a degree of physical effort during the class, as well as engage in cognitive activity beforehand, selecting the most appropriate class to attend. As a result, much of management's attention in service organisations is devoted to devising strategies for managing customer participation. Different tactics may be used by the instructor, for example, to influence both forms of participation. Loud music might be played to encourage physical participation during the class, and an advertisement placed in the local paper to encourage people to attend.

Because customers themselves can play such a crucial role in the delivery process, a number of writers advocate that they should be treated as 'partial employees' and the same strategies that are used to control and motivate employees should be used with customers; they should be given clear instructions as to what is expected of them and appropriate rewards for their contribution. Another strategy for controlling the level of customer involvement in the service delivery system is simply to replace human with machine-based inputs. Although machines are generally more predictable than humans, this is not an option considered by many of the service providers described in this book, as human contact is considered by customers to be a key component of service quality.

Strategies used to manage customer involvement are discussed in more detail in Chapter 4.

Attention to contact personnel

Contact personnel feature prominently in the service system and are perceived as being part of the service product. With many services there is often little or no tangible evidence available to the consumer before purchase to help them make an assessment about the quality of what they are paying for. Where this is the case, customers often use the appearance and manner of service employees as a first point of reference when deciding whether or not to make a purchase. Although a restaurant may be listed in the *Yellow Pages*, a new customer cannot make an assessment about the quality of the food or the standard of service simply from the telephone listing. However, a brief telephone conversation with a restaurant employee can have a vital impact on the customer's decision to visit that restaurant instead of another. Faced with uncertainty about the purchase decision, customers turn to service employees for reassurance and to form quality perceptions before, during and after the service experience. Effective human resource management strategies are therefore very important in service organisations and are considered in more detail in Chapter 7. The task of managing employees is clearly problematic. Bateson[10] notes that 'unlike physical goods people are not inanimate objects but have feelings and emotions'.

One approach to managing the human resources of the organisation (both service employees and, to a certain extent, customers) is to present them with 'scripts' to follow during the service encounter, to ensure that they know exactly what to expect and how to behave. Many organisations favour the use of a set 'script' by employees in an effort to standardise the quality of service delivery (for example, servers at McDonald's who are encouraged to invite all customers to 'have a nice day'). (McGrath[11] notes, in her study of service encounters in a small gift shop, how employees frequently have different scripts for their frontstage and backstage activities which, although they may be contradictory in content, are considered to be acceptable business practice and part of their role as sales assistants. She notes how, onstage, sales assistants reassure customers about their purchase with comments like 'that's wonderful' or 'lovely', yet as soon as they go backstage they comment to fellow employees 'I didn't think we'd ever sell that!' and 'That is one of the few things in this store that I personally cannot stand.') Other service organisations may 'empower' employees to adapt their script to the behaviour and personality of the individual customers in an effort to improve the quality of the service encounter. This is where the theatre/drama metaphor can help clarify the strategies of service managers (see next section). Empowerment of employees is discussed in more detail in Chapter 7.

Multiple points of contact

Although clearly the customers' contact with employees is very important, the structural models highlight the importance of every 'point of contact' in the delivery system. Where these are considered by customers to be especially satisfying or dissatisfying, they have been defined as 'critical' incidents.[12] All points of contact in this context present customers with an opportunity to evaluate the service provider and form an opinion of service quality. In a restaurant, the 'critical' dissatisfying incident could be a telephone call with an employee, the smell of food being prepared in the kitchen, or the seating arrangements inside. A critical incident for one customer may go unnoticed by another. The exterior decor may be enough to prevent some customers from entering a restaurant, while others will not make an assessment of service quality until they actually taste the food. It becomes very important that the service provider is aware of each point of contact in the system and, more importantly, the impact it has on the customer's perception of service quality.

Many firms underestimate the number of potentially critical incidents that exist within the system. A simple analysis of the points of contact between a client and an accountant, for example, reveals the following pattern of critical incidents and highlights potential problem areas that relate to other elements of the service besides interaction with contact personnel.

Initial enquiry:

- read advertisement in local paper
- contact with receptionist
- contact with accountant's building/offices

First meeting:

- exposure of interior of building and facilities
- second contact with receptionist
- meeting with accountant
- contact with other employees of the firm
- exposure to physical evidence of service quality (e.g. accounts prepared for other clients)

Subsequent meetings:

- receive completed work
- further telephone conversations with employees of firm
- exposure to word of mouth from other clients
- contact with related suppliers and buyers
- exposure to payment schemes

Although this is clearly not a comprehensive list of potential interactions, and will vary from one client to another, it illustrates the number of opportunities that the client has to make an assessment of the quality of the service being provided. The process of service design, discussed in Chapter 6, explicitly acknowledges the many points of contact in a visual form. It is one way of identifying, and designing out, potential service failure points.

Marketing effectiveness versus operational efficiency

A trade-off has to be made, in many service organisations, between marketing effectiveness and operational efficiency. Looking at Figure 3.1, where should investments or savings be made – in the Service Marketing System or the Service Operation System?

The success of many of the small operators described in the cases in this book depends on providing a personal service for customers; that is, a concentration on the service marketing system. This clearly has benefits from a marketing perspective as it enables the service provider to respond quickly to the changing needs and requirements of individual customers. However, the greater the degree of customisation in the service offer, the less opportunity there is for cross-utilisation of resources. If there is a loss of production efficiency caused by the provision of tailor-made services (for example, where a first-class restaurant provides a personalised menu for special client groups), large organisations will often compensate for this by charging a higher price. This is a simple concept that is often forgotten by smaller operators who struggle to identify the real costs associated with the service operation system and consequently find it difficult to price accordingly.

Concern with timing of consumption

The service manager needs to be concerned about when the customer consumes the service as he/she is part of the system when consuming. A manufacturer of chocolate bars, in contrast, is more concerned about the location of purchase than the time of ultimate consumption (except perhaps to assist in the new product development process), as it has no immediate impact on the production process. The timing of consumption becomes a problem for many service organisations as demand levels are rarely stable and predictable. Most services experience fluctuations in demand that often vary from week to week and year to year. For example, although a tour operator may plan for an increase in demand for holidays to Turkey during the summer months, a sudden change in the stability of the economy in the country in May could dramatically change the level of demand. Unlike a manufacturing organisation, the tour operator cannot store up holidays to Turkey until the economy stabilises and demand returns. Strategies have to be devised to retain customers during the summer months, perhaps by offering alternative holiday destinations. This would be one instance of how service organisations manage the supply of their service to match the pattern of demand. Similarly, the hairdresser can reschedule working hours of staff to account for the fact that few customers want their hair cutting on a Monday. Top stylists are given a day off on Monday in return for working on Saturday, one of the hairdresser's busiest days of the week. An alternative strategy facing service business is to attempt to influence the pattern of customer demand to suit supply. The hairdresser might offer customers the opportunity to get a free haircut if they visit between nine and twelve on a Tuesday morning.

Many service providers find it very difficult to match demand and supply on all occasions and, where demand exceeds supply, queuing and reservation systems are put into operation. Customer feedback highlights the fact that delays in service delivery, often characterised by long queues, can have a negative impact on customer evaluations of the service.[13,14] The ideal solution would be to eliminate queues completely by careful operations management. However, where this is not possible, service providers are advised to 'change the customer's wait experience (by perceptions management) so that it results in less uncertainty and anger'.[15] Customers become most annoyed and frustrated when they are forced to wait for a service without being given an explanation for the delay. Service providers are advised to communicate to customers as quickly as possible why they are being asked to wait. Where the reason can be clearly identified by customers themselves, for example, waiting for a ride at a funfair or to pay for goods at a supermarket checkout, strategies must be put in place to make the wait as pleasant as possible for customers. Magazines that are provided in dentists' waiting rooms for customers to read, and videos played to customers waiting in a queue for a funfair ride, are both examples of tactics used by service organisations to help consumers pass the inevitable 'waiting' time pleasurably.

Growth limitation

Customer participation in the system limits the growth opportunities available to the service firm. Where customers have to travel to the service organisation to benefit from the service (for example, hairdresser, colour consultant), the location of the service becomes critically important and a major source of competitive advantage. Where there is very little perceived difference between the components of the offer (for example, dentistry), a convenient location can make all the difference. When trying to expand a service business, owners are faced with problems that stem largely from the intangible components of the offer.

Although it may be possible to open several physically identical hair-dressing studios in different locations, it is not possible to replicate the personality and skills of one particular stylist in all the salons. As a result, organisations are constantly looking for ways to expand their target market that do not involve a physical change in location. George Ball and Son, the funeral director (Case Study 2), for example, has become the nominated funeral director for the UK's largest prepayment plan 'Chosen Heritage'. This enables the company to gain access to a new target market without physically having to move location.

Using the theatre/drama metaphor: the service as a performance

Grove and Fisk[16] present a perspective that considers services as 'drama', with features present at a service encounter being likened to those contributing to a theatrical production. They identify the key components of the service experience as being the setting, the actors, the audience and the performance. The actors and audience are the various human participants (for example, the salon employees and customers, in a hairdressing context), the setting is the physical environment (for example, the salon itself, decor, lighting, and so on) and the performance, the process of service assembly. All three components are closely interrelated.

In the context of the funeral service, management attention would need to focus on the parts played by the various players in the team – the ministers, doctors, gravediggers, as well as direct employees of the company – in order to control the whole performance. While the actual funeral itself might only last for a few hours, as with a play, the audience has difficulty appreciating the amount of preparation that has gone on backstage to get ready for the 'performance', namely coffin engraving, bereavement counselling, gown hire, and so on. All too often customers relate the price charged solely to the actual funeral ceremony itself without considering the costs of the backstage activities.

Although Grove and Fisk acknowledge that the service as drama metaphor cannot be applied equally well to all service businesses, they consider it to be a simpler and more powerful concept than the service factory. It draws management attention to the importance of managing customer (audience) involvement in the service experience, as well as managing the production itself – the stage design, layout and the performance of the actors (employees). The notion of 'role playing' can be used in this context to examine the interpersonal relationships between service customers and employees. Both sets of participants can be seen to be working to a script that is determined by their respective role expectations. Coffin bearers, for example, are expected by their employer to dress and speak to customers in a manner that is appropriate to their role. Their script is closely controlled to ensure that it conforms to customer expectations. In these circumstances, although the unpredictability of demand for the service itself necessitates the use of casual labour for such jobs, a disproportionate amount of time is spent recruiting bearers because of the importance of their contribution in terms of meeting customer expectations. If just one coffin bearer were to act 'out of character' for a small part of the ceremony, it could significantly lower the customers' perception of the quality of the entire service.

Lessons from the theatre

Services marketing can learn from the many different theatrical movements that have been developed to create distinct audience responses. Many retail organisations, in particular, do claim to be offering 'retail theatre', but their public statements betray a lack of awareness of true theatre.[17] Table 3.1 demonstrates that a study of the main theatrical movements of the twentieth century – theatrical realism, political realism, surrealism and absurd theatre – can provide a focus for retail service managers who acknowledge the potentially different customer roles, and aim to create appropriate intended effects to match them.

Table 3.1 Classification of customer roles and intended effects: retail applications

Theatrical movement	Role of the customer	Intended effect	Retail management focus
Theatrical realism (practitioner: Stanislavski)	Voyeur	● The customer recognises a realistic setting. 'I am observing "a slice of real life".'	● Present merchandise in a realistic setting.
		● The customer has no sense of involvement. 'I am observing the performance from a distance.'	● Maintain a distance between the customer and the presentation.
Political realism (practitioner: Brecht)	Spect-actor	● The customer's role is transparent and clearly understood by both parties. 'I am fully aware that this retailer is trying to sell me something.'	● Present merchandise in a simple, open and honest environment. Empower employees to be open and honest about their roles and feelings towards the merchandise.

Table 3.1 *contd.*

		● The customer has the opportunity on-site, to be critical of the offer and the way that it is presented. 'I feel comfortable challenging any aspect of what's on offer.'	● Provide extensive opportunities for customer participation. Develop mechanisms to encourage customers to be critical of merchandise.
Surrealism (practitioner: Artaud)	Sense-ceptor	● The customer has a sensory experience. 'I feel as if I have been through this experience. I know what it feels like.'	● Provide opportunities for customers to 'experience' events. ● Provide stimulus to arouse depth of affective response.
Absurd theatre (practitioner: Craig)	Connoisseur	● The customer is intellectually challenged by what is presented. 'I don't know what this means but I will try to make sense of it.'	● Present merchandise in a 'thought provoking', but minimalist, way. No attempt to be made to explain logic behind the presentation. Little information to be provided.
		● The customer response is an individual response. 'In my opinion this is about ... but I will keep it to myself.'	● No opportunities to be provided for customer–employee or customer–customer interactions.

Source: Adapted from Baron, Harris and Harris (2001) (see note 17).

Table 3.1 can help retail and service management to focus their offer according to what they would like to be the intended effect of the 'perform-ance' on their customers. Take, for example, the retailing of computer soft-ware. Traditionally, the merchandising of such products has simply involved making shelves and shelves of CDs and manuals accessible to the self-service customer. In the Microsoft store in San Francisco, they have tried a different formula. According to the business manager, the store is an attempt to get the software out of the box and present it in a lifestyle environment. The store is split into 'successful living', 'small business', 'creative publishing', and 'road warrior' areas. In the 'successful living' area, for instance, boxes of software (for example, 'Family Lawyer') are placed on shelves with silk, beanbag wrist rests, etched glass vases and mugs with definitions of 'passionate' written on them.

Using Table 3.1, managers could consider strategies for merchandising such products, based on each of the four theatrical movements, and the corresponding *defined* customer role.

- Customer as voyeur

For the customers to adopt this role, they must see a totally realistic setting from a safe distance. This could be achieved through introducing even more realism in working, living, learning and playing areas in the store, with employees playing appropriate parts – for example, drinking coffee in the living area, playing computer and other games in the playing area. Guidelines as to how to create the 'customer as voyeur' role can be gained from a study of Stanislavski's use of theatrical stage settings in theatrical realism.

- Customer as spect-actor

For the customers to adopt this role (that is, of critical participants in the service), their role must be transparent and understood by both parties, and they must have the on-site opportunity to be critical of the product and merchandising. This could be achieved by creating rooms in the store explicitly for debates about the product, where customers can share knowledge about the products, and by having regular on-site IT educational sessions. Guidelines as to how to create the 'customer as spect-actor' role can be gained from a study of Brecht's use of theatrical stage settings in political realism.

- Customer as sense-ceptor

For the customers to adopt this role, they must receive, and be immersed in a sensory experience. This could most readily be achieved by a section of the software store entirely devoted to virtual reality experiences. However, care must be taken to ensure all the activities contribute to an unambiguous intended effect. Guidelines as to how to create the 'customer as sense-ceptor' role can be gained from a study of Artaud's use of theatrical stage settings in surrealist theatre.

- Customer as connoisseur

For the customers to adopt this role, they must be intellectually challenged by what is presented, and be able to give an individual interpretation of the performance. This could be achieved by ensuring that the combination of artefacts in the display area has no real explanation, and customers could be challenged (electronically) to reach their purchase goals. Guidelines as to how to create the 'customer as connoisseur' role can be gained from a study of Craig's use of theatrical stage settings in absurd theatre.

The example of retailing of software shows how, by using the theatre metaphor, the service experience surrounding the display of physical products can be varied. The same principles can be applied to the retailing of other goods and services. Some formats may more readily lend themselves to particular customer roles. For example, retailers of sports goods, such as Niketown, are giving customers a sensory experience – what it is like to be a top sportsperson. The theatre/drama metaphor, and Table 3.1, provides ideas for innovation in service content, and segmentation of customers, which can complement the structural insights provided in Figure 3.1. To paraphrase Goodwin,[18] drama can be moved into the service factory.

SUMMARY

Some fundamental theory and frameworks for the marketing of services have been inspired by two common metaphors: the factory metaphor and the theatre/drama metaphor. If the metaphors are understood, and used appropriately, they add to our understanding of services marketing. The metaphors can even be mixed as argued in the previous section. In this way, both the structure and content of services are given due regard. A summary of the use of these two popular metaphors is provided in Table 3.2.

Table 3.2 The use of the factory and theatre/drama metaphors

	Factory metaphor	Theatre/drama metaphor
Strategic goals	Efficiency	Rave reviews from audiences
Focus of attention	Structure and process	Performance
Assumptions about consumers	Inputs contributing to production	Audience requiring cues from actors
Assumptions about the service	Automated factory	Stage play
Recommendations to management	Design systems and procedures	Coach actors and write scripts
Potential areas of application	Airlines, fast food, rail travel	Theme parks, pubs, restaurants, retailers

Summarising the factory metaphor

It is assumed that the goal of a service is efficiency. Therefore, we try to get consumers through the system quickly, reduce bottlenecks and queues, and acknowledge the importance of quality control. The focus of attention is the structure and total process through the system. For example, with rail travel, we should examine all the points of contact the passenger has with the service, from the purchase of the ticket right through to the ordering of the taxi at the destination point. The consumers are assumed to be contributors to production, but also the cause of bottlenecks. They are seen as 'partial employees' who can help with service production. For example, regular hospital patients can help new patients familiarise themselves with the environment and systems. The service itself is likened to an automatic factory and terms such as 'inputs', 'process', 'outputs' and 'productivity' become part of the language.

Summarising the theatre/drama metaphor

It is assumed that the goal of the service is to receive 'rave reviews' from the audience (customers). There is a need to acknowledge explicitly that customers evaluate their experiences individually. The focus of attention is on the content of the service; that is, the interactions that take place involving the actors (contact personnel) and audience. Roles and scripts of both actors and audience are of prime importance, as is the design of the service setting. The consumers, being likened to an audience, require cues, leading to stimulation and an 'experience'. The service itself is compared to a stage play, incorporating all the hedonistic elements of service consumption, with attention being drawn to the performance, rather than the process. Terms such as 'front- and backstage', 'settings', 'roles' and 'scripts' become part of the language.

As is seen in the final two rows of Table 3.2, the recommendations to management may depend on the features of a particular service which determine which of these two metaphors is predominant.

LEARNING OUTCOMES

Having read this chapter, you should be able to

- apply conceptual frameworks, emanating from the use of factory and drama/theatre metaphors, to explore key issues affecting service management

- understand the implications, for strategy, HRM and operations, of adopting the factory or drama/theatre metaphors, and the assumptions made about the customers

- appreciate the origin of terms, such as delivery, process, productivity, setting, roles and scripts, which are part of the language of services marketing and management research.

DISCUSSION QUESTIONS AND EXERCISES

1. Draw a Services Marketing System for George Ball and Son (Case Study 2). What difficulties did you experience in employing the Services Marketing System for a funeral service?

2. Outline some 'scripts' that employees have employed with you in service encounters.

3. Try searching the internet to find details on marketing courses that they offer. How many clicks on the mouse did it take to find the information?

4. To what extent do customers in an open street market play the role of 'spectactor'?

5. What should the goal of lectures be – efficiency or the subject of rave reviews?

Notes and references

1. Morgan, G., *Imaginization: The Creative Art of Management*, Sage Publications, Newbury Park, Ca., 1993.

2. Monin, M. and Monin, D. J., 'Rhetoric and Action: When a Literary Drama Tells the Organization's Story', *Journal of Organizational Change Management*, vol. 10, no. 1, 1997, pp. 47–60.

3. Goodwin, C., 'Moving the Drama into the Factory: The Contribution of Metaphors to Services Research', *European Journal of Marketing*, vol. 30. no.9, 1996, pp. 13–36.

4. Tynan, C., 'A review of the marriage analogy in Relationship Marketing,' *Journal of Marketing Management*, vol. 13, no. 7, pp. 695–704.

5. Hunt, S. D. and Menon, A., 'Metaphors and Competitive Advantage: Evaluating the Use of Metaphors in Theories of Competitive Strategy', *Journal of Business Research*, vol. 33, 1995, pp. 81-90.

6. Monin, M. and Monin, D. J. 'Rhetoric and Action: When a Literary Drama Tells the Organization's Story'.

7. Bateson, J. E. G., Managing Services Marketing: Text and Readings, 2nd edn., The Dryden Press 1992.

8. Lovelock, C. H., *Managing Services Marketing, Operations, and Human Resources*, 2nd edn., Prentice Hall International, Englewood Cliffs, NJ, 1992.

9. Bateson, J. E. G., Managing Services Marketing: Text and Readings, 2nd edn., The Dryden Press 1992.

10. Ibid.

11. McGrath, M. A., 'An Ethnography of a Gift Store: Trappings, Wrappings and Rapture', *Journal of Retailing*, vol. 65, no. 4, 1989, pp. 421–49.

12. Bitner, M. J., Booms, B. H. and Tetreault, M. S., 'The Service Encounter: Diagnosing Favourable and Unfavourable Incidents', *Journal of Marketing*, vol. 54, January 1990.

13. Scotland, R., 'Customer Service: A Waiting Game', *Marketing*, 11 March 1992, pp. 1–3.

14. Taylor, S., 'Waiting for Service: The Relationship Between Delays and Evaluations of Service', *Journal of Marketing*, vol. 58, April 1994, pp. 56–69.

15. Ibid.

16. Grove, S. J. and Fisk, R. P., 'The Dramaturgy of Services Exchange: An Analytical Framework for Services Marketing', in L. L. Berry, G. L. Shostack and G. D. Upah (eds), *Emerging Perspectives on Services Marketing*, American Marketing Association, Chicago, 1983.

17. Baron, S., Harris, K and Harris, R. 'Retail Theatre: The Intended Effect of the Performance', Journal of Service Research, vol. 4, no. 2, pp. 102–117.

18. Goodwin, C., 'Moving the Drama into the Factory: The Contribution of Metaphors to Services Research'.

Service encounters

LEARNING OBJECTIVES

Overall aim of the chapter:
To provide a comprehensive evaluation of the encounters that a customer has, in a service context, with contact personnel, other customers and equipment/technology.
  In particular, the *chapter objectives* are

- to demonstrate both the frequency and variety of interactions faced by a customer in the service encounter

- to emphasise the significance and managerial implications associated with customer interactions in the service encounter

- to outline the distinguishing features of interpersonal interactions between customers and employees and the principal causes of satisfaction and dissatisfaction with these interactions

- to provide an insight into the frequency and importance of customer-to-customer interactions, and some methods for compatibility management

- to present recent research on customer interactions with technology-based services and the principal causes of satisfaction and dissatisfaction with the interactions.

Introduction

'Service encounters' has been identified as a key component of the current agenda for service marketers.[1] As noted in the previous chapter, every time customers come into contact with any aspect of the service delivery system they are presented with an opportunity to evaluate the service provider and form an opinion of service quality. A customer may form an impression about the quality of a dentist's work, for example, from a brief conversation with another patient in the waiting room, or simply from a glance at the wallpaper in the surgery. Irrespective of the nature and length of the contact, each 'encounter' represents an important 'moment of truth' for the customer. The latter term, originally introduced by Normann[2] has more recently been termed the 'bullfight metaphor' by Mattsson[3] as it underlines strongly 'the uniqueness and the importance of every encounter between the customer and the service provider'.

Shostack[4] provides a helpful definition of the service encounter, referring to it as the 'period of time during which a customer directly interacts with a service'. This acknowledges the notion, from Chapter 3, that customers have multiple points of contact. Furthermore, customers relate to the 'period of time' when asked to recall incidents with the service. Two examples are now given.

Example 1 – Mother takes 5-year-old daughter to 'kiddies' fun and fitness class' at a leisure centre.

- Saw details of kiddies' fun and fitness class on leisure centre website

- Rang leisure centre to enquire about this 'new' service

- Parked the car outside the leisure centre

- Met the girl running the class, and talked about what would happen

- Saw new fitness studio

- Met other kids in the class

- Sat outside with other mothers, while the class took place

Example 2 – Adult male requires quick repair on car.
- Rang dealer where car last serviced, found new dealership taken over

- Rang new dealership

- Dropped car off at dealership, parking spaces available

- Explained problem to man at dealership, (his role not clear)

- Rang up later – not contacted as promised

- Saw female receptionist.

- Chatted to another customer while receptionist in back office

- Talked over repairs, bill less than expected, exhaust adjusted 'free of charge'

- Picked up car and drove home

The examples fit Shostack's definition of the encounter. Her definition includes interpersonal interactions and also customer contact with physical facilities, technology and other tangible elements – interactions that were highlighted in the Service Delivery System in Chapter 3. Because of the inseparability characteristic of services, encounters will be *frequent* in the service delivery system. Because of the intangibility characteristic of services, the *tangible* aspects are important, that is, the people the customers meet, as well as the physical surroundings and equipment. Because of the hetero-geneity characteristic of services, there will be *differences* in the nature and customer perceptions of encounters.

In this chapter we examine the significance of service encounters, as well as the related managerial issues. This is followed by a detailed look at the first three of the following types of interactions:

- customer with service employees
- customer with fellow customers
- customer with technology/equipment
- customer with the physical environment.

The customer interactions with the physical environment will be covered in Chapter 6, as part of service design.

Given the nature of the four types of interaction, the theory on service encounters draws on elements of communication theory, interpersonal skills, sociology, environmental and cognitive psychology, ergonomics and human–machine interfaces.

Significance of service encounters

Why, then, has 'service encounters' been identified as such a key com-ponent of the current agenda? It is because:

- service encounters are seen to influence customers' perceptions of service quality
- there are opportunities to *manage* service encounters.

All the interactions that take place during the 'period of time' have the potential to influence quality perceptions, and the greater the number of interactions, the more chances there are for customers to judge the service (and spot mistakes!). Even relatively straightforward services, such as those described in Examples 1 and 2, consist of a mix of customer interactions with service employees, fellow customers, technology and physical surround-ings. If services are designed to reduce the potential number of customer interactions, those that remain are critical. The words of advice to webpage designers are apt. Go for fewer clicks, but enhance the encounters.

Not all the interactions are equally critical. In Example 1, according to the mother, the two things that really mattered were the manner of the girl instructor (who checked the daughter's prior experience, and treated her as someone special), and her daughter's interaction with the other children. In Example 2, the most important elements were the attitude of the person on the phone at the new dealership (welcoming), and the explanation of the bill at the end, which helped recover some ill feeling about not being contacted when the car was ready to be picked up. At a more extreme level, a bad landing in an aeroplane is likely to be the most critical memory, however good the rest of the flight had been – good food, pleasant conversation, polite airline staff.

Despite the mix and some of the complexities of the interactions in service encounters, there are seemingly obvious ways of managing them. Employees can be trained to act and react appropriately. Physical surroundings and equipment/technology can be designed to create appropriate environments and way-finding. Even customer–customer interactions can be controlled or encouraged. Most research on service encounters, therefore, is significant in that there are easily understood management implications resulting from it.

Before examining the different types of customer interactions in more detail, we outline some of the more general managerial issues associated with each of them.

Customer interacts with service employee(s) – managerial issues

● How do we train employees to increase customers' levels of satisfaction and perceived quality of the service?

First of all, we need to know what *customers themselves* find satisfying and dissatisfying about services. There is a variety of consumer research techniques that can be used; qualitative methods such as interviews, observation, critical incident stories, and quantitative methods such as surveys and controlled experiments. Second, we need to assess whether the incidents that customers find (dis)satisfying are generic across a range of services, or whether they are situation specific. Third, we need to examine different styles of employee training methods. Some are appropriate for training employees to 'follow the rule book'. Others are more appropriate for encouraging improvisation.

● To what extent, and in what circumstances, should employees be empowered?

As customers, we can often feel frustrated when a service employee seems unable to carry out what seems like a very straightforward adaptation to a service element without first gaining authority from a more senior person. For example, the railway train guard may not be empowered to allow passengers to use empty first-class carriages even when they are causing potentially dangerous congestion by having to stand up in the aisles of the economy class. Or the administrative assistant may not be authorised to accept a student assignment after the 'due time', whatever the circumstances. Clearly, as these examples imply, there is often a trade-off between employees applying rigidly a set of fair rules, and employees adapting and improvising without the need for higher-level approval.

Customer interacts with fellow customers – managerial issues

- How can we manage customer compatibility?

As many services take place in the presence of other customers, the fellow customers (often strangers) may affect perceptions of the service. This is quite normal in services such as air travel, aerobics classes, coach tour holidays and tutorials. It is in the interest of service management to keep together customers with similar behaviours and tastes, and separate those with different behaviours and tastes.

- To what extent do customer-to-customer interactions determine the service experience?

Although it may be more difficult for service providers to identify and control interpersonal exchanges between customers in the service environment, such exchanges have the potential to affect the customer's perception of the quality[5] of the service provided and are easily recalled by customers.[6,7]

- To what extent can/should we encourage/discourage customer-to-customer interactions?

Martin and Pranter[8] are anxious to point out that compatibility management is more important in some service environments than others. For example, careful management of the encounter is needed when customers are expected to share time, space or service equipment with one another. Where the service experience necessitates that customers are in close proximity with each other for a period of time, there may be advantages to be gained by encouraging customer-to-customer interactions. Customers travelling on long train journeys often hold conversations with the person sitting in the seat next to them, which passes the time pleasantly. As we see later, the extent to which managers should encourage or discourage customer-to-customer interactions is linked with customer involvement and participation in services.

Customer interacts with technology/equipment – managerial issues

- What are the gains and losses involved in replacing interpersonal service with self-service?

The heterogeneity characteristic of services arises mainly from variations associated with the human service employee. Much of this variation could be eliminated by replacing the human-based contribution with technology-based services. Examples are automatic teller machines for banking transactions, 'pay at the pump' options for petrol purchases, book/music purchases using the internet, and airline ticket machines. While there are gains in the consistency, and possibly reliability through the use of technology-based services, many customers do value human contact,[9] and attention must be given to clarifying customers' roles with self-service systems.[10]

- What are the attitudes and behaviours of customers with regard to technology-based services (especially the Internet)?

It has been suggested that customers' sources of satisfaction and dissatisfaction with technology-based services may be different from those associated with interpersonal services.[11] With the increasing use of the internet,[12] in particular, there is a need for management to use creative research techniques to understand more fully the customer needs of, and experiences with the technology.

Customer interacts with the physical surroundings – managerial issues

- How do we design the physical setting of a service to encourage 'approach' rather than 'avoidance' behaviours of customers?

As consumers, we encounter many types of designed 'servicescapes'. Some are designed to create experiences for us (for example, 'theme bars'). Some are designed to support direction finding (for example, airports). Some are designed to support the comfort of the occupants (for example, children's wards in hospitals). Some are designed to suit the purposes of an event (for example, the layout of a seminar room or lecture theatre). Some are designed to attract and retain potential customers (for example, shopping malls and retail stores). We have all probably avoided certain service settings, or wished to leave them at the earliest opportunity, or in contrast 'felt at home' in other settings. The design of the 'servicescape' can be particularly important, as customers' *first* encounter with a service is often with the physical environment.

- Can 'servicescape' design ideas be transferable across different types of services?

The majority of servicescapes cater for interpersonal services, with both customers and employees on-site. Others cater for self-service operations, where only customers are on-site. There are also remote services, such as 'helplines', where only employees are on-site.[13] Rather than each type of service 'starting from scratch', can ideas from one type of service be transferred to another where on-site presence is similar? Examples of transfer of ideas can be seen with some interpersonal services: 'theatre' being applied to retail stores, and theme park activities present in shopping malls.

Customer interactions in service encounters

The managerial issues raised in the previous section have resulted in research that has been undertaken to increase our understanding of customer interactions in services. We now summarise some of the work relating to customer interactions with *service employees*, *fellow customers* and *technology/equipment*.

Interactions between customers and employees

Distinguishing characteristics of service encounters

Czepiel *et al.*[14] identify a number of distinguishing characteristics of service encounters; that is, how they may differ from other types of interpersonal interactions such as those with friends. The characteristics may not always be the case for all services, and not always desirable, but do apply to customer–employee service encounters in many different services, and so are important to recognise. They are outlined below.

● Service encounters are purposeful.

Contact generally takes place for a particular reason so that at least one party can achieve a specific goal. This is clearly the case when a patient comes into contact with a doctor in the surgery, or when a customer calls a waiter to his/her table for advice on a menu. The specific purpose of many encounters may not be immediately obvious as it often relates to deeper psychological goals such as relieving boredom, demonstrating superior product knowledge, or simply seeking reassurance about a purchase decision.

● Service providers for their part are not generally altruistic.

They are providing a service because they are being paid to do so. This clearly has implications for the way employees and customers approach the service encounter. As McGrath[15] found, in her study of retailing in a gift shop, many employees consider it to be part of their job to give customers a false opinion about products being sold in an effort to increase sales. Customers for their part expect this to happen. For example, a recent study of the conversations that took place between customers in a retail furniture store in the North of England[16] revealed that customers preferred to ask other customers (whom they had never previously met before entering the store) for personal opinions about products rather than ask sales assistants. It would appear that staff could not be trusted to give an honest opinion in their role as store employees.

● In the service encounter, prior acquaintance between participants is not required.

As consumers, we can go into a bar, hairdressers, shop or hotel and interact with a service employee without ever meeting them before. Czepiel *et al.* describe the relationship as a 'special kind of stranger relationship' that operates within a certain set of limitations and boundaries. Because of the clear understanding of the boundaries of the relationship, they note that customers often engage in a higher level of self-disclosure than they would in any other social relationship. This is the case, for example, with clients of a colour consultant or wardrobe advisor, who realise that in order to get the most out of the encounter they must reveal a great deal about their personal lives to the service provider, who is in effect a complete stranger. However, where there is prior acquaintance, 'regulars' may receive a special type of service.

- In most encounters task related information exchange dominates.

Although service employees may be encouraged to engage initially in pleasantries with customers, the important conversations always relate to the service being provided. The train passenger will ask from which platform the train leaves. The bank customer will simply want to know the exchange rate when changing dollars to sterling. The owner of a funeral business acknowledges that, although customers can be very distraught and vulnerable a week after the death of a relative or close friend and need bereavement counselling, it is an important part of the job is to draw attention to the practical issues relating to the funeral early in the proceedings.

- Service encounters are 'limited in scope', with the scope of the interchange being 'restricted by the nature and content of the service to be delivered'.

There are mutually understood boundaries for a service, often relating to the price being charged, and what the customer receives for the money. A provider of guitar lessons in the home may charge £20 for half an hour's tuition. He/she would not expect to become involved in teaching other aspects of musical training.

- Following on from the characteristic identified above, the roles played by the service provider and the client, in the encounter, are generally well defined and understood by both parties.

Pupils attending music lessons, for example, will expect to be set homework each week and understand that they need to practise on their instrument in the time between lessons. Dissatisfaction with the encounter often arises when either party fails to abide by the rules and adopt the appropriate role. A checkout assistant in a food supermarket was overheard complaining to a customer in the queue about the behaviour of an earlier customer. 'He just stood there and expected me to pack his shopping for him. I was very annoyed. He should know that when we are very busy we just don't have time for that.' Service provider roles may also be unclear or even unrealistic, however. For example, sales assistants in a DIY shop having over 40,000 product lines cannot possibly have knowledge of every product, and yet customers do expect answers to their own product enquiries.

- A temporary suspension of the 'normal' social status of participants often occurs in service encounters.

Accountants and dentists, normally considered to occupy high-status positions in society, carry out a large amount of their work for clients with lower-status occupations. This inversion of the normal social order can add an interesting dimension to service exchanges; that is, 'a degree of role ambiguity or piquancy to the interaction'.[17]

Features of satisfactory and unsatisfactory incidents

According to Bitner *et al.*,[18] 'effective management of the service encounter involves understanding the often complex behaviours of employees that can distinguish a highly satisfactory service encounter from a dissatisfactory one, and then training, motivating and rewarding employees to exhibit those behaviours'.

In this context, one of the first tasks facing service management is to identify which encounters with service personnel customers find most satisfying and/or dissatisfying. Bitner *et al.* used the 'critical incident' technique to help to identify the sources of satisfaction and dissatisfaction. Customers across three 'high contact' service industries (hotels, restaurants and airlines) were asked to describe a specific instance, during the service that they had received, in which particularly good or poor service interaction had occurred. The study identified 699 incidents; 347 satisfactory and 352 dissatisfactory. Of the 347 satisfactory incidents, 86 were from airlines, 165 from restaurants and 96 from hotels. Of the 352 dissatisfactory incidents, 77 were from airlines, 191 from restaurants and 84 from hotels.

The analysis of the results revealed a number of *employee behaviours* that directly influenced customer satisfaction and dissatisfaction with their service experience. The largest proportion of *satisfying* incidents occurred as a result of unprompted and unsolicited actions by employees which generally gave customers a pleasant surprise; for example, going to your regular restaurant to find that the seating has been arranged in advance especially for you, just as you would want it. On other occasions customers unexpectedly received special or individual treatment for another reason. For instance, they may have been given a vegan menu even though the restaurant had not been notified beforehand of special requirements. The largest proportion of *dissatisfactory* encounters related to 'employees inability or unwillingness to respond in service failure situations'. To illustrate this, if customers had been allocated an unsuitable hotel room by mistake, employees did not appear to be either concerned about the situation or prepared to do anything about it. They would frequently communicate their reluctance to act by non-verbal as well as verbal communication, shrugging their shoulders, for example, to indicate that there was nothing that they could do about the situation.

In general, most of the satisfactory and unsatisfactory incidents related to the presence or absence, respectively, of employees' abilities to:

● recover service delivery system failures

● be adaptable in responding to special customer needs or requests

● take spontaneous actions.

Table 4.1 provides examples of appropriate and inappropriate employee actions relating to the three categories.

In a follow-up survey which analysed *employees'* critical incidents,[19] the same three categories above were identified, together with a fourth category, 'coping with difficult customers'. It is reassuring to service managers that similar sources of satisfaction and dissatisfaction have been confirmed by both customers and employees. Furthermore, each category represents a source of *both satisfaction and dissatisfaction*. Management effort can be channelled into improving customer satisfaction by concentrating on these categories.

Table 4.1   Customer sources of satisfaction and dissatisfaction with customer–employee interactions

Category	Type of service issue facing employee	Exemplar	Example of a satisfactory employee response	Example of an un-satisfactory employee response
Recovery of service system failure	● Unavailable service.	Customer tries to pick up hire car. The one ordered is not available.	Upgrade the car (often followed by positive word of mouth).	Imply it was the customer's fault – didn't fill in the necessary paperwork.
	● Unreasonably slow service.	Train delayed one hour.	Offer free tea/coffee and biscuits while waiting; allow free phone calls.	Standard script: 'We apologise for the delay in service … a buffet service is available on the train for the sale of hot drinks.'
	● Other core service failures.	Dead mouse found in hotel swimming pool.	Move to another hotel (upgrade).	'Will get rid of it when I finish serving dinner for other guests.'
Responding to special customer needs or requests	● Customer has 'special' needs.	Child with nut allergy at restaurant. Parents ask which meals are OK.	Check with chef or manager and run through menu with customers.	Don't know the answer and unable to find out.
	● Customer has preferences.	Customer wants a Big Mac breakfast with no egg.	Adapt, and give two sausages and no egg.	'Sorry, you'll have to pick the eggs out yourself.'
	● Customer admits to making an error.	Customer misses flight through misreading check-in time.	Put on next available flight.	Missed the flight. Tough!
Taking spontaneous actions	● Opportunity for unprompted or unsolicited action.	Waiter notices that customer has a cold.	Brings over a 'hot toddy on the house'.	Asks customer to leave if he cannot stop coughing.
	● Opportunity for demonstrating extraordinary behaviour.	Customer conversation with hotel employee.	Give hotel guest a vase of flowers she admired.	Show exasperation through swearing, yelling or rudeness.

Source: Adapted from Bitner *et al.*, 1990 (see note 18).

Critical incident studies can provide a lot more detail about specific events and behaviours that underlie service encounter dissatisfaction than can standard customer satisfaction surveys. However, the technique only tends to focus on incidents leading to customer delight, at the top end of the scale, and dissatisfaction at the bottom, and may miss out the merely satisfactory encounters in the middle.

The next stage in the successful management of this form of encounter is to train, motivate and reward staff to exhibit the behaviours that lead to the satisfying encounter. The results of the above study highlight the important role employees have to play in keeping customers informed about what is happening in the service system. In order to be able to do this effectively, employees themselves need to know what is going on and have a shared understanding of what the organisation is trying to achieve. They need to possess knowledge about the service provided as well being able to demonstrate a wide range of interpersonal skills. In order to be able to respond appropriately in service failure situations, front-line employees need to be given the power to take action without continued reference to a higher authority. Many of these ideas are encapsulated in the notion of employee empowerment that is discussed more fully in Chapter 7. In their capacity as 'relationship managers', employees have the power significantly to reduce perceived uncertainty for the customer and consequently improve 'relationship quality'.[20]

Managerial implications

Arising out of the research above, there are two actions, in particular, which should lead to an improvement in customer satisfaction.

1. *Plan* for effective service recovery.

Interestingly, 23 per cent of the accounts of *satisfactory* incidents relate to employee responses to service failures. Even if there was initial customer disappointment with a service failure, a successful recovery of the situation by an employee can lead to a high level of ultimate customer satisfaction. Clearly, service failures should be avoided, but equally clearly they do happen, and service recovery policies can be designed and planned. Where customers perceive that an organisation has not thought through its responses to service failures, this leads to dissatisfaction and negative word-of-mouth. For example, it is not unusual (especially at the time of writing) for UK railway trains to break down or be delayed. Given the frequency of such occurrences, passengers expect the train operators to have effective recovery systems in place. If they do not, the negative word-of-mouth that follows affects the whole transport system.

2. Communicate with employees about *all* parts of the business.

Employees need to be flexible and give flexible responses when anything even slightly unusual occurs in interactions with customers. To do so, employees need to know the implications of their actions on all parts of the business. For example, the kind gesture of giving the hotel guest a vase of flowers (Table 4.1) may not be wise unless the employee knows who pays for another one, whether there is a budget code, and who is responsible for the replacement. Similarly, the new schoolteacher could be given the flexibility to rearrange a classroom in an open-plan environment to meet pupil needs, but only in the full knowledge of its effect on other classes, teachers and administrative staff.

Customer-to-customer interactions

Although it may be more difficult for service providers to identify and control interpersonal exchanges between customers in the service environment, such exchanges have the potential to affect the customer's perception of the quality[21] of the service provided and therefore merit some consideration. As many services take place in the presence of other customers, customer-to-customer interactions inevitably occur. It may be just a casual conversation, such as the chat at the desk in the car showroom (Example 2, p. 55). However, it may be the key to a service purchase, as in Example 1, p. 55, where the demonstration by the daughter of the enjoyment of being with the other children was a very important element of the service encounter. Despite the potentially significant effect on service encounters, customer-to-customer interactions have tended to be the neglected dimension of the service experience.[22] However, there are helpful research findings in this area, which yield a number of managerial implications.

We start with a summary of research findings.

Forms of customer-to-customer interactions

There are two types of participation:

1.   Interactions between acquaintances.

People often consume services with friends and/or relatives. They carry out shopping with 'purchase pals'.[23] In the context of furniture shopping, for example, a survey showed that only 27.3 per cent of the sample of consumers shopped alone, while over 50 per cent shopped in pairs.[24] For some people, interacting with acquaintances is an integral part of a service. 'Regulars' sit in the same seats at the bar or pub every night, or sit at the same table in the bingo hall every Thursday night. In these cases, service organisations provide the premises for the 'third places' for acquaintances to meet.[25]

The behaviour of acquaintances in a given service setting may vary in different countries. This can be observed with respect to the role of the male partner in female clothing outlets. In Marks & Spencer in the UK, for example, males will sit in a waiting area outside the female fitting rooms, and in many cases may not even see the proposed purchase being tried on by their female partner. In contrast, in Greece, the couples wish the male to have a more active say in the purchase, and a waiting area for the males would be redundant.

There is some evidence that service companies may wish to facilitate interactions between acquaintances. For example, hairdressers will encourage you to bring a friend to enhance the social aspects of the service. Equally, the provision of 'adult crèches', where people can wait while their companions are trying on garments, is an acknowledgement that people often shop in pairs or groups. However, there is surprisingly little published research on the interactions between purchase pals and the effect of such interactions on purchase behaviour, despite the fact that it is acknowledged that 'one purchase behaviour that it is easy for salespeople to identify ... is the utilisation of a shopping/buying companion or "purchase pal"'.[26] In the car salesroom context, for example, it is believed that customer utilisation of a companion indicates a lack of experience and a greater susceptibility to salesperson influence.[27]

2.   Interactions between strangers (or unacquainted influencers).

People often consume services in the presence of other consumers, and interact with them. A stranger may recommend a certain type of beer in a public house or a holiday destination in a travel agent. More annoyingly, a stranger may blow smoke in your face in a restaurant. Often strangers are very knowledgeable about services that you are sharing or about the products available in a service environment. For example, a lady who was thinking of buying a puppy obtained sufficient quality advice from fellow customers in the waiting room at a veterinary practice that the risk of purchase was reduced considerably. She was advised on issues such as 'hip counts', reliable local breeders and insurance plans and it only took half an hour.

Some consumers are more likely to interact with fellow consumers than others. McGrath and Otnes[28] identified categories of consumers who are the most likely to engage in on-site conversations with strangers in retail settings. The 'overt interpersonal influencers' were categorised as being 'helpseekers', 'reactive helpers' and 'proactive helpers'. Helpseekers actively seek information by questioning other shoppers. Reactive helpers respond readily to requests from other shoppers for information. Proactive helpers go out of their way to engage in conversations and offer advice to fellow shoppers. Some shoppers play more than one of these roles. Interestingly, there is some evidence that people who regularly find themselves acting in the role of reactive helper do, in fact, have the ability to respond to requests by other shoppers for product-related information.[29] Consumers seem to be able to identify responsive and knowledgeable fellow shoppers.

Interactions between strangers can be viewed positively or negatively by the participants. In a study of interactions in Florida theme parks, consumers were asked to recall, in their own words, any critical incidents they had encountered with strangers.[30] There were almost equal numbers of positive (49 per cent) and negative (51 per cent) interactions. Many of the incidents described related to sociability (meeting another couple, and spending some time with them in the pub) or to matters of protocol (annoyance with queue-jumpers). In a garden centre context in the UK, conversations with fellow customers were almost always viewed positively.[31]

In the remainder of this section, we concentrate on *customer-to-customer interactions between strangers*.[32]

Frequency of occurrence of customer-to-customer interactions

There are several types of services for which customer-to-customer interactions are central to successful operation. Services such as group coach or walking holidays, aerobic or language classes, and spectator sports or music concerts depend on interactions between customers to provide a social dimension, share knowledge/experience, or simply create an atmosphere.

However, customer-to-customer interactions occur frequently in service environments that are not necessarily designed to encourage them. In a study of a US shopping mall, it was found that 23 per cent of a sample of consumers had had a conversation with a person that they had just met in the mall that day. In the UK, 13 per cent of a sample of consumers had talked to 'stranger' consumers in a garden centre on the day of the survey, and almost 33 per cent of consumers could recall such conversations on previous visits.[33] The percentages, when multiplied by consumer throughput in these environments and the many similar ones, demonstrate that there are millions of, often spontaneous, customer-to-customer interactions taking place each day in service settings.

Factors stimulating customer-to-customer interactions

Risk reduction is often a stimulus for engaging in on-site conversations with strangers in service settings, with consumers, adopting the role of help-seeker, seeking credible opinions and information – Does this scarf go with this top? Is this the right platform for the train to the airport? Do I sit here to wait for the doctor?

Quite often, interactions start with some form of physical assistance. It is common in train or air travel for passengers to help others with bags and luggage, and this acts as an 'ice-breaker' for prolonged conversations which can last the length of the journey. Hospital patients use the pretext of lending a newspaper or helping to clear up the food trays to start conversations with new arrivals on the ward. In each of these examples, it is possible for strangers to get to know each other in a 'safe conversation' about the service environment. Travel-related conversations are very common between passengers on a train or plane, whereas accounts of illnesses are commonplace between patients in a hospital ward. It is not unusual for people in such environments to share negative experiences about the service. To be able to have a mutual moan about train delays, hospital food, or queueing for service is often beneficial to the people concerned, and these interactions can act as 'safety valves' for the service organisations.

Just as the service environment itself can be a stimulus for customer-to-customer interactions, so can physical products on display. In a customer survey in an IKEA store in the north west of England, almost 50 per cent of conversations between strangers were product-related.[34] For example, one customer would ask another if a bed quilt would suit a certain room setting, or where she purchased the product she was carrying in her bag.

Managerial implications

From the research findings, especially those on customer-to-customer inter-actions between strangers, there are actions that service organisations can take which recognise the customer satisfaction to be gained from positive interactions, and the dissatisfaction associated with negative interactions.

1.   View consumers as a human resource.

In a discussion of social support in the service sector, it has been maintained that, by supporting each other, consumers may carry out functions nor-mally associated with employees. 'Sometimes consumers will be even more effective than paid employees; they are more readily available, and the absence of a profit motive will lend credibility to their advice.'[35] Retail and service managers will need to accept that on-site consumers represent a credible, willing and able human resource, and that their own employees can learn from consumers.[36] Rather than directing their management efforts at keeping consumers apart, or at training employees to intervene to make a sale, service companies could concentrate on training staff to be facili-tators of consumer-to-consumer interactions and how *not* to intervene in consumer conversations.[37]

2.   Plan to facilitate interactions.

The process of actively managing customer-to-customer encounters in such a way as to enhance satisfying encounters and minimise dissatisfying encounters is one part of what Martin and Pranter[38] call 'compatibility management'. They identify a number of roles a service provider may play in managing customer compatibility.[39]

● Rifleman

This role involves targeting the organisation's marketing activity at cus-tomer segments that are likely to demonstrate 'compatible behaviours' during the service experience. Holiday companies, for example, stress in their brochures that certain resort destinations are 'quiet and particularly suitable for young children'. This is designed to discourage younger travellers who might be looking for exciting nightlife and the opportunity to meet others of a similar age with the same interests. Tour operators realise that even a few negative encounters between these two customer groups could potentially damage their perception of the quality of the service provided.

● Environmental engineer

Assuming this role, the service provider would design the service setting before the customers arrive to produce compatible behaviours when they are present. This might include offering separate seating to smokers and non-smokers in a restaurant, and dimmed lights and special booths for romantic meetings between couples.

● Legislator

In this role, the service provider lays down certain rules that customers have to abide by to receive the service. For instance, a golf club may expect all its members to sign a 'members book' every time they use the course and wear evening dress for all official club functions. Having a clearly defined set of behavioural rules immediately gives members a point of reference for their dealings with others in the club.

● Matchmaker

Here the service provider actively promotes the service to specific groups that are likely to share common experiences and problems, and consequently are more likely to benefit in the same way from the service experience. A beauty consultant, for example, offers a special consultancy service to young mothers with newborn babies. They are often uncertain about how to make the most of their appearance when trying to regain their shape after childbirth. They frequently also experience the same skin problems and benefit from specialist make-up advice. The consultant is able to use the experiences of the group members when presenting her material.

● Teacher

Teachers have the responsibility of educating customers into their role in the service encounter, thus avoiding any confusion or potential conflict between customers. Flight attendants, for example, play the role of teacher when they transfer customers from the waiting lounge onto the plane. They request that customers board the plane in order of the row number allocated on the ticket. Although this clearly has operational benefits, it also avoids potential interpersonal conflict between waiting passengers who might accuse each other of queue-jumping.

● Santa Claus

In this role the service provider rewards customers who exhibit behaviour that results in positive encounters between customers. For example, one customer found telling another how to place a monetary deposit in a shopping trolley to release it for use, might be rewarded with a discount on his/her own grocery purchases. Alternatively, a customer recommending a product to another in the store might be rewarded with a free gift.

● Police officer

Here the service provider is responsible for ensuring that the designated rules and codes of conduct are being followed by all customers. The doorman at a nightclub, for instance, might operate in this capacity, turning away customers who do not conform to the appropriate dress code.

● Cheerleader

As the title suggests, this role involves encouraging customers in the service environment to work together and share common experiences that relate to the service being provided. For example, the receptionist in the dentist's waiting room might be asked by an anxious patient whether a particular treatment is painful. If the receptionist has never had the treatment she might ask another patient who has had the treatment to offer reassurance to the first customer. The receptionist is acting as a 'facilitator' in the exchange between the two customers. A more overt example of cheerleader behaviour is demonstrated by holiday couriers, whose main task is to encourage a 'good time' atmosphere among customers sharing the same holiday package.

As customers are involved in both forms of interpersonal encounter identified above – in exchanges with employees and with other customers – service managers are concerned about what motivates customers to take part in the encounter and how their general contribution can be controlled and managed. The nature and extent of customer participation in service delivery systems is clearly very important, as are the strategies to manage customer contributions. These issues are discussed in Chapter 5.

Interactions between customers and technology/equipment

Interpersonal interactions have received the most attention in the services marketing literature. However, advances in technology and equipment have resulted in a greater likelihood that customers will interact with 'machines' during the period of time they are in contact with a service (as in Example 2, p. 55, where the first interaction was with the website of the leisure club). Indeed, as was described in Chapter 2, one of the key dimensions of a service-oriented business is that it should enhance service capabilities through the use of 'state-of-the-art' technology. The impact of the Internet on service provision is wide-ranging. In the service sector, it is used most for travel, entertainment and financial services purchases. In the retail sector, it is used most for purchases of books and music, office products, toys and computers.[40]

We concentrate here, therefore, on:

- consumer sources of satisfaction and dissatisfaction with technology-based services, and the managerial implications
- strategies for services via the Internet.

Consumer sources of satisfaction and dissatisfaction with technology-based services

A further critical incident research study was carried out to determine consumer sources of satisfaction and dissatisfaction with technology-based services.[41] Technologies included in the survey were automated airline ticket machines, automated hotel checkouts, car rental machines, ATMs, internet shopping, Internet information searches and 'pay at the pump' terminals. An analysis of the critical incidents revealed three categories of sources of satisfaction, and four categories of sources of dissatisfaction (see Table 4.2).

Table 4.2 Sources of satisfaction and dissatisfaction with technology-based services

Sources of satisfaction	Sources of dissatisfaction
● Solves an immediate problem	● Technology failure
● Perceived as better than the interpersonal alternative	● Process failure
● Performed operation successfully	● Poor design
	● Customer driven failure

Source: Adapted from Meuter *et al.*, 2000 (see note 11).

The most frequently cited source of satisfaction with technology-based services was the perception that it was better than the interpersonal alternative (68 per cent). Consumers perceived savings in time and/or money, especially when they did not find the need to deal with a salesperson, for example at the 'pay at the pump' terminal. A further 21 per cent of the incidents were described as satisfactory because the technology performed the service operation successfully; that is, it did what it was supposed to do. That this is a source of satisfaction is probably a reflection of relief (or even mistrust in technology). As expectations with technology and machines change over time, this particular source of satisfaction may become less frequent. The other source of satisfaction was the solving of an immediate problem (11 per cent). For example, birthday greetings can be emailed to a friend/relative even after the last post has gone, or money can be drawn out of an ATM to pay for the midnight taxi home.

The most frequently cited source of dissatisfaction with technology-based services was the failure of the technology (43 per cent). The airline ticket machine was out of order, for example, or the ATM swallowed the card for no apparent reason. 'Poor design', especially of internet websites, was cited in 36 per cent of the unsatisfactory incidents. Either the system was confusing to the consumer, resulting, for example, in ordering the same book twice, or it was inflexible, for example giving the option of gift deliveries only to the cardholder's address. Process failures (17 per cent) occurred where the technology was fine, but there were other problems such as items that were ordered over the internet being delivered to the wrong address, or on the wrong day. Occasionally, consumers admit responsibility for unsatisfactory incidents. Customer-driven failures (4 per cent) have resulted from demagnetised strips on credit cards, and annoyance/carelessness with a music ordering website (resulting in 200 copies of the same CD!).

Managerial implications

Managers can learn not only from the categories in Table 4.2, but also from a comparison with the sources of (dis)satisfaction with interpersonal services outlined in Table 4.1. Three implications for managers of technology-based services are now discussed.

1.   Plan for effective *service recovery*.

If it is accepted that some breakdowns or failures are inevitable, strategies for service recovery need to be in place. It was seen that empowerment of employees was an option with interpersonal interactions, and also that effective service recovery resulted in customer satisfaction. With technology-based services (and the absence of service employees), the key to service recovery will lie in enabling the customers themselves to resolve the problems. To do this, service organisations require an in-depth understanding of problem situations experienced by consumers. What are their frustrations? What are the issues associated with remembering order numbers, account names and passwords? What are the main navigation problems consumers have with Internet shopping? To obtain such depth of understanding, and the subsequent development of self-recovery systems, is likely to require 'shopping with consumers' style research[42] in the context of internet or other technology-based encounters, rather than survey-based research.

2.   *Involve* customers.

The inseparability characteristic of services entails levels of customer involvement in service encounters. In interpersonal encounters in retail environments, it has been established that customers often have product and process knowledge that is better than that of employees, and are prepared to share the expertise under certain conditions.[43] Actively encouraging customer involvement can be advantageous to the service provider. But do customers understand *how* they are expected to perform? Are they *able* to perform as expected? Are there valued rewards for performing as expected?

With technology-based services, there is evidence that those who design the technology do not appreciate the lack of consumer understanding of how they are expected to perform. There is even a designated website for 'silly' consumer queries received at computer help lines[44]. Some of the stories are very amusing, but the overriding impression, on reading them, is of a lack of empathy with consumer role clarity, abilities and motivations. There is a consumer experience gap.[45] Where consumers want simplicity, they may get complexity. Where they want service, they may get technology. Where they want to accomplish their goals, they may get 'compelling features'. With technology-based services, it is even more important to view customers as human resources for the service organisation, empathise with them, and involve them in the human resource strategies, in order to reduce the consumer experience gap.

3.   *Customise* the service.

With interpersonal services, many of the recorded sources of customer satisfaction related to employees' abilities to respond to *special* customer needs or requests, or to employees acting spontaneously for *individual* customers. Customers are highly satisfied where it has been demonstrated that the service organisation, or its representatives, has tailored the service to them. With technology-based services, there is an opportunity for services to be customised as a matter of course, which may lead to them being perceived as better than the interpersonal alternative. The most obvious examples of customised services are the Internet book retailers who will notify individual customers when a book has arrived in their preferred category. Customisation is an option, however, with all technology-based services where a particular customer's frequency and types of purchases are routinely recorded.

The danger here is one of complacency. Is the service really providing customisation that leads to satisfaction and repeat purchases? Service companies will still need to carry out research into sources of customer loyalty, as well as customer satisfaction, with technology-based services.

Strategies for services via the internet

For some products (services and/or goods) the potential for selling over the Internet is much greater than for others. What are the criteria that make a product a candidate for successful Internet selling? Rosen and Howard[46] list the following:

- tactility less important
- generally unpleasant in-store experience
- customisation important
- personal nature
- high margin
- cheap to ship
- instant gratification less important
- standard
- price sensitive
- gift oriented
- info-intense.

Financial and travel services fit most of the criteria, as do goods such as music and books. Other services, such as medical or educational, and other goods, such as clothing or furniture, tend to fit fewer of the criteria, and consequently have less of a presence on the Internet.

Where a service or good does have potential for Internet selling, companies' strategies for internet usage can vary. Largely, they fall into two camps:

- on-line or on-site, i.e. 'clicks *or* bricks'
- on-line and on-site, i.e. 'clicks *and* bricks'.

With a 'clicks or bricks' strategy, companies favour either on-line or on-site product selling. The on-line option offers the advantages of 24-hour access times for customers, and a global customer base. However, for physical goods, the selection and picking service is once again the responsibility of the retailer. There are still consumer trust problems to do with security of payment and the lack of sensory experience (sight, smell, human contact) may be a disadvantage. For retailers of goods, the backstage logistics and delivery systems are complex and costly.[47]

With a 'clicks and bricks' strategy, companies are using the Internet as an effective shop window to support on-site retail or service offers. The Internet is integrated into retail and services marketing strategy, as opposed to being an alternative channel for direct sales. Borders Bookstores, for example, make their Internet service available in their stores to facilitate ordering. B&Q, in the UK, use their websites to provide general DIY help, and information as to which products can be bought in-store, to both the general public and traders. In the United States, there is some evidence that retailers expanding virtually through an Internet presence are also growing physically through store expansion.[48]

SUMMARY

The service encounter has received considerable attention from academics and managers alike because it is believed that:

- a single interaction can affect a customer's total perception of a service organisation

- the service encounter has distinct elements which can be controlled and managed.

There are a number of characteristics that distinguish interpersonal service encounter interactions from other forms of human interaction. Knowledge of these distinguishing characteristics helps service providers to identify, understand, and subsequently manage, interpersonal interactions between and among employees and customers, and to assess critically the level of customer participation in the service encounter. Technology-based services are becoming more commonplace, and it is noted that, by the nature of the interaction, sources of satisfaction and dissatisfaction with such services are different to those associated with interpersonal services. Companies, particularly those adopting 'clicks and bricks' strategies, can benefit from understanding the differences.

Customer interactions, in service encounters, with the physical environment, or servicescape, are discussed in Chapter 6.

LEARNING OUTCOMES

Having read this chapter, you should be able to

- define the service encounter and categorise the various types of interaction the customer may have during the encounter

- break down service encounters into the multiple points of contact the customer has with the service

- appreciate the managerial implications associated with customer interactions with employees, with other customers and with technology and equipment

- categorise the causes of customer satisfaction and dissatisfaction through interactions with employees and technology-based services

- understand the significance of 'other customers' as part of the human resource present in service encounters.

DISCUSSION QUESTIONS AND EXERCISES

1. Can increased empowerment of employees lead to customer dissatisfaction?

2. Name three types of service where customer compatibility is an important issue.

3. Why might the distinguishing characteristics of service encounters (p. 60) not always be desirable for certain services?

4. Provide an example of service recovery as applied to you as a customer. How did the manner of the recovery affect your view of the service organisation?

5. Provide specific, personal examples that illustrate the 3 sources of satisfaction and 4 sources of dissatisfaction listed in Table 4.2.

Notes and references

1.   Martin, C. L., 'The History, Evolution and Principles of Services Marketing: Poised for the New Millennium', *Marketing Intelligence and Planning*, vol. 17, issue 7, 1999, pp. 324–8.
2.   Normann, R., *Service Management*, Wiley, New York, 1984.
3.   Mattsson, J., 'Improving Service Quality in Person-to-Person Encounters: Integrating Findings from a Multidisciplinary Review', *Service Industries Journal*, vol. 14, 1994.
4.   Shostack, G. L., 'Planning the Service Encounter', in J. A. Czepiel, M. R. Solomon and C. F. Surprenant (eds), *The Service Encounter*, Lexington Books, Lexington, Mass., 1985.
5.   Bitner, M. J., 'Evaluating Service Encounters: The Effects of Physical Surroundings and Employee Responses', *Journal of Marketing*, vol. 54, April 1990, pp. 69–82.
6.   Harris, K., Baron, S. and Ratcliffe, J., 'Customers as Oral Participants in a Service Setting', *Journal of Services Marketing*, vol. 9, no. 4, 1995, pp. 64–76.
7.   Parker, C. and Ward, P., 'An Analysis of Role Adoptions and Scripts During Customer-to-Customer Encounters', *European Journal of Marketing*, vol. 34, no. 3-4, 2000, pp. 341–58.
8.   Martin, C. L. and Pranter, C. A., 'Compatibility Management: Customer to Customer Relationships in Service Environments', *Journal of Services Marketing*, vol. 3, no. 3, Summer 1989, pp. 5–15.
9.   Milne, J., 'Someone to talk to', *Internet Business*, March 2000, pp. 75–83.
10. Bowen, D. E., 'Customers as Human Resources in Service Organisations', *Human Resource Management*, vol. 25, no. 3, Fall 1986, pp. 371–83.
11. Meuter, M. L., Ostrom, A. L., Roundtree, R. I. and Bitner, M. J., 'Self-Service Technologies: Understanding Customer Satisfaction with Technology-Based Service Encounters', *Journal of Marketing*, vol. 64, July 2000, pp. 50–64.
12. Forecasts of internet usage vary, but at the time of writing, in the USA, Internet sales are expected to be 4.4 per cent of all retail sales ($108billion) by 2003 (source: Rosen and Howard, below), while in the UK, retail sales via the Internet are expected to be 5 per cent of all retail sales (£12.5billion) by 2005 (source: Verdict 2000).

13. Bitner, M. J., 'Servicescapes: The Impact of Physical Surroundings on Customers and Employees', *Journal of Marketing*, vol. 56, no. 2, pp. 57–71.

14. Czepiel, J. A., Solomon, M. R. and Surprenant, C. F. (eds), *The Service Encounter: Managing Employee/Customer Interaction in Service Businesses*, Lexington Books, Lexington, Mass., 1985.

15. McGrath, M. A., 'An Ethnography of a Gift Shop: Trappings, Wrappings and Rapture', *Journal of Retailing*, vol. 65, no. 4, 1989, pp. 421–49.

16. Baron, S., Harris, K. and Davies, B. J., 'Oral Participation in Retail Service Delivery: A Comparison of the Roles of Contact Personnel and Customers', *European Journal of Marketing*, vol. 30, no. 9, 1996, pp. 75–90.

17. Czepiel, J. A., Solomon, M. R. and Surprenant, C. F. (eds), *The Service Encounter: Managing Employee/Customer Interaction in Service Businesses*.

18. Bitner, M. J., Booms, B. H. and Tetreault, M., 'The Service Encounter: Diagnosing Favourable and Unfavourable Incidents', *Journal of Marketing*, vol. 54, January 1990, pp. 71–84.

19. Bitner, M. J., Booms, B. H. and Mohr, L. A., 'Critical Service Encounters: The Employee's View', *Journal of Marketing*, Vol. 58, October 1994, pp. 95–106.

20. Crosby, L. A., Evans, K. R. and Cowles, D., 'Relationship Quality in Services Selling: An Interpersonal Influence Perspective', *Journal of Marketing*, vol. 54, July 1990, pp. 68–81.

21. Bitner, 'Evaluating Service Encounters'.

22. Baron, S., 'Customer Interactions: A Neglected Dimension of Service Encounters', Inaugural Professorial Lecture, Manchester Metropolitan University, February 2000.

23. Woodside, A. G. and Sims, T. J., 'Retail Sales Transactions and Customer "Purchase Pal" Effects on Buying Behavior', *Journal of Retailing*, vol. 52, Fall 1976, pp. 57–64.

24. Baron, Harris, and Davies, 'Oral Participation in Retail Service Delivery'.

25. Oldenburg, R., *The Great Good Place*, Marlowe and Company, New York, 1999.

26. Goff, B. G., Bellenger, D. N. and Stojack, C., 'Cues to Consumer Susceptibility To Salesperson Influence: Implications for Adaptive Retail Selling', *Journal of Personal Selling and Sales Management*, vol. xiv, no. 2, Spring 1994, pp. 25–39.

27. Ibid.

28. McGrath, M. A. and Otnes, C., 'Unacquainted Influencers: When Strangers Interact in the Retail Setting', *Journal of Business Research*, vol. 32, 1995, pp. 261–72.

29. Harris, K., Baron, S. and Davies, B., 'What Sort of Soil Do Rhododendrons Like? Comparing Customer and Employee Responses to Requests for Product-Related Information', *Journal of Services Marketing*, vol. 13, no. 1, 1999, pp. 21–37.

30. Grove, S. J. and Fisk, R. P., 'The Impact of Other Customers on Service Exchanges: A Critical Incident Examination of "Getting Along"', *Journal of Retailing*, vol. 73, no. 1, 1997, pp. 63–85.

31. Parker, C. and Ward, P., 'An Analysis of Role Adoptions and Scripts During Customer-to-Customer Encounters'.

32. More details on this section can be found in Harris, K., Baron, S. and Parker, D., 'Understanding the Consumer Experience: It's "Good to Talk"', *Journal of Marketing Management*, vol. 16, no. 1–3, 2000, pp. 111–27.

33. Parker, C. and Ward, P., 'An Analysis of Role Adoptions and Scripts During Customer-to-Customer Encounters'.

34. Baron, Harris, and Davies, 'Oral Participation in Retail Service Delivery'.

35. Adelman, M. B., Ahuvia, A. and Goodwin, C., 'Beyond Smiling: Social Support and Service Quality', in *Service Quality: New Directions in Theory and Practice*. R. Rust and R. Oliver (eds), Sage, Thousand Oaks, Cal., 1994, pp. 139–72.

36. Harris, Baron, and Davies, 'What Sort of Soil do Rhododendrons Like?'.

37. McGrath and Otnes, 'Unacquainted Influencers'.

38. Pranter, C. A. and Martin, C. L., 'Compatibility Management: Roles in Service Performers', *Journal of Services Marketing*, vol. 5, no. 2, Spring 1991, pp. 143–53.

39. Pranter and Martin, 'Compatibility Management'.

40. Rosen, K. T. and Howard, A. L., 'E-Retail: Gold Rush or Fool's Gold?', *California Management Review*, vol. 42, no. 3, Spring 2000, pp. 72–100.

41. Meuter, Ostrom, Roundtree and Bitner, 'Self-Service Technologies'.

42. Otnes, C., McGrath, M. A. and Lowrey, T. M., 'Shopping with Consumers: Usage as Past, Present and Future Research Technique', *Journal of Retailing and Consumer Services*, vol. 2, no. 2, 1995, pp. 97–110.

43. Harris, Baron, and Davies, 'What Sort of Soil do Rhododendrons Like?'

44. http://rinkworks.com

45. www.zdinternet.com

46. Rosen and Howard, 'E-Retail: Gold Rush or Fool's Gold?'.

47. Burt, S., 'E-Commerce and the High Street: Threat or Hype?', *Contemporary Issues in Retail Marketing*, Manchester Metropolitan University, September 2000.

48. Rosen and Howard, 'E-Retail: Gold Rush or Fool's Gold?'.

Consumer experiences

LEARNING OBJECTIVES

Overall aim of the chapter:
To create an awareness of the notion of the consumer experience, and the reasons for the increased interest in the notion by both academics and practitioners.

In particular, the *chapter objectives* are

- to illustrate the notion of a memorable consumer experience

- to outline the three main reasons for the current interest in consumer experiences

- to compare and contrast the perspectives on the consumer experience of consumers, services marketers and academics

- to summarise the implications for service management who wish to create and stage consumer experiences.

Introduction

After receiving services, consumers sometimes simply forget them or regard them as so 'ordinary' that they just do not talk about them, even when the services have been regarded positively. Yet, after receiving other services, they feel they want to recount their service story to anyone who will listen.

What is it that can make a consumer service into an *experience* worth recounting?

In the late 1990s, there was a significant interest in consumer experiences within the field of marketing.[1,2,3] In this chapter, the reasons for the interest are outlined, different perspectives on the consumer experience are discussed, and some implications for service management are identified.

But first, let us examine (in this case in the context of higher education) how service providers give clues that they wish to provide something more than simply the core product. The UK's Open University (OU), in an advertisement in 2000, listed the advantages of studying for a degree by open learning, and demonstrated their leading-edge technology. However, both the photograph and the final message were about how studying with the OU is an 'unforgettable experience' where students can 'make new friends' from all walks of life. Both the OU providers and the students have acknowledged that the total experience is far greater that the studying and passing of modules, and that the social element is often the most memorable.

Academic conferences are an opportunity for academics to disseminate their research and learn from other researchers. However, conference organisers recognise that delegates expect more than just this core element of the service in order to make the conference worth talking about. For example, the organising committee of the American Marketing Association 1999 Winter Educators' Conference promoted 'a conference that offers great collegial interaction, a super location, and an exciting program'. In the UK Academy of Marketing 2000 Conference Programme, delegates were advised that 'One of the principal factors of past conferences that makes them memorable has been the friendliness and hospitality that delegates have received. Our conference aims to maintain such a tradition. You will find a full conference programme, both daytime and evenings, with many opportunities to renew old acquaintances and make new ones.'

In all these examples, there is a recognition that, in order for the experience to be memorable, consumers need to be given the opportunity to *engage* in the service, not merely to be a player in a service transaction. In the story in Chapter 1, John Townsend can be seen to be engaging in the airline flight service more than his son Jack, and would be more likely, therefore, to talk about his service experience. Even UK high street retailers, who have traditionally focused on selling merchandise, have begun to devote display space to sell packaged experiences. For example, UK shoppers can buy a James Bond Experience from Boots, or a Big Boys Toy adventure from WH Smith. These, perhaps, are the most obvious examples of services becoming consumer experience; that is, when consumers engage in something out of the ordinary.[4]

A consumer experience

Exhibit 5.1 provides an illustration of a consumer experience where a considerable amount of money was paid for a service that proved to be memorable. It provides a reference point for the later sections of the chapter. It is written by Peter, who, with his wife Christine, flew from the UK for an Easter holiday in Las Vegas with the tour operator 'Airtours'. It starts with the Airtours welcome meeting, held in the 'Planet Hollywood' store.

Exhibit 5.1 Consumer account of the 'Sunset Trail Ride and Barbecue Dinner' experience

'At the welcome meeting, we were given details of all the tours/shows we could book through Airtours – flight over the Grand Canyon, visit to the Hoover Dam, and various variety shows. The Airtours rep. went through them all in a presentation, complete with slides. The particular tour that she really got excited about, however, was the 'Sunset trail ride' tour[5]. It involved a short drive to the Red Rock Canyons to a ranch, followed by a 2-hour horse ride with the cowboys, and then a meal of barbecued steak, beans and corn on the cob, enjoyed whilst sitting around the campfire under the desert stars. We had originally planned to revisit the Grand Canyon, but Christine and I both liked the idea of the canyon ride, although neither of us had ever ridden a horse before. It seemed like many others at the presentation had the same idea and similar reservations. Most of the questions were about the canyon ride, and we were reassured that it was possible for novices "from four to 94 years of age". Being in our fifties, therefore, appeared not to be a drawback. It seemed, however, quite expensive at $139 per person, so we didn't book on the spot. Two days later, we decided to opt for the canyon ride and sacrifice the Grand Canyon tour (which we were told, by another couple, was a bit disappointing with just a flight for 20 minutes around a small part of the Grand Canyon).

   The day came, and we arrived at the pick-up point at the Excalibur Hotel. The bus driver handed out two-page insurance disclaimers to us all, and we had to tick and sign at least 20 boxes. We began to wonder what we'd let ourselves in for. He went on to warn us not to over-claim our riding skills as the cowboys might put us on a horse that we could not control. This seemed to cause a stir, and so he quickly responded by saying complete novices would get the gentle horses, such as "Buttercup" and "Smiler", rather than "Thunder" or "Bullet". With hindsight, this was part of the experience – a wind-up of the group to get them talking. Soon the scenery became spectacular, with the beautiful red rocks, and we arrived at the ranch. The driver could not resist one last dig at us, by pointing out a trail high into the mountains that we were going to ride on. At the ranch, we all had to pay up front (it seemed strange to be paying by credit card in such an environment), including a generous tip to the, as yet, unknown cowboys/girls. They then came along and introduced themselves – Big Jim, Hawk, Randy, Jodie, etc. – ten in all, all wearing hats and with spurs on their boots. There were 50 customers on this trail ride. Others were turned away whilst we were there. We could see the horses in a fenced area. This was it, then. No turning back. Big Jim asked if anyone was nervous. Five women, including Christine, confessed, and were made a fuss of, and fixed up with horses. No men confessed any trepidation and I wasn't going to be the first. Big Jim, did, however, draw attention to the lack of male honesty, which relieved the tension a bit. Christine was on "Dusty", and I was given "Cherokee", but we were separated, and could not share our misgivings. The cowboys/girls briefly demonstrated how we should steer and stop the horse with the reins. This was hard to take in, and quite scary. When we set off, I over-used the reins, and was shouted at "Don't pull hard on Cherokee. He's got a sensitive mouth." Not a good start. The next part is taken from Christine's diary of the holiday.

> My horse was an Albino with blue eyes called Dusty, Peter's a brown one with piebald markings (Cherokee). We had to ride *on our own* (no-one walking beside us) up a very steep hill, along very rocky and sometimes sandy terrain. Very frightening at first, and my stirrups were too high (+ one higher than the other), so my legs were really aching and rigid the whole time. Stopped for photos on the way up, and at the top for one with Peter. My horse was right at the end of a sheer drop. Stunning views, but sunset hampered by a few clouds. At top, Nicole (cowgirl) adjusted my stirrups, but I was still aching. Saw a coyote. When we got back, I couldn't get off the horse, so Peter and a cowboy lifted me off – my legs were like jelly. Then we had enormous steaks, corn on the cob, jacket potato, beans and lettuce, and then toasted marshmallows on the camp-fire. Finally, a drive back with a view of Las Vegas lights, quite spectacular.

The whole account seems fairly negative, but our legs began to function properly only five minutes after getting off the horse, and round the camp-fire, everyone was in high spirits sharing their experiences and fears. Christine said that we would get a lot of mileage out of this, back home. The photos have been out with all our friends, embellished with stories of our ride up the canyon. It was certainly the highlight of the Las Vegas holiday. Even silly things take on a greater meaning – such as cowboys on horseback communicating by mobile phone, and us sitting around the campfire (after singing "Home on the range") and being given the ranch's website.'

It is interesting that the pain and fear (the latter no doubt orchestrated to a certain extent by the service provider) contributed greatly to Christine and Peter's experiences. The satisfaction and relief of conquering the pain and fear, and sharing it with other customers, was positive. The scenery and context will have made the experience possible, but their participation and engagement in the service was the key to their evaluations. The photographs, taken by the cowboys/girls, were the tangible items that jogged the memories.

What has been said so far in this chapter is probably not too surprising. So why is the topic of consumer experience capturing the interest of academics and practitioners at the start of the twenty-first century?

Reasons for the interest in consumer experiences

There are three main, interrelated reasons for the upsurge in interest in consumer experiences:

- the economics of selling experiences
- the move towards providing 'theatrical' retail/service offers
- the closure of 'third' or 'great good places'.

The economics of selling experiences

As was mentioned briefly in Chapter 1, Pine and Gilmore[6] have advocated that advanced economies have moved to what they call the *Experience Economy*. The arrival at this position is via a historical progression of economic value from extracting commodities to making goods, to delivering services, to staging experiences (see the coffee example on p. 24). This progression is shown in Figure 5.1.

As we move along Figure 5.1, from left to right, Pine and Gilmore argue the offer moves from being undifferentiated to being differentiated, and from being irrelevant to customer needs to being relevant to customer needs. But, importantly for them, it moves from cheap (market) pricing to premium pricing. One can charge a premium price in the experience economy for staging a differentiated experience which is relevant to customer needs. Support for their argument can be seen, for example, in the 'Christmas service' being offered by event planners to families in the USA. For prices of up to £30,000, families can 'enjoy the Christmas festivities, by avoiding the fuss'.[7] For around £27,000 the deal may include three Christmas trees, decoration of seven fireplaces, crystal tableware, shopping for presents, cooking the turkey and signing Christmas cards with a look-alike signature. This is to provide what the purchasers regard as the real Christmas experience; something they could not provide for themselves. According to the providers, the business had taken off in December 2000 'as never before'.

Similarly, customers are willing to pay $139 each for a trail ride in the canyons, with all the cowboy, camp-fire ambience (an experience), whereas a 2-hour horse ride (a service) could normally be purchased for less than half that amount.

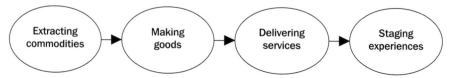

Source: Adapted from Pine and Gilmore, 1999 (see note 2).

Figure 5.1 The progression of economic value

A UK consumer behaviourist consultant advises that 'people are telling us that they're oversupplied with merchandise and undersupplied with experiences … their houses are full of the stuff. And there's a feeling that an experience lasts a lifetime, while a product wears out.'[8] If, indeed, consumers are expressing needs for staged experiences rather than manufactured goods, then Pine and Gilmore reckon that organisations, such as retailers or shopping centre managers, could stage consumer experiences and *charge an entry fee*. This may not be too far-fetched given the propensity of consumers to pay for tangible mementoes, such as 'Rainforest Café' tee shirts after a dining experience, despite being oversupplied with merchandise. It is quite possible that Peter, Christine or any of their fellow customers would have purchased Red Rock Canyon Trail Ride tee shirts or cowboy hats, had they been available, in their post-ride euphoria (or even via the internet!).

The move towards providing 'theatrical' retail/service offers

A Verdict Report, written in 1999, stated that

> *Retail theatre is more than a fancy layout and slick decoration. The most successful involve real inter-activity with the consumer, making them active, rather than passive, participants. Only in this way can consumers actually feel involved and the shopping experience made more memorable and interesting. For the retailer there are significant bonuses to be gained as a result – shoppers stay in the store for longer, they come back more often and they (probably) tell their friends about the experience.*[9]

Consumer experiences are often seen as the outcome of the offer of 'theatre' in services, none more so than in the retail sector where many firms across the whole spectrum of retailing claim to be offering *retail theatre*.[10] The use of the theatre metaphor in services has been discussed in Chapter 3.[11] Some examples of the claims of retail theatre show superficiality, in that the idea of theatre seems indistinguishable from selling, (for example, the US home furnishing retailer, Tag's Hardware, state 'We treat retail like theater: come in, be entertained and spend money on your way out'), or merchandising (for example, the UK supermarket group Safeway where they are reported to want 'to bring in the idea of retail theatre, where you have such a fantastic display of apples, for example, that you cannot resist loading into your trolley').

Nevertheless, others do acknowledge that 'theatre' includes the engagement of the consumer and the encouragement of consumer participation in the creation of consumer experiences, as advocated in the Verdict report above. For example, the key to retail theatre for the UK electrical retailer, Comet, is to allow 'the customer to touch, feel and experience the product', and the Levi's jeans retail store in San Francisco, with children in mind, 'hopes to captivate youthful shoppers partly through sensory immersion (surround sound! flickering video projections! DJ/VJ listening stations! tub of warm water)'.[12]

A catalyst for the creation of on-site retail consumer experiences has been the competition of on-line shopping alternatives (see Chapter 4). Through internet shopping, consumers can meet convenience, speed of purchase, and low price needs when shopping for many types of goods. On-site shopping, therefore, has to provide something different – experiences through theatre – in order to encourage longer stays, repatronage and positive word of mouth. In parallel with consumer experiences with on-site retail/service providers, research is being undertaken on consumer experiences with retail/service websites, the E-Xperience.[13] Here the emphasis is on creating hassle-free, seamless experiences for consumers.

It is not only in retail, however, where theatrical techniques are used to create consumer experiences. The most blatant example in the hotel sector is the Venetian Hotel in Las Vegas, which is said to have cost $2 billion to build.[14] As with other Las Vegas hotels, it has a Casino and over 5000 bedrooms. It also has 17 restaurants, and a spectacular themed presence on Las Vegas Boulevard, complete with Rialto Bridge, a canal and a replica of the St Mark's Campanile bell tower. The main experience for consumers, most of whom are visitors not residents, is to be found, however, in the 'Grand Canal Shoppes' inside the hotel. The shops are in a themed setting, with gondola rides (at $15 per person) on the canal running through them to a replica St Mark's Square complete with cafes, bars, and so on, all under a painted blue sky with small white clouds. The gondoliers are all trained singers, dressed authentically, who serenade their passengers at the canal turning point, heard, of course, by all the passing shoppers. There are scheduled operatic performances and concerts on the canal bridges and in the square, and mime artists act as statues in the wider spaces of the shopping mall.

The closure of 'third' or 'great good places'

It may seem, from the above, that the creation and provision of consumer experiences is only available to well-funded service organisations in the retail and leisure service sectors. However, it is recognised that many much smaller service organisations provide a social consumer experience, playing the role of a 'third place', or what has become to be known as a 'great good place'[15] – a meeting place for people (whose other two places are home and work). Consider the following report[16] on the reaction of the American public to the end of a television series:

> When the final episode of Cheers aired in 1993 after 11 years of warming America's barstools, 80 million people tuned in to bid farewell to the cozy saloon where, as the theme song had it, 'everyone knows your name'. The audience wasn't just saying good-bye to a TV show; it was mourning the passing of 'the great good place' of modern life, as sociologist Ray Oldenburg called the gathering places where communities refresh and sustain themselves. Yes, the old-time saloon and lodges and even the barbershops that once provided places for socializing are mostly gone.

It would seem that the end of a fictitious bar had been mourned in a nostalgic reflection on the reduction in places to meet and socialise, most of which were made available by service providers. Oldenburg[17] listed these great good places:

- cafés
- coffee shops

- bookstores
- bars
- hair salons
- other hangouts at the heart of a community.

In great good places, Oldenburg points out, 'the entertainment is provided by the people themselves. The sustaining activity is conversation, which is variously passionate and light-hearted, serious and witty, informative and silly.'

The notion of the consumer engaging with the service to create an experience again is paramount.

Some service organisations have reacted to the public mourning of the demise of great good places by proclaiming positively that they are a great good place, standing up for the values that Oldenburg proclaims they possess. For example, Bobby Byrne's restaurants and pubs,[18] in Cape Cod USA, refer to themselves as 'An Eating, Drinking and Talking Establishment' and as 'Cape Cod's "great good place" to raise a glass, break bread, and share a great good thought'. Their message to the 'gentle customer' is that 'the pub is about more than food and drink ... we hope that we nourish your spirit and enable you to experience not only another great place but also a great good thought'.

In the UK, 'other hangouts at the heart of a community' would include the thousands of small shops and service businesses that serve the communities with their 'high streets'.[19] They provide the locations for consumer experiences brought about through social conversations.[20] Their numbers are decreasing year by year, and there are calls for government intervention to maintain a healthy independent retail sector, as independent retailers contribute significantly to the preservation of local communities.[21] The potential closure of these great good places has raised awareness of what would be missing, much of which relates to the perceived lack of opportunities for consumers to have the experience of socialising.

Perspectives on the consumer experience

To what extent is there a common understanding of a consumer experience?

Both the word 'experience' and the phrase 'consumer experience' are used often in the context of services marketing, but the meanings and connotations may differ according to the user.

The consumer perspective

Taking the perspective of consumers and their representatives, it is noticeable that, on balance, a consumer experience means a *bad experience* with the purchase of a good or service. On the internet, for example, one of the well-known search engines, Yahoo!, lists 30 websites dealing with consumer experiences. Some of them, such as 'weBBBox.com', acknowledge that consumers have both good and bad stories to relate – 'If you tell us about your good and bad experiences, with your favorite and not-so-favorite businesses, we'll post them here in the webBbox for all the world to read.' However, the majority of the websites, by their very name, assume a negative stance on consumer experiences, and their addresses vary, from the obvious 'complaints.com' or 'The Complaint Station' to the more provocative 'bitchaboutit.com', 'Gripenet' and 'MadNow.com'.

Even in government reports consumer experiences are juxtaposed with consumers' rights of complaint. A report by the General Consumer Council for Northern Ireland,[22] for example, states that 'we tracked the *experiences* of Northern Ireland consumers in the previous 12 months from having reason to complain to seeking advice and taking action in relation to their complaint ...'.

This commonly held view of a consumer experience regards experience as relating to *a particular incident that a consumer has undergone with a service provider*, and furthermore, often one that may have been unpleasant. The voicing and sharing of complaints also implies that different consumers may have similar experiences with the same service provider. The bad experience of purchasing a VCR from Company X with malfunctioning remote control, and the subsequent hassle in replacing it, may be a familiar story for several consumers. In Peter and Christine's story of the trail ride, there were many separate incidents, and their particular interchange with the service providers over the issue of 'tips' would have been a (rather negative) consumer experience, according to the view above.

The services marketer perspective

In contrast, service marketers take the perspective that a consumer experience is a *memorable episode based on a consumer's direct personal participation or observation*.

Pine and Gilmore distinguish experiences from the other elements of Figure 5.1 as follows (see Table 5.1).

They emphasise that experiences 'occur within any individual who has been engaged on an emotional, physical, intellectual, or even spiritual level. The result? No two people can have the same experience.'[23] From their perspective, experiences are not simply particular incidents that consumers undergo with service providers, they are memorable events that engage the consumers. So, Peter and Christine's consumer experiences would relate to their engagement with the trail ride on the emotional (fear, sense of achievement), physical (discomfort on ride, satisfied hunger) and intellectual (learnt

Table 5.1 Distinctive characteristics of experiences

Economic units	Distinctive characteristics
Commodities	Basic materials extracted from the natural world
Goods	Tangible products that companies standardise and then inventory
Services	Intangible activities performed for a particular customer
Experiences	Memorable events that engage individuals in a personal way

riding skills, knowledge of the terrain flora and fauna) levels over the whole event. Furthermore, they would each have different experiences.

Schmitt,[24] a proponent of 'experiential marketing', agrees with Pine and Gilmore's definition of experience, pointing out that experiences require some stimulation, and that the marketer needs to provide the stimulant in order to create desired customer experiences. He argues that 'as a manager, rather than being concerned with any particular individual experience, you need to ask yourself the more important strategic question of what type of experiences you want to provide and how you can provide them with perpetually fresh appeal'. Such a strategic underpinning of experiential marketing can, he believes, be achieved by addressing five components of customer experiences:

- sense
- feel
- think
- act
- relate.

Table 5.2 gives a brief contextual description of the components, which are derived from the consumer behaviour field. The trail ride experience in Exhibit 5.1 can be analysed according to the five components.

Sensory experiences of all types were demonstrated on the trail ride. The service providers had quite a lot of control over this aspect. They chose the particular route or trail to provide stunning views. They gave instructions on how to ride. They ensured trail ride sounds of horses going over authentic terrain, and encouraged singing and 'hollering'. They cooked huge barbecued steaks, and they ensured that all consumers experienced the smell of the camp-fire.

According to both Peter's account and Christine's diary, there were many individual emotions and feelings experienced during the whole event, ranging from feelings of fear to relief and high spirits. The learning to ride a horse was certainly a problem-solving exercise that challenged them, especially when the horse was walking next to the sheer drop. Similarly the

Table 5.2 Schmitt's five components of the customer experience

Component	Description
Sense	Creation of sensory experiences through sight, touch, sound, taste and smell
Feel	Creation of affective experiences during consumption
Think	Creation of cognitive, problem-solving experiences that engage customers creatively
Act	Enhancement of customers' physical experiences
Relate	Creation of 'individual experiences' relating the customer to his or her ideal self, other people, or cultures

Source: Adapted from Schmitt, 1999 (see note 3).

two-hour ride was a physical ordeal that neither of them had previously experienced. At the end they had learnt something about a different culture and enjoyed recounting their stories back home in the UK.

Academic perspectives

There is an academic interest in examining how individuals describe their own experiences.[25] There is value in understanding the symbolic meanings attached to consumer experiences in the act of consumption. Here, the assumption is that consumers' 'reality' is complicated by a reliance on sign perceptions, interpretations and uses. An understanding of how individual consumers perceive marketing stimuli, and how they interpret and use them, should then provide insights for marketing management. In a study of the consumer experience of the British pub, for example, a semiotic analysis of consumers' experiences in, and of public houses, concluded that the pub concept is associated (by consumers) with individuality and personal choice, rather than a mass-marketing approach.[26] The strategies of the multiple pub operators, that involved uniform pub brands, were therefore seriously questioned in the light of these interpretations of consumers' accounts of their pub experiences.

We have seen reference, in Chapter 1, to services which have *experience attributes*, as distinct from search or credence attributes. In this sense, experience refers to the accumulated knowledge consumers gain through undertaking a service that allows them to evaluate the service after the event. However, from an academic perspective, the notion of *a consumer experience as Gestalt* tends to prevail over the notion of it being related to a particular incident with a service provider, or to the accumulation of knowledge only. This is why theatre, in its true sense, can aid service marketers in the creation of experiences for consumers. In theatre, each performance is designed to achieve a specific audience reaction, with a detailed consideration given to *all the elements* that create the reaction (improvisation, casting, role play and rehearsal associated with actors, together with stage management, lighting, sound, and costume and props associated with the setting) and to how they work together. The role of the audience, in addition to the role of the actors, is always considered explicitly, and the audience role is different in different forms of theatre.[27] We have seen, from Chapter 3, that audience roles in theatre can be transposed to customer roles in services (refer back to Table 3.1). The experiences of customers playing the role of voyeurs, for example, would be different from those playing the roles of spect-actors, sense-ceptors or connoisseurs. This brings us back to Schmitt's strategic question about what type of experiences you should provide and how you can provide them.

The use of theatrical techniques to create consumer experiences provides an opportunity to go beyond the superficiality that surrounds much of the popular conception of retail or service theatre, and at the same time explore a type of experience in some detail, together with the ways of providing it. To illustrate, let us suppose a retail or service provider wishes to provide an experience with consumers in the role of spect-actor. As a spect-actor

- the customer's role is transparent and clearly understood by both the customer and service provider(s)
- the customer has the opportunity on-site to be critical of the offer and the way it is presented.

It is seen from Table 3.1 that the role of the consumer as spect-actor was informed by the work of the theatre practitioner Bertolt Brecht. A rich source of ideas can be generated for service providers, that wish to offer different, engaging experiences to consumers (in their roles as spect-actors), from a detailed examination of three aspects of theatre that Brecht directed:

1. methods for managing and developing the roles and performances of actors,

2. techniques for providing planned opportunities for audiences to influence performances, and

3. arrangement of the staging and mechanics for stimulating audience participation.[28]

There are parallels in human resource management (with 1 and 2 above) and operations management (with 3 above) in the creation of these experiences with large organisations, such as the Venetian Hotel, or with smaller operations such as the Trail Ride or even the UK corner shop.

Implications for service management

Whether or not we are living in an experience economy, there is evidence that consumers are willing and able to pay for experiences. Three implications for service management who wish to create consumer experiences arise from the discussion above.

1. *There seem to be different perspectives on the meaning of experience, and these perspectives need to be acknowledged and addressed by management.* There is evidence that, in popular parlance, a consumer experience is synonymous with a critical incident of the type described in Chapter 4, and as with consumer accounts of critical incidents, the majority of such experiences are 'bad'. Bad experiences lead to complaints and an 'us and them' mentality between the consumer and provider. Notions of co-production of an experience between consumer and producer are undermined. It is therefore in the interests of service management to reinforce the view of their offered experience as an engaging event or episode – something to which consumers contribute part of themselves. An eating and drinking establishment may be an adequate descriptor, but an eating, drinking and talking establishment may change the perception of dining at Bobby Byrnes from a functional service (with many incidents and encounters) to a place where the consumer is an integral part of an experience.

2. *All the evidence suggests that the creation of an experience should be highly focused, with great attention to detail.* The intended effect on the consumer must be absolutely clear with all stimuli reinforcing the effect.

This applies equally to theme-related virtual experiences, such as the Grand Canal Shoppes in the Venetian Hotel, and social experiences in places such as the local butcher's shop. In the former case, the shops, restaurants and the 'actors' must conform to visitors' perceptions of Venice; for example, pasta restaurants in 'St Mark's Square'. In the latter, employees can be trained to talk to customers and encourage customer-to-customer interactions in the shop to provide the opportunity for social exchanges and the dissemination of local news. Help in creating and sustaining a focus can be gained through reproducing ideas that emanate from theatre practice for generating audience reactions, or by using the components in Table 5.2 as a checklist for engaging individuals on emotional, physical and intellectual levels.

3. *Much can still be learnt about the pricing of experiences.* Pine and Gilmore argue strongly that organisations can charge premium prices. But how much can/should organisations charge? Could the Trail Ride operators have charged more than $139, given that potential customers were being turned away? It should be noted that prices for the Gondola rides in the Venetian Hotel went up 50 per cent, from $10 to $15 between two visits to the website in April and May 2001. There does seem to be the potential for companies to charge premium prices, as for many experiences that are on offer, demand is exceeding supply. The record amount paid for an experience no doubt goes to American businessman, Dennis Tito – £14 million for a week's holiday on the Russian Soyuz spacecraft in May 2001. It was to be 'the fulfilment of a life's dream to fly into space'.[29]

Pricing strategies such as cost-plus, or prepayment plans, which tend to be associated with services that are personnel based and which rely on 'experience evaluations',[30] do not appear to be appropriate for Gestalt experiences. It seems to depend on what consumers are prepared to pay, and inventive market research is needed to establish pricing structures that reflect consumers' spending thresholds.

SUMMARY

It has been argued that consumers wish to purchase experiences and that we may be at the beginning of an experience economy. For the service provider, there are benefits to be gained, in creating differentiated (out-of-the-ordinary) experiences that meet consumer needs, through premium pricing. The interest in creating on-site 'theatre' for consumers is a response to this challenge and also to the competition of online services. In parallel, there is evidence that consumers also value traditional social experiences provided by the great good places which are managed by service providers.

An experience may relate to a particular incident with a service provider, to accumulated knowledge, or to the Gestalt. In the latter case, the *engagement* of the consumer is the distinguishing feature. Organisations wishing to offer an experience therefore must consider in detail how to focus on creating a clear intended effect on consumers. Lessons on how to do this can be borrowed from theatre practice, with especial attention being given to engaging consumers on an emotional, physical and intellectual level. The pricing of out-of-the-ordinary experiences is neither straightforward nor easy to justify, and requires further research.

LEARNING OUTCOMES

Having read this chapter, you should be able to

- appreciate and critically evaluate the reasons for the upsurge in interest in consumer experiences

- understand the distinctive characteristics of engaging experiences and the components that make up such experiences

- distinguish between various definitions of 'experience', and how they offer different perspectives on consumer experiences

- evaluate the implications for service management arising from the discussion of consumer experiences.

DISCUSSION QUESTIONS AND EXERCISES

1. What makes a consumer *experience*?

2. Use search engines with the words 'retail theatre' or 'retail theater'. From the results of the search, what appear to be the elements of theatre as applied in retailing?

3. What great good places do you frequent?

4. Explain the different perspectives on the meaning of 'experience'.

5. What advantages might there be for customers to be active, rather than passive participants?

Notes and references

1. Pine, B. H. II and Gilmore, J. H., 'Welcome to the Experience Economy', *Harvard Business Review*, July-August, 1998, pp. 97–105.
2. Pine, B. H. II and Gilmore, J. H., *The Experience Economy: Work is Theater and Every Business a Stage*, HBS Press, Boston Mass., 1999.
3. Schmitt, B. H., *Experiential Marketing*, The Free Press, New York, 1999.
4. Arnould, E. J. and Price, L. L., 'River Magic: Extraordinary Experience and the Extended Service Encounter', *Journal of Consumer Research*, vol. 20, June 1993, pp. 24–45.

5. Can be seen on the website http://rockytrails.com/trail.html

6. Pine and Gilmore, *The Experience Economy*.

7. Rhodes, T., 'US Buys Off-the-shelf Christmas', *The Sunday Times*, London, 24 December 2000.

8. Bray, P., 'Times Change, but People Don't', *The Sunday Times*, London, 13 June 2000.

9. Retail Verdict UK, A Monthly Newsletter, 'Retail Theatre: Interaction Ups Footfall', Verdict Research Limited, October 1999.

10. Baron, S., Harris, K. and Harris, R., 'Retail Theatre: The "Intended Effect" of the Performance', *Journal of Service Research*, November 2001.

11. Pine and Gilmore argue, however, that 'work *is* theater', and would not want to present work *as* theater, i.e. in a metaphorical sense (Pine and Gilmore, *The Experience Economy*, chapter 6).

12. These and other quotes of retail theatre can be found in Baron, Harris and Harris, 'Retail Theatre: The "Intended Effect" of the Performance'.

13. Notes by Doug Hoffman, as circulated to SERVNET subscribers on 1 May 2001 from *Doug.Hoffman@mail,biz.colostate.edu*

14. See http://www.venetian.com

15. Oldenburg, R., *The Great Good Place*, Marlowe & Company, New York, 1999.

16. Levine, J., 'A Place to Chat', *Forbes*, 9 September 1996.

17. Oldenburg, R., *The Great Good Place*.

18. See http://www.bobbybyrnes.com

19. Parker, C. and Byrom, J., 'Towards a Healthy High Street: Training the Independent Retailer', Manchester Metropolitan University, Summer 2000.

20. Baron, S., Leaver, D., Oldfield, B. M. and Cassidy, K., 'Independent Food and Grocery Retailers: Attitudes and Opinions in the Year 2000', Manchester Metropolitan University, June 2000.

21. Pickering, J. F., Greene, F. J. and Cockerill, T. A. J., 'The Future of the Neighbourhood Store', Durham University Business School Publications, September 1998.

22. General Consumer Council for Northern Ireland, *Consumers in the Dark: Rights, Redress and Proficiency*, 1998.

23. Pine and Gilmore, *The Experience Economy*, p. 12.

24. Schmitt, *Experiential Marketing*.

25. Giorgi, A., 'Concerning the Possibility of Phenomological Research', *Journal of Phenomological Research*, vol. 14, Autumn 1983, pp. 129–70.

26. Clarke, I., Kell, I., Schmidt, R. and Vignali, C., 'Thinking the Thoughts They Do: Symbolism and Meaning in the Consumer Experience of the "British Pub"', *British Food Journal*, vol. 102, no. 9, 2000, pp. 692–710.

27. Baron, Harris, and Harris, 'Retail Theatre: The "Intended Effect" of the Performance'.

28. Harris, K., Harris, R. and Baron, S., 'Customer Participation in Retail Service: Lessons from Brecht', *International Journal of Retail and Distribution Management*, April 2001.

29. Meek, J., 'Attention Houston, Tito Has Boarded', *The Guardian*, Manchester, UK, 1 May 2001.

30. Guiltinan, J. P., 'A Conceptual Framework for Pricing Consumer Services', Proceedings of the 7th Annual Services Marketing Conference, American Marketing Association, Chicago, pp. 11–15.

Service design

LEARNING OBJECTIVES

Overall aim of the chapter:
To provide a comprehensive outline and evaluation of research on the design of the service process and the design of the physical service environment.

In particular, the *chapter objectives* are

- to demonstrate the place of service design in the expanded services marketing mix

- to provide an overview of the techniques of service blueprinting and service mapping used in service process design

- to summarise the strategic and operational applications of service blueprinting and mapping

- to introduce the environmental dimensions of the 'servicescape', and the effects on customer and employee responses

- to provide a classification of physical service environments

- to summarise research on the effects of ambient conditions on human behaviour.

Introduction

When we speak of service design, we may be speaking of the design of the *process*, or the design of the *physical environment*. The earlier chapters have shown the importance of process and the physical environment (a major component of physical evidence) in the services marketing mix. The additional 3Ps – process, people and physical evidence – are often more prominent in customers' perceptions of services than the traditional 4Ps. (Refer back to the critical incident accounts in Table 2.1.) In this chapter, we summarise the main contributions to theory regarding the *design* of

● the service process

● the physical service environment.

This does not mean that P for people is being ignored. For example, it is strongly advocated that consumers should be actively involved in designing a service process 'regardless of whether consumers are privy to, or even aware of all parts of the process, their awareness of its results and evidence makes them potentially valuable participants in the design of the entire system'.[1] In a similar vein, design of physical service environments is significantly underpinned by an understanding of consumer and employee approach and avoidance behaviours.[2]

Figure 6.1 shows the structure of this chapter. It links the material of Chapter 3 with the two strands of service design. It should be stressed that the two strands are not mutually exclusive. For example, the design of the physical environment of a hotel would need to acknowledge the processes undertaken by guests, who arrive (need reception area), use rooms (need easy access to rooms), and possibly eat/drink/swim, and so on (need signage and access to facilities). However, by separating the two strands, we can concentrate on the essential components of each of them.

Starting from the top of Figure 6.1, the services marketing system, introduced in Figure 3.1, focused management attention on obtaining a balance between operational efficiency and marketing effectiveness. By and large, operational efficiency can be addressed through the design of the process,

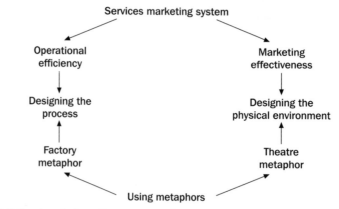

Figure 6.1 Service design: the two strands

whereas the design of the physical service environment is concerned with marketing effectiveness. Starting at the bottom of Figure 6.1, the application of the factory metaphor implies an efficiency goal, while the application of the theatre metaphor implies a marketing effectiveness goal – 'rave reviews from audiences'. In general, the factory metaphor provides ideas for the design of the process, whereas the theatre metaphor provides ideas for the design of the physical service environment.

Designing the process

As already stated, service is a process not a tangible product. It is worth reflecting, however, that in the development of many tangible products, there is usually a design stage prior to production and distribution. For example:

- a new model of car will require engineering drawings
- a house will require architects' plans
- sketches will be drawn of fashion or furniture prototypes.

When we think of a design stage, it is normally carried out with reference to a visual or diagrammatic representation of the tangible product. Let us consider the task of designing a house as an example. Architects' drawings may take the form of front, side and top elevations of the proposed building. Without these commonly understood visual references, discussions about specifications or modifications of the house would be difficult, if not impossible. Imagine using words only to communicate about plumbing, electrical supply and kitchen cupboard requirements. Words on their own, whether written or spoken, may lack the desired level of precision or be unclear in terms of context. The visual front, side and top elevations reduce imprecision and potential misunderstandings, thereby preventing potentially expensive mistakes.

For tangible products, therefore

- the design stage is an importa⁀ ᵃˢᵖᵉᶜᵗ ᵒᶠ product development. Design is sometimes synonymous wi
- sketches, diagrams or drawin₂ be indispensable.

Tangible products exist in time sketches, diagrams and drawings the product (that is, its existence processes, and which exist only iı in a similar manner to that appli

We demonstrate some of the ı consequences of applying desigı by blueprinting is described, anɑ prints is given. Second, we descri is a logical extension to the bluer design methods to reduce the ris; potential applications of the blu

Blueprinting

A technique for structural process design, called blueprinting, was developed by Shostack in 1987.[3] As we shall see, the service blueprint is a very important and effective management tool in its own right. However, in addition, the interest in blueprinting

- highlighted the importance of service design
- focused attention on process modelling
- encouraged the development of other diagrammatic techniques in particular, service mapping.[4]

There were already in existence techniques for charting processes or flows. For example, PERT (Program Evaluation and Review Technique) and Critical Path Analysis were commonplace visual scheduling aids for project planning, and the use of flowcharting to visualise input, output and iterative processes in computer program design was the norm. The value of the early work on blueprinting was the use and selection of the existing techniques to facilitate, specifically, the design of services.

Stages in blueprint preparation

A comprehensive visual model of a service process, in the form of a blueprint, provides the means for management more readily to identify strong and weak links in the process, and to discuss the effects of potential structural changes such as greater customisation or an expanded range of services. It should be emphasised that it is not only a new service which has to be designed. It is often worth taking a closer look at the design of existing services. In each case, the preparation of a service blueprint requires a series of stages. Normally, they are:

1. Represent the (service) product in the form of its molecular structure;
2. Break down the process into logical steps;
3. Recognise the variability in the process;
4. Identify the 'invisible' elements in the process.

Within the context of hairdressing services, we will discuss each stage in greater detail.

1. Representing a (service) product in the form of its molecular structure.

Most products are a combination of intangible and tangible elements. For products classified as 'services', the intangible elements predominate. Representing intangible elements by circles, and tangible elements by squares, the molecular structures of two service providers of hairdressing – a gents' barber and a unisex hairdresser – are shown in Figures 6.2 and 6.3 respectively.

diagram such as Figure 6.2 it is possible to give more prominence to believed to have greater importance in the product offering. The for the 'haircutting skills' indicates that this is deemed to be the

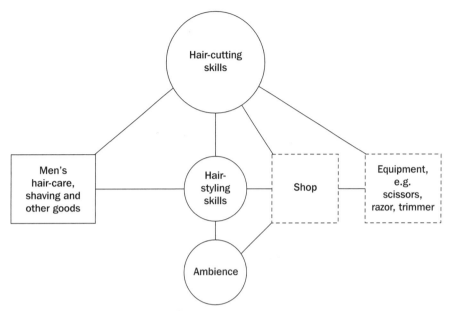

Figure 6.2 One-man gents' barber

key intangible element of the service. 'Hair-styling skills', 'ambience' and the range of tangible goods on sale are felt to be subsidiary to the customers' needs for a haircut.

It is also possible to identify what Shostack terms 'essential service evidence', by broken-line squares. An essential service element is a physical element which is essential to the service provided, but which cannot be purchased by the customer. (In a different context, the aeroplane, for any scheduled or package flight, constitutes essential service evidence.) Essential service evidence may have a significant effect on the service purchase.

Additionally, there may be many examples of peripheral (tangible) evidence such as newspapers or magazines to read, appointment cards, or coat-hangers. These are not essential for the operation of the core services, but may add to, or detract from, a customer's satisfaction with the service.

In Figure 6.3, we see that for the unisex hairdresser the relative importance of hair-styling and hair-cutting skills is reversed. Also the offer of hair-washing skills, manicure skills and advice/consultancy is available and important.

Although, arguably, the molecular structure stage could be omitted in the production of a service blueprint, and the final version of a molecular diagram may seem very obvious, we would argue strongly that it should be undertaken for the following reasons:

● It concentrates the mind and provokes valuable discussion.

Even for the relatively straightforward one-man gents' barber business, a keen debate centred around the intangible elements. Eventually, the original 'hair-cut' and 'hair-style' were replaced by 'hair-cutting skills' and 'hair-styling skills'.

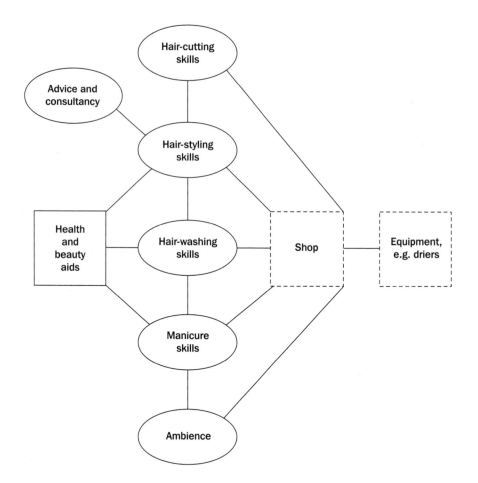

Figure 6.3 Multi-staffed unisex hairdresser

● It increases understanding of the service being offered.

For the multi-staffed unisex hairdresser, two aspects were worthy of debate. First, the relative sizes of the circles were considered in great detail. In particular, how important is advice and consultancy? Second, after a question was raised about how a unisex salon differs from a female hairdresser, the element 'ambience' was added to the diagram. This provoked further debate.

Clearly there is a subjective element to any molecular structure. However, the identification of basic elements and essential evidence is, we feel, necessary before beginning the construction of any subsequent process diagram.

2. Breaking down the process into logical steps.

Taking the gents' barber as the example, we can trace the steps of a typical customer from arrival at the barber's shop to his departure.

- When the customer arrives, he is greeted by the barber, who directs him to a seated waiting area unless there are no other customers. In such a case the customer will be directed to the barber's chair.
- Once in the barber's chair, the customer is asked his requirements.
- The customer's hair is then cut in a way which (hopefully) meets his requirements.
- The barber, on finishing, will ask if the customer requires anything else (e.g. hair-care products).
- The customer will then pay and depart.
- The barber thanks the customer for payment (and possibly a tip), and in his goodbye statement infers a repeat visit.

Once agreement is reached on the sequence of basic steps, it is possible to represent the process visually. This is shown in the top half of Figure 6.4, and represents the element of the service that is normally in the customer's line of visibility (and within hearing distance).

3. Recognising the variability in the process.

In Figure 6.4, you will notice that in three places the symbol (a fan) appears. The fan is used to denote variability within the process. Variability can be either

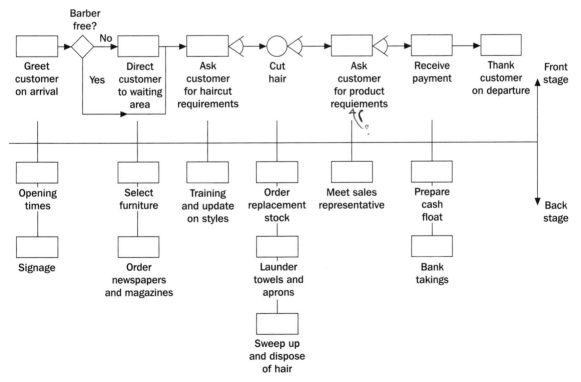

Figure 6.4 Blueprint of one-man gents' barber

- planned and controlled by the service provider, i.e. a range of potential actions that may be taken or
- unplanned, i.e. a range of potential events that might occur.

In the former case, the fan follows a rectangle. The first example is when the barber asks the customer for haircut requirements. The range of offers open to the customer is controlled by the barber. The barber may plan, for example, to offer only a limited number of options ('short-back-and-sides' or 'trim'; square neck or tapered), or to offer a wide range of the latest styles. Although customers may request different cuts, the variability in the requests is controlled by the barber. In the second example, where customers are asked whether they require any (hair-care) products, the variability of responses is controlled by what the barber has on offer on the shelves.

In the latter case, where variability is unplanned, the fan follows a circle. When the barber cuts a 'short-back-and-sides', it will not be an identical cut for all customers because of human error, and so a range of potential outcomes may occur. Within reason, customers may accept variability with a certain type of cut. There is an acceptable tolerance band within which a 'trim' or 'square neck' can fall. However, a 'trim' which more resembles a 'short-back-and-sides' would represent a deviation from tolerance standards which is unacceptable. Such deviations would be treated as quality issues and represent service failures.

It is important at this stage in the service design process to recognise where unplanned variation may occur and to anticipate potential service failure points.

4. Identifying the 'invisible' elements in the process.

The lower half of Figure 6.4 shows the elements of the barber's operation that are normally outside the customer's line of visibility, and how they are linked to the visible elements of the process. If greater detail is required, many of the invisible elements themselves can be represented as processes. For example, the element 'order replacement stock' is a process involving a number of stages, beginning with the initial contract with the supplier and ending with delivery and settlement of the invoice.

In total, Figure 6.4 provides a blueprint for the gents' barber. His case is somewhat unusual in that the barber himself is involved in all the visible and invisible elements and processes. He may find the blueprint useful mainly as a means of enhancing the service and determining potential future actions or strategies. In most services, however, the various contact personnel may only be involved in a limited part of the visible or invisible activities. In a theme park, for example, where seasonal employment is high, a blueprint of the whole operation provides an understandable visual reference to all employees, who may otherwise have a very blinkered view of the product offer. Newly employed or part-time staff can more readily be shown how their role fits into the whole operation, and that it is recognised to the same extent as other job roles.

Before moving on to discuss service mapping, it is worth emphasising three features of blueprint construction.

1. It is very difficult to do, even following the four stages above. It may involve a large investment in time. Apparently, Shostack herself found it very difficult to blueprint a new bank service because of its complexity. She therefore turned to a shoeshine stand service, developed the blueprint, and only then moved on to the more complex service.[5]

2. Those involved with the blueprint construction are forced to understand and discuss the basic elements of the service and to reach agreements about relative importance of elements, planned and unplanned variability and service failure points. Serious debate on such fundamentals, forcing participants to step back and take a bird's-eye view of the operation, may be considered a considerable benefit in its own right.

3. It is important that the visible element of a blueprint is constructed from the customer's perspective. Yet, in practice, service processes are often 'documented from a manager's or service designer's perspective, rather than a customer's perspective'.[6] Some suggested techniques which focus on the customer perspective include 'service journey audits',[7] and 'service transaction analysis'.[8]

Overall, the benefits of blueprinting must be weighed against the time investment.

Service mapping

Service maps build on blueprints and provide two additional features to add to management information.

●   They pay greater attention to customer interaction with the service organisation.

Clear diagrammatic distinctions are made between actions of customers and of service contact personnel. In effect, more detail is provided on the visible activities in blueprints such as Figure 6.4.

●   Additional vertical layers to the diagram are drawn in service maps to provide a visual representation of the structure of the service.

In particular, the 'invisible' activities are divided into those provided by frontline employees, support staff and management services.

In a service map (Figure 6.5), therefore, the horizontal axis denotes the process, going from left to right, and the vertical axis denotes the structure of the service provided. The larger the service organisation, the greater the need to make clear the structure in order that the service logic is understood by all employees.

In the blueprinting examples, one horizontal line divides the visible from the invisible elements. Consequently, it is commonly known as the line of visibility. In service maps, the organisation structure, denoted on the vertical axis, is made clearer through more dividing lines. There are four lines in total.

1. *The line of interaction.* This denotes the distinction between the customer's and frontline employee's parts in the service encounter.

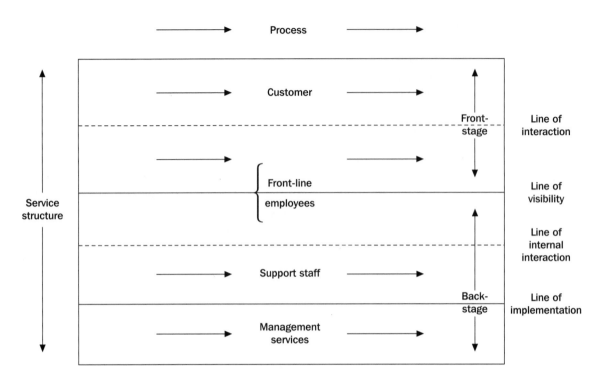

Figure 6.5 The layers and features of the service map

2. *The line of visibility.* Note here, that whilst much of the work of frontline employees is concerned with the service encounter, which is above the line of visibility, some of their work is carried out below the line of visibility, that is, out of sight of the customer.

3. *The line of internal interaction.* This denotes the division between the frontline employees and the operations support staff. Such internal interactions normally occur out of sight of customers.

4. *The line of implementation.* This denotes the division between operations support staff and general management services. It may be the case that the latter are located physically at a distance from the former and are not therefore directly involved with implementing the service.

To illustrate the vertical dimension of a service map (Figure 6.6), let us examine one element of a process: the payment for goods in an outlet of a multiple grocery retailer. Figure 6.6 is only a snapshot of a vertical portion of a much larger, complete service map.

Complete maps can be drawn of

● Specific services, such as that provided by a multiple grocery retailer or by a unisex hairdresser. Such maps will generally be large and complicated and the investment in time will be even greater than for blueprinting.

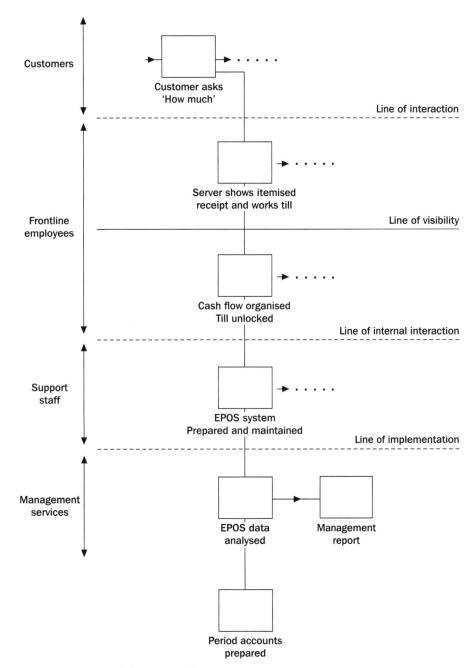

Figure 6.6 Vertical dimension of service map

● Concepts. In a concept service map, general issues are highlighted, but within the layered structure. An example is given in Figure 6.7, where five service quality dimensions are considered in the row below the line of interaction. (The five service quality dimensions will be discussed in greater detail in Chapter 8.)

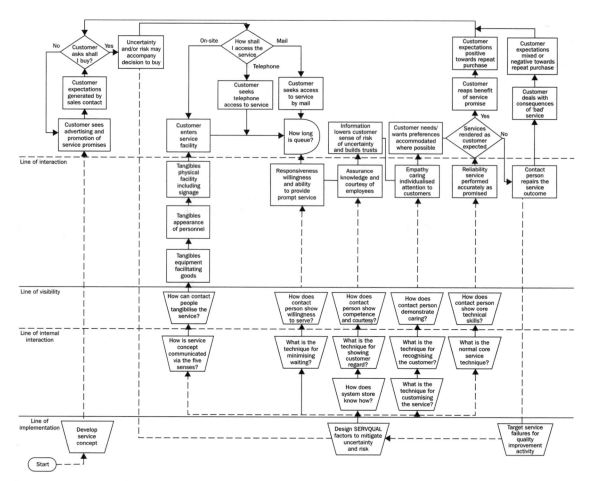

Figure 6.7   Concept service map

Applications of blueprinting and service mapping

1. Service failures and fail-safing

Whatever the diagrammatic form of a service design – whether it be a blueprint, a specific service map or a concept service map – one of the main aims will be to identify the potential points in the process which may result in a service failure. It is probably inevitable that on some occasion either the customer or the server will make some mistake. If these occasions can be anticipated, and the mistake prevented from turning into a service 'defect' and hence a service failure, then the effort spent in service design may be justified. Once points of potential service failures have been identified, failsafes can be designed to reduce the risk of human mistakes turning into actual service failures.

In the 'Waymark Holiday' case (Case Study 5), for example, an account is given of how a holiday in Greece, at Easter, did not match the expectations of three customers. Although, arguably, the poor experience may have been largely the fault of the customers in being inadequately prepared for such a holiday, the company have responded by taking the responsibility, and introducing a fail-safe, in the form of an expanded checklist of questions to ask new customers, in order to avert the possibility of similar experiences being repeated.

Due to customer participation in services, mistakes or errors that may lead to service failures can be made by servers or by customers. Chase and Stewart[9] provide a very useful classification of server errors and customer errors, and the remainder of this section draws heavily on their work.

Server errors are conveniently described as task, treatment or tangibles.

- Task errors include doing work incorrectly or work not requested, or doing work in the wrong order or too slowly.
- Treatment errors include failure to acknowledge, listen to, or react appropriately to a customer.
- Tangible errors may be caused by failure to clean facilities or provide clean uniforms, or by failure to control ambient conditions in the physical environment.

Being aware of potential server errors is important. What is also needed, in order to fail-safe the server, is imaginative but simple means of preventing the errors reoccurring. A church minister may prevent the error of failing to mention family members by name during a funeral by always completing a pro forma prior to the service, or by going over a checklist with the funeral director. A consultant surgeon in a hospital could always talk to patients after examinations as part of a routine. Fail-safes are often simple mechanisms, but their absence can be damaging.

Customer errors can be classified as relating to preparation for the service encounter, the encounter itself, or to the resolution of the encounter.

- Preparation errors may result from the failure of customers to bring the necessary materials to the encounter, or to understand their roles in the service encounter.
- Encounter errors include failure of customers to remember steps in the service process, to follow the system flow or to specify desires or follow instructions.
- Resolution errors include failure of customers to signal service failures, learn from experience, adjust expectations or execute appropriate post-encounter actions.

The dentist's patients may miss appointments through forgetfulness. The accountant's clients may fail to produce necessary receipts. The lead violinist of the school orchestra may forget her music! Each of these are customer preparation errors, but it is obviously in the service provider's interest to devise ways of minimising the frequency of such errors through some fail-safe device, such as timely reminders or clear instructions to clients prior to the encounter. The Thai restaurant owner may prevent customer encounter errors with the lunchtime buffet feast (resulting in customer confusion and crowding) by providing diners with clear details of the routes round the buffet tables and recommended menu mixes. The follow-up customer call after a car service represents a means of ensuring that the customer has the opportunity to engage in appropriate post-encounter activities.

Chase and Stewart,[10] using a service map of the standard car service at a car dealership as a reference, identify many potential service failure points. Those which represent customer errors are denoted above the service map, and those which represent server errors are denoted below the map. Although, once drawn to the attention, most potential service failures are obvious, they are easily overlooked without a comprehensive diagram of the service design. Of equal importance to the car dealership management is that most fail-safes are relatively inexpensive to employ. The failure to notice that a customer has arrived, for example, can easily be averted by the use of a bell chain. This must be followed by the acknowledgement of the customer's arrival by a frontline employee. Such simple devices may avoid loss of business through customer frustration on confusion. Proper attention to detail such as this throughout the process is facilitated by use of the service map as a point of reference.

2. Ensuring safety

For many services, for example air travel, theme parks, and hospitals, safety of the consumer is paramount, and a significant element of the service operation. Any consequences resulting from a perceived lack of appropriate attention to safety issues are normally highly publicised. Take, for instance, the following pieces from *The Times* of 9 January, 2001:

> *Hospitals are dangerous places. Around 5,000 patients die each year from infections caught after arriving in hospital. Yet these death traps continue to accept admissions, even stacking up their customers in corridors.*[11]

> *... a damning survey [of hospitals] ... that found overflowing lavatories, soiled tissues lying around the ward, carpets ripped up, and even pigeons in a canteen. A third of hospitals failed basic hygiene checks, including wards, lavatories, décor, furniture linen and 'smells'.*[12]

These are cases where there is visible evidence that the invisible elements of the service operation are not being undertaken effectively.

Clearly, a blueprinting or service mapping approach cannot, in itself, enhance safety. But, as can be seen below, with an illustration of a study of butchers' services, the linking of the consumer-centred process (the visible part of a blueprint) with the 'invisible' practices of the service providers, can highlight important safety issues that may otherwise have been overlooked.

The service provided by butchers in the UK had received considerable publicity in the late 1990s especially through an outbreak of E. coli food poisoning resulting in fatalities. The butcher's shop at the centre of the outbreak had failed to separate raw and cooked meats, and did not provide separate knives/tools, separate tables/work surfaces, scales or vacuum packers. To understand more clearly the practices carried out by butchers, an observational study was undertaken in 1999/2000 of 91 businesses that sold both raw and cooked meats.[13]

Observation of the consumer process, which includes paying for the purchased meats, immediately highlighted the issue of hand-washing practices of the employees. Hand washing was seen not to be routine after handling money or using the cash till. Indeed, for a minority of the businesses observed, hand-washing facilities were deemed unsatisfactory, where, for example, there was no dedicated wash-hand basin, no hot water, or soiled bars of soap. In all, the study was able to highlight specific areas for hygiene concern:

● the meat slicer
● the cooked meat scale pan
● the hand tap at the wash-hand basin
● the cooked meat chiller handle
● the vacuum packer
● the keys of the cash till
● a cleaning cloth used for cooked meat surfaces
● the butcher's apron.

The study had, in effect, undertaken the stages of blueprint construction outlined at the beginning of this section. The blueprint itself is an effective way of visualising the process, and the links between the visible and invisible elements.

3. Using blueprints to identify complexity and divergence and address service positioning

Once an acceptable blueprint has been drawn, in what ways can it aid understanding and determine potential actions?

Shostack proposed that, initially, two features of the process should be examined.[14]

● Level of complexity
● Degree of divergence

The level of complexity relates directly to the number of steps and sequences, and the interrelationships between them. The more steps and intricacies, the greater the complexity. The degree of divergence refers to the amount of planned scope or latitude which contact personnel are given. Low divergence results in a high level of standardisation. The fans on the blueprint indicate points where varying degrees of divergences can be considered.

Figure 6.8 provides a means for an initial classification of a service in terms of the two dimensions – complexity and divergence. According to this matrix, the gents' barber would fall into the north-west cell, that is, low in both complexity and divergence. The multi-staff unisex hairdresser is arguably more complex, because of services such as consultancy and advice, and hair-styling could be deliberately made as highly divergent, involving a high degree of customisation.

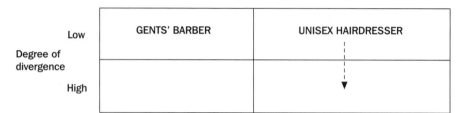

Level of complexity

Degree of
divergence

| | Low | GENTS' BARBER | UNISEX HAIRDRESSER |
| | High | | |

Figure 6.8 Classification of services according to level of complexity and degree of divergence

In Figures 6.9, 6.10 and 6.11, Shostack provides examples of blueprints of services which differ according to the two dimensions of complexity and divergence. In each case, complexity is related to the size and number of elements in the blueprint, and divergence depends on the number of fans in the diagram.

Returning to our hairdressing examples, both the gents' barber and the unisex hairdresser can ask how they might increase or reduce complexity or divergence, and how this might alter their positioning in the market. The gents' barber, for example, could increase complexity in a number of ways. He could

- employ an assistant
- increase the range of goods to be sold
- deal with several suppliers, rather than one representative.

Each of these potential actions would result in a repositioning of his offer.

He could reduce complexity (to an even lower level) by, for example

- not stocking any goods at all
- not supplying reading material for waiting customers.

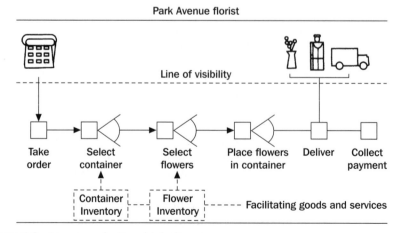

Figure 6.9 Low complexity – high divergence

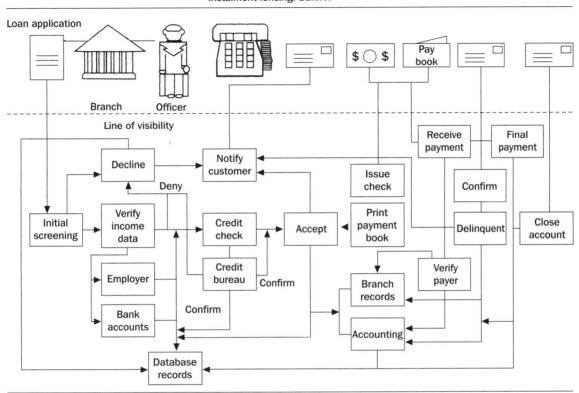

Figure 6.10 High complexity – low divergence, i.e. standardised

He could increase divergence by giving a greater emphasis to hair-styling. He could reduce divergence further by only offering, say, 'short-back-and-sides' cuts with two neckline levels.

Any change in complexity and divergence will reflect the barber's judgement of the current and potential customer base. Both the molecular diagram and the blueprint will enable him to focus on the elements of the process which affect positioning and operation.

4. Stimulating creativity

In our experience, the presentation of the visible component of a blueprint to a group of service providers or professionals acts as a catalyst for ideas and innovations with the service. The consumer process which underpins the visible part of the process does not necessarily have to be complex. For example, for a group of veterinary surgeons, the client experience involved with taking their dog or cat for a routine vaccination, presented as a non-complicated sequence of events (see Figure 6.12), provided the catalyst. For a group of dentists, the visible process showing the patient experience

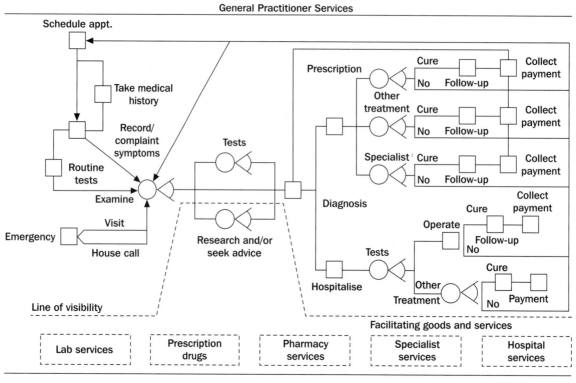

Figure 6.11   High complexity – high divergence

associated with a visit to the dentist for a routine check-up had the same effect.

Let us take the dog/cat vaccination process (Figure 6.12). Although the individual stages, and the sequence of stages itself seem straightforward, there are many ways in which veterinary practitioners respond to the questions below the line of visibility, and creativity does not require huge changes to existing practice. Even stage 1, (ensuring that clients receives appropriate reminders) can be done in several ways – from a conventional letter to the client to a cartoon-based reminder card addressed to the pet. However, the more cheerful reminder cards only add insult to injury if the pet has died in the interim, thus highlighting another key aspect of the service (efficient record keeping). Posing the questions in the shaded area, for all the stages of the process, usually generates discussions and new ideas from groups of interested people (for example, all employees in a veterinary practice).

Blueprints can also be used to aid *new* service development. A study of the development of nine new services identified 'lack of systematic reporting and feedback' and 'rudimentary documentation' as two of the factors contributing to problems and their symptoms in service development processes.[15] Both of these drawbacks can be overcome to a great extent by drawing and modifying the blueprint of the proposed new service as a means of communication. It can facilitate a balance between creativity and formal planning and control.

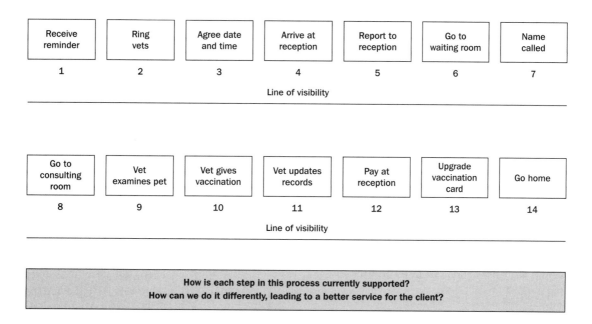

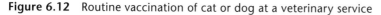

Figure 6.12 Routine vaccination of cat or dog at a veterinary service

Designing the physical environment
The servicescape

As noted in Chapter 4, service managers need to consider not only the impact of interpersonal interactions on customer perceptions and behaviour, but also the impact of what Bitner refers to as the 'Servicescape'.[16] The 'servicescape' describes elements of the built environment (that is, the man-made, physical surroundings) that constitute part of the service, as opposed to the natural or social environment – specific dimensions of the service-scape of a dentist, for example, including the lighting in the waiting rooms and the surgery, the wall decor, the signage and the temperature. Service providers demonstrate that they believe that servicescape dimensions can influence the cognitive and emotional responses of consumers to their service experience. A dentist, for example, may colour surgery walls pink in the belief that it helps to reduce the anxiety felt by patients, and may scatter small, cuddly toys around the surgery to help to put children at ease. Similarly, the supermarket operator may think that the smell of freshly baked bread pumped through the store will influence customers to buy bread. These components can potentially have as great an influence on customer behaviour as interpersonal encounters. For example, a customer may have a positive encounter with a sales assistant on entering a food store and be able to locate the ideal product, but may find waiting in a queue in a stifling atmosphere unbearable and consequently leave before making a purchase. The physical environment can also have a dramatic impact on the employee's approach to the service encounter. Research suggests that the same physical environment that can potentially affect consumers' reactions to their experience can affect the motivation and performance of service employees.[17]

Bitner presented a framework that illustrates how customer and employee internal responses and behaviours (that is, 'approach' or 'avoid') are influenced by servicescape elements. The servicescape environmental dimensions, referred to in the model, include:

- ambient conditions (air quality, temperature, noise, smell, etc.)
- spacial and functional features (layout, equipment, furnishings, etc.) and
- signs, symbols and artifacts (style of decor, signage).

The model illustrates how these elements can affect the consumers' and employees' emotional, cognitive and physiological state and their subsequent behaviour.

The physical service environment and customer satisfaction

Research, in a retail context, which examined customer behaviour in a pleasant and a not so pleasant store atmosphere, found that: 'Customer satisfaction with the store was greater in the pleasant store' and 'Customers in the pleasant store spontaneously spent more money on articles they simply liked'.[18] (The pleasantness of the store was based on its condition, layout/way-finding, and information rate; that is, the degree to which the merchandise presentation was out of the ordinary, yet integrated.)

Research, in the context of leisure services such as sporting events, concluded that: 'when the subjects perceived the servicescape to be of higher quality, they were more satisfied with the servicescape, and were therefore more inclined to want to go to games at the stadium', and 'What this servicescape quality/satisfaction/repatronage relationship means for owners and managers of leisure services is that careful attention should be given to each aspect of the servicescape to ensure that customers are satisfied, not only with the primary service, but also with the entire leisure service experience.'[19]

It is seen, therefore, that relationships between servicescape design and positive customer behaviours are being made in specific service sectors. Table 6.1 provides a classification of services by consumption purpose and time spent in the service facility, which highlights the types of services where the design of the physical environment is particularly important.

The more that services are viewed as hedonistic, and greater the amount of time the customer spends within the service facility, the greater the potential influence of the physical environment on customer affective responses, attitudes and repatronage behaviour.

So, whereas the design of the physical environment of a dry-cleaner may require most of the attention being given to the utilitarian service efficiency aspects, the design of the physical environment of a theme park would

Table 6.1 Classification of physical service environments

Time spent in facility	Purpose of consumption		
	Utilitarian		**Hedonic**
Minutes	● Dry-cleaner ● Taxi-cab ● Post-office ● Bank branch	● Barber's shop ● Coffee bar ● Lecture room ● Vets	● Games arcade ● Clairvoyant ● Sauna ● Children's playground
Hours	● Pre-natal class ● Law office ● Hospital out-patients ● Supermarket	● Restaurant/public house ● Airline/airport ● Museum ● Garden centre	● Shopping mall ● Football stadium ● Theatre ● Leisure centre
Days	● School ● Hospital ● Law court ● Training centre	● Hotel ● Conference Centre ● Health spa ● Caravan park	● Cruise liner ● Theme park ● Holiday villa ● Coach tour

require much greater attention to generation of customer excitement, fun and entertainment. As with other service classification systems outlined in Chapter 2, service providers in a given cell of Table 6.1 can draw on ideas of servicescape designs from other service providers in the same cell.

Additionally, those service providers that are wishing to concentrate more on consumer experiences, as outlined in Chapter 5, may look to moving from left to right in Table 6.1. For example, if an airport is to become more of a hedonic experience for customers, the airport designers could look to the kinds of physical environments which are created by the services in the far right column of Table 6.1. In Changi Airport in Singapore, for example, in addition to a very large shopping mall, the destination lounge contains an interactive science centre, a large games arcade, and a themed indoor orchid garden complete with streams, bridges, seats and tropical fish.

Physical environment design considerations

In designing the physical service environment, a balance has to be struck between enabling operational efficiency, and providing marketing effectiveness through offering opportunities for customers to engage in an experience. For the services, in the left column of Table 6.1, operational efficiency may determine the design of the physical environment. The design of hospital out-patients' departments, bank branches, schools, and even supermarkets are created to accommodate the main business function. In contrast, for the services in the right-hand column of Table 6.1, the design of the physical environment should encourage 'rave reviews from the customers', in keeping with the theatre metaphor (Chapter 3). The designs of the services in the middle column of Table 6.1 are the most challenging in obtaining an appropriate balance between operational efficiency and marketing effectiveness.

Take airports, for example.
The example of Changi Airport, above, demonstrates the opportunities for airport designs which go way beyond the utilitarian, having already succeeded in meeting the efficiency requirements of customers. In a similar vein, the company responsible for the design of the Dubai Duty Free Shopping area claim that by 'combining years of duty free experience with skills of visitor attractions, we introduce "retail theatre"'.[21] However, it would be inappropriate for airports to aim for 'theatre' until customers are satisfied with the environmental dimensions highlighted by Bitner; that is, ambient conditions, spacial and functional features, and the airport signs, symbols and artefacts. In a study of airport departure lounges, for example, Rowley and Slack[22] provided details of one particular lounge that 'did not succeed in conveying the message that the passenger was a valued customer'. The servicescape evidence for this conclusion included:

- departure board not working
- insufficient space between seating areas and insufficient numbers of seats
- hot and confined space
- high level of noise, due to background music and high density of people talking and moving
- people flows crossing each other
- only two ladies' toilet cubicles
- luggage left in locations that obstruct people movement because there is nowhere else to leave it.

The design of hotels is equally challenging. Many are designed in a utilitarian way that has attracted criticism. 'In them, one is nowhere: in Manchester, or in Verona, in Groningen, or in Roissy ... the room is a place of protection and the foyer is a non-place resembling an airport lounge.'[23] The purely functional design of a hotel can prevent guests from any meaningful exposure to other guests, and pays no regard to the consumer being an active part of the environment. To position itself more to the right of Table 6.1, hotel designers could, for example, 'reintroduce recesses, corners and curves, fuzziness, enabling people to meet, to get together in a part-open and part-closed space that favours community encounters'.[24] Such elements of hotel servicescape designs would be driven by the aim of getting people together rather than cocooning them.

The ambient conditions

The ambient conditions of a physical service environment include air quality, temperature, noise and smells. We are all aware that service providers can, and do, manipulate the ambient conditions in service environments – air conditioning in cars and hotel rooms, background music in restaurants and shopping malls, and the smell of potpourri in craft shops. What is less well known is the effect of these manipulations on consumer behaviour in the environment. Some recent studies on the effect of smell and/or music on consumer responses can be summarised as follows.

Smell/scent

Bone and Ellen[25] provided a model of the 'conventional wisdom' of the effect of smells, scents or odours on consumers in various service environments, and then reviewed the academic research findings relating to the model. The model links three olfactory features – scent *presence*, scent *pleasantness*, and scent *congruity* (that is, how well the olfactory cue complements other stimuli, such as music) – to the effects on the person:

- approach or avoidance
- mood (arousal and valence)
- cognitive effort

and to responses to the stimulus:

- affective and evaluative responses
- purchase intentions
- behaviour (time spent in facility, information search, variety seeking/ switching).

The relationships are believed to be moderated by individual differences and the task/content effects.

Bone and Ellen's overall conclusion, based on the existing research, was that 'the conventional wisdom is not significantly upheld in the empirical results'. For example, the research to date does not support the view that scent presence affects a retail customer's behaviour. Clearly, there is something of a mismatch, at the moment, between practitioner 'gut feel' as to the consumer responses to smell/scents, and the findings from academic research. More research, particularly on-site studies, would help service providers.

Music

Oakes[26] provided a structure, which he calls the musicscape, that relates background music features – *compositional* (tempo, harmony, volume) and *genre* (classical, popular, jazz) – to internal customer responses in the service environment:

- cognitive (expectations, perceived duration)
- emotional (elicited mood)

and behavioural outcomes in the environment:

- consumption speed
- actual stay duration
- purchase behaviour.

In the musicscape, the moderating variables are believed to be customer age, gender and social class, and familiarity with the music.

Research relating to these relationships suggests that:

● slower tempos tend to make consumers shop at a more leisurely pace, and sometimes to spend more money than do faster tempos

● shopper behaviour might differ according to the type of music played.[27]

However, it is again very difficult to generalise, and some studies have shown that the 'no music' option has yielded the most favourable customer responses and behavioural outcomes! At the same time, in Coventry in the UK, background music has been introduced for the *complete city centre shopping area*, with both tempo and genre being varied according to the time of day. The choice of classical music in the mornings, pop music at (the busier) lunchtime, and country-and-western music in the afternoon is presumably based on a 'conventional wisdom' view of the effects of background music on shopping behaviour. However, as with the olfactory effects, the empirical studies on the musical effects are contradictory, and situation specific, and do not necessarily support the conventional wisdom.

Current research is focusing on the combined effects of environmental cues; that is, lavender scents with classical music, on customer responses and behaviours.[28]

SUMMARY

In this chapter, two separate, but related aspects of service design have been introduced – design of the service process, and design of the physical service environment – both of which recognise the important people element of services.

As has been argued earlier, the process, physical evidence and people elements of the services marketing mix have significant parts to play in consumer accounts of satisfying and dissatisfying service encounters.

In designing the service process, for both existing and new service businesses, the service blueprint, and its derivatives, provide an informative visual aid. The applications of blueprinting include the reduction of service failure situations through fail-safing, the enhancement of core service safety, the identification of complexity and divergence in a service with a view to repositioning, and the provision of a visual catalyst for creativity in services. The design of a service process is influenced strongly by the factory metaphor, and the notion of operational efficiency (Chapter 3).

The design of the physical service environment or 'servicescape' is important to both customers and employees who frequent a service environment. In general, the environment should encourage 'approach' behaviours; that is, be comfortable and fit for purpose in the eyes of customers and employees. A useful classification of servicescapes is by purpose of consumption and typical time a customer spends in the service facility (shown in Table 6.1). As a rule of thumb, the more time a customer typically spends in the facility, and the more likely that the purpose of the visit is hedonic, the more the servicescape should be designed to encourage affective responses in customers. Likewise, the less time a customer typically spends in the facility, and the more likely that the purpose of the visit is utilitarian, the more the servicescape should be designed for speedy throughput of customers. Ambient conditions in the servicescape, that is, scent, music, lighting, can be manipulated but the effects of the manipulation of scents and music on customer responses and behaviours are not generalisable. The design of the servicescape is clearly influenced by the drama metaphor (Chapter 3), and the notion of 'experience' (Chapter 5).

LEARNING OUTCOMES

Having read this chapter, you should be able to

- draw a simple service blueprint
- appreciate the importance of the 'invisible' elements contributing to the service process
- identify potential service failure points in a process, and plan for fail-safing or effective recovery
- link servicescape features to approach/avoidance behaviours
- classify servicescapes according to the time spent in the facility and the purpose of consumption, and appreciate the scope for transfer of servicescape ideas
- evaluate the 'conventional wisdom' of ambient condition manipulation in the light of research findings.

DISCUSSION QUESTIONS AND EXERCISES

1. Prepare the visible part of a blueprint for the patient's time in the outpatients' department in Case Study 6.

2. What are the main differences between a service blueprint and a service map?

3. Can service failures be prevented through service design?

4. Examine your lecture and tutorial rooms and the student café/bar. What aspects of the ambient conditions are (dis)pleasing to you?

5. Outline how Table 6.1 allows the transfer of servicescape ideas between contexts.

Notes and references

1. Schneider, B. and Bowen, D. E., 'New Service Design, Development and Implementation', in *Developing New Services*, (eds) George, W.R. and Marshall, C., American Marketing Association Proceedings Series, Chicago, 1984, pp. 82–102.

2. Bitner, 'Servicescapes: The Impact of Physical Surroundings on Customers and Employees', *Journal of Marketing*, April 1992.

3. Shostack, G. L., 'Service Positioning through Structural Change', *Journal of Marketing*, vol. 51, 1987, pp. 34–43.

4. Kingman-Brundage, J., 'Technology, Design and Service Quality', *International Journal of Service Industry Management*, vol. 2, 1991, pp. 47–59.

5. Shostack, G. L., 'How to Design a Service', *European Journal of Marketing*, vol. 16, 1982, pp. 49–63.

6. Johnston, R., 'Service Transaction Analysis: Assessing and Improving the Customer's Experience', *Managing Service Quality*, vol. 9, issue 2, 1999, pp. 102–9.

7. Gyimothy, S., 'Odysseys: Analysing Service Journeys from the Customer's Perspective', *Managing Service Quality*, vol. 10, issue 6, 2000, pp. 389–96.

8. Johnston, 'Service Transaction Analysis'.

9. Chase, R. B. and Stewart, D. M., 'Make your Service Fail-Safe', *Sloan Management Review*, Spring 1994, pp. 35–44.

10. Ibid.

11. Wheatcroft, P., 'Sickly Hospitals are Far More Dangerous than Fragile Railways', *The Times*, London, 9 Jan, 2001.

12. Charter, D., 'Hit Squads Threat as Hospitals get Deadline to Clean Up Filthy Wards', *The Times*, London, 9 Jan, 2001.

13. Worsfold, D., 'Food Safety Behaviour in Butchers' Shops', *Nutrition and Food Science*, vol. 31, issue 1, 2001, pp 13–19.

14. Shostack, 'Service Positioning through Structural Change'.

15. Edvardsson, B. , Haglund, L. and Mattson, J., 'Analysis, Planning, Improvisation and Control in the Development of New Services', *International Journal of Service Industry Management*, vol. 6, no. 2, 1995, pp 24–35.

16. Bitner, M. J., 'Servicescapes: The Impact of Physical Surroundings on Customers and Employees', *Journal of Marketing*, April 1992, pp. 57–71.

17. Sundstrom, E. and Altman, I., 'Physical Environments and Work-Group Effectiveness', *Research in Organizational Behaviour*, vol.11, 1989, pp. 175–209.

18. Spies, K., Hesse, F. and Loesch, K., 'Store Atmosphere, Mood and Purchasing Behavior', *International Journal of Research in Marketing*, vol. 14, 1997, pp. 1–17.

19. Wakefield, K. L. and Blodgett, J. G., 'The Importance of Servicescapes in Leisure Service Settings', *Journal of Services Marketing*, vol. 8, no. 3, 1994, pp. 66–76.

20. Wakefield, K. L. and Blodgett, J. G., 'Customer Response to Intangible and Tangible Service Factors', *Psychology and Marketing*, vol. 16, no.1, 1999, pp. 51–68.

21. www.haley-sharpe.co.uk

22. Rowley, J. and Slack, F., 'The Retail Experience in Airport Departure Lounges: Reaching for Timelessness and Placelessness', *International Marketing Review*, vol. 16, issue 4/5, 1999, pp. 363–76.

23. Aubert-Gamet, V. and Cova, B., 'Servicescapes: From Modern Non-Places to Postmodern Common Places', *Journal of Business Research*, vol. 44, no.1, 1999, pp. 37–45.

24. Ibid.

25. Bone, P. F. and Ellen, P. S., 'Scents in the Marketplace: Explaining a Fraction of Olfaction', *Journal of Retailing*, vol. 75, no. 2, 1999, pp. 243–62.

26. Oakes, S., 'The Influence of the Musicscape within Service Environments', *Journal of Services Marketing*, vol. 14, no. 7, 2000, pp. 539–56.

27. Mattila, A. and Wirtz, J., 'Congruency of Scent and Music as a Driver of In-store Evaluations and Behavior', *Journal of Retailing*, Summer 2001, vol. 77, issue 2, pp. 273–289.

28. Ibid.

Internal marketing

Introduction

Effective human resource management is vital in service organisations. The inseparability of production and consumption for many services means that customers are actively involved in the service delivery system and frequently exposed to the actions and attitudes of service employees. As we noted in Chapter 4, each interaction between customer and employee, or 'moment of truth', can potentially influence that customer's satisfaction/dissatisfaction with the service experience, and ultimately the profitability of the service organisation. In a manufacturing situation, although a dissatisfied employee may have the opportunity deliberately to produce a faulty product, normal methods of supervision and quality control would ensure that the fault is corrected before it reaches the final consumer. In a service context, the damage caused by a dissatisfied employee could be potentially much more serious. A one-minute telephone conversation with a disgruntled service operator could easily lead a customer, thinking of purchasing a skiing holiday, to switch to a competitor organisation.

In research into customer attitudes towards banks, a number of reasons why customers choose to terminate their relationship with a bank were identified.[1] Some 13 per cent of customers close their accounts because of an encounter with a rude or unhelpful employee, 11 per cent terminate because they feel that their bank is cold and impersonal, and another 16 per cent close accounts because of a general perception of poor service. All three reasons are directly or indirectly linked to negative employee attitudes and/or behaviour. Employee behaviour in services can have an equally significant positive impact on customer satisfaction. In Exhibit 7.1 below, a customer describes a particularly satisfactory experience with a veterinary practice – one that is almost entirely attributable to positive employee behaviour.

Exhibit 7.1 Customer experience with a veterinary practice

> 'The only reason that I stayed so long at one vet's, was the back-up staff, the fantastic nurses, who were really enthusiastic about the animals and the receptionists. They used to come out and play with the dogs and they knew all of their names. For me this is a very important part of the overall feeling, knowing that these people care.'

In highly competitive service industries, such as the airline industry, where service innovations quickly get copied, the attitude and behaviour of employees can provide a key point of difference. Although British Airways introduced a range of new services for its travellers, including 'flying beds', and a 'raid the larder' flexible food offering, a statement by the Brand Manager of the airlines business class, Alison Maxwell, highlights the crucial role played by employees: *'We are proud to be innovators but these ideas do get copied so we must rely on our staff and the style and delivery of the service.'*

The link between employee satisfaction, loyalty and productivity, and customer loyalty and company growth and profitability is neatly conceptualised in the 'service–profit chain'.[2] (The service profit chain is covered in greater detail in Chapter 10; see also Figure 10.3.) The chain, which was developed from an analysis of successful service organisations in America, has seven components and shows how internal service quality and employee satisfaction, retention and productivity (components of the operating strategy and service delivery system) are linked to organisational growth and profitability.

Within the chain

- profit and growth are stimulated primarily by customer loyalty
- loyalty is a direct result of customer satisfaction
- satisfaction is largely influenced by the value of services provided to customers
- value is created by satisfied, loyal and productive employees
- employee satisfaction, in turn results primarily from high-quality support services and policies that enable employees to deliver results to customers.[3]

The chain highlights the critical role played by human resource management in developing 'internal service quality', which in turn generates employee satisfaction and productivity and external service value for consumers. Internal service quality relates to aspects of the workplace/job design, policies for employee selection and development and reward systems, but it is measured by the feelings and attitudes that employees have about their jobs, other people that work with them in the organisation, and the organisation itself.

A simplified version of the chain, derived by the Gallup Organisation to be relevant to employees of a retail organisation, is shown in Figure 7.1.

Employee–Customer–Profit Chain

What gets measured, gets done

Figure 7.1 Service–profit chain as applied to a retail organisation

We have already noted, in Chapter 4, that a service organisation can consider its customers as 'partial employees' and consequently develop human resource strategies to manage their contribution. The focus of this chapter, however, is on approaches put forward to *manage effectively the paid employees' contribution in service organisations*. Although, clearly, traditional human resource management strategies aimed at attracting, selecting, training, motivating, directing, evaluating and rewarding service personnel may be relevant to a greater or lesser extent in service organisations, we concentrate in this chapter on the concept of 'internal marketing', which advocates a consideration of a slightly different perspective when managing internal service employees.

There are several forms of internal marketing. What they all share in common is the notion that customers exist within a service organisation as well as outside. Service employees, for example, should be treated as internal 'customers' if they are to deal effectively with the organisation's external customers and, as such, could be 'managed' using the same marketing tools and techniques that are used with external customers.

The chapter is divided into three sections. The first section begins by outlining some of the main ideas underlying the concept of internal marketing. Although it has been accepted by academics and practitioners as being a useful addition to traditional human resource management strategies, there are a number of criticisms of the internal approach which are presented in the second section. In the third section, we consider specific ways of increasing job satisfaction for service employees. We focus on employee empowerment as one particular strategy used frequently by service organisations to increase levels of both customer and employee satisfaction, and ultimately the profit of the service organisation.

Defining internal marketing

There are numerous definitions of the concept of internal marketing. It has been variously described as referring to 'those activities that improve internal communications and customer consciousness among employees, and the links between these activities and external market place performance'[4]; or 'the development of an internal marketing orientation, a culture which most effectively and efficiently creates the behaviours that lead to the provision of superior customer value'.[5]

We can think of internal marketing as 'viewing employees as internal customers, viewing jobs as internal products and then endeavouring to offer internal products that satisfy the needs and wants of these internal customers while addressing the objectives of the organisation'.[6]

There are two basic ideas that underlie the concept of internal marketing:

1. The notion that every individual in a service organisation should recognise that they have customers to serve (both inside and outside the organisation);

2. To achieve 1, all internal customers (employees) must be convinced about the quality of the service being provided, and be happy in their work.

Both ideas that underlie the concept of internal marketing focus attention on the vital role played by service employees in the service system. As our case studies illustrate, the employees of a service firm are frequently in contact with the organisation's external and internal customers. They are consequently an integral part of the image that is presented of the service and can play a key role in determining the success of the business. Berry feels that internal marketing is especially important in labour-intensive services where the performance of the employee is the product which the external customer buys. For many customers, for example, 'a rude or incompetent teller is a rude or incompetent bank'.[7] As we have already noted, with very little else that distinguishes the service of one bank from another, the quality of the people can act as a crucial point of difference.

- *Every individual should recognise that they have customers to serve.*

In order that the ultimate consumer receives a quality service, every individual and every department within the organisation must also provide and receive a quality service. Employees should be encouraged to regard their successor in the service chain as not merely a colleague but as an internal customer.[8] The provision of a five-star service for hotel customers, for example, relies on quality being provided by all the individuals working in the supply chain. The chambermaids need to be given immaculate linen by the laundry agent, the chef needs quality ingredients from the fresh-fruit trader and well-trained kitchen assistants need to give a quality service to the ultimate customer. Every employee connected with the service organisation needs to recognise that there is someone whom he or she must serve: an internal customer. Within a traditional human resource management framework, this idea focuses on relationships between functions in the company as well as on the relationship between the contact personnel and consumers.

In a retail environment, for example, the focus of management attention might be on improving the traditionally adversarial relationship between head office personnel; that is, buyers and store managers. Buyers would be encouraged to treat complaints from store managers about buying discrepancies with the same level of attention that they would devote to customer complaints, and provide them with the same level of service as that received by the ultimate consumer. In a reciprocal manner, store managers should be encouraged to treat head office personnel in the same way. In a qualitative study of internal marketing in a UK bank, the absence of such mutual respect was found to be a major barrier to the successful implementation of the concept.[9] Although it was acknowledged that 'support staff' in the bank should provide a level of service to front-line sales personnel, 'there was no evidence that interviewees felt that any form of reciprocal action might be necessary'. As one sales manager commented, 'I can see cash coming in when I sell a product, they don't do anything. They have to support us but the support just isn't there.'

- *All internal customers (employees) must be convinced about the quality of the service being provided, and be happy in their work.*

In order to be effective employees, the internal marketing approach recognises that all staff need to understand and approve of the mission of the organisation so that everyone is working towards a common goal. To achieve this, the services offered by the company need to be promoted to internal customers as well as to external customers. Berry[10] advocates that the best way to achieve such employee motivation is to use traditional marketing tools and concepts *internally* with employees. For example, just as marketers use advertising programmes to influence customers to behave in desired ways, for instance to buy a particular product, the same tools could be used to influence the behaviour of employees, for example to get them to approach external customers in a certain way. Employees are treated like customers and provided with 'job products' that satisfy their needs.[11] The people who buy goods and services in the role of the consumer, and the people who buy jobs in the role of the employee are the same people. Whereas consumers exchange economic resources for goods and services, employees exchange human resources for jobs that provide among other things economic resources.[12]

Some of the traditional marketing tools that could be used internally with employees would include the following.

Market research

This traditionally involves identifying the needs and wants of consumers in a systematic manner, and monitoring the impact of marketing activities on consumers. The same process can be used with employees. Service personnel can regularly be given the opportunity to give feedback to service management about working conditions, company policies generally, as well as their understanding about what comprises service quality for the customer. The information might be obtained by using questionnaires or focus groups, or in-depth interviews with employers. Although employee surveys may often need to be handled with more care than customer surveys, because of the fear of negative comeback for employees, they not only provide employees with a measure of satisfaction but also can identify early breakdowns in internal communication.

Marketing offers an array of research techniques that might not have been considered by the personnel function. For example, the critical incident technique, which has been used extensively in services to identify sources of satisfaction and dissatisfaction for customers in their encounters with employees, could also be used to develop an understanding of problem areas for employees. A survey of 1220 UK bar staff recently revealed a range of customer behaviours that staff found particularly unpleasant. According to the survey, more than two-thirds of those interviewed regularly and deliberately ignored rude customers waiting at the bar to be served. According to the employees, the key to getting served quickly for customers was to have 'a good position, a pensive expression and a polite approach'. Market research has also been used innovatively with front-line employees of a DIY chain, to profile the segments of customers that visited the outlets. Although profiles were generated by ten separate employee focus groups, the profile descriptors were remarkably consistent, highlighting the value of employees as internal sources of information.

Segmentation techniques

By grouping together employees with certain similarities, for example those of the same age, ambitions, previous employment, and so on, the service employer is in a better position to design an appropriate service package (or job specification) for that employee. As Berry notes, internal marketing of this form is behind many of the commonly used personnel concepts such as 'job share', 'flexitime' and 'fast track graduate training schemes' within companies.

Targeting

When initially recruiting employees, service providers can target suitable candidates in the same way that a successful company might target potential customers. A company with limited skills or resources might decide to serve just one or two consumer segments and therefore be selective about the people to whom it presents goods and services. In the same way, a service company might be selective about where it advertises vacancies for positions. Many of the jobs in service businesses involve constant liaison with external and internal customers and therefore require employees to possess high-level interpersonal skills. Not every interested party will possess these skills. Therefore, service businesses can use marketing techniques to match the right employee to the right job. The Waymark Holidays case study (Case Study 5) illustrates the important role played by a holiday group leader and the potential impact of getting the wrong person for the job.

Promotion

There are traditionally four basic forms of promotion available to marketing managers trying to influence the behaviour and attitudes of current and potential customers towards products and services: advertising, sales promotion, personal selling and publicity. Each form can help the organisation achieve slightly different promotion objectives. Sales promotion techniques, for example, are defined as short-term incentives designed to encourage customers to try new products or to increase short-term sales of existing products. They might include money-off tokens on products or free trial sized packs of new products attached to a standard product. Similar mechanisms are used to motivate service employees. For example, a bonus might be given to employees who receive the largest number of customer 'thank you' letters in a month. Another alternative would be to offer incentives to employees who were prepared to swap jobs with colleagues in different positions within the organisation albeit for a short period of time. This would improve the employees' understanding of difficulties and challenges faced by others in the supply chain.

All of these marketing tools could be used primarily to improve the fit between the requirements of the internal customer (the employee) and the organisation. However, if employees are to be further convinced about the quality of service being provided, as the company wants its external customers to be, other steps can be taken. Employees could experience the service and be actively involved in the formulation of marketing strategy.

It is often entirely feasible for employees to be given the opportunity to experience using the organisation's goods and services *as external customers*. This might involve giving leisure club staff unlimited access to the club's facilities, or giving staff in a DIY store a selection of new products to use. Although this occurs automatically in a number of service industries (that is, financial services), it is still viewed as a benefit for the employee rather than seen as adding value to the organisation. Research on positive customer word of mouth in services continues to highlight the impact it can have on loyalty and purchase behaviour.[13] Little attention, however, appears to have been given to the potential impact of positive *employee* word of mouth (stimulated by product/service experiences) on organisational performance. Another alternative would be to encourage staff to shadow customers as they experience the service. For example, in an educational environment, lecturers could 'spend a week as a student' attending the full range of lectures and tutorials. Where organisations positively seek employee feedbacks from such initiatives, the employees are involved in the development of marketing strategy and consequently have more responsibility for the outcome and impact of customer-focused decisions. This, in turn, can result in employees gaining a fuller understanding of the company's marketing 'vision'.

Evaluating the usefulness of the internal marketing approach

In theory

Problems with the approach

Rafiq and Ahmed[14] presented a critique of the ideas behind the concept of internal marketing, and drew some comparisons between the marketing approach to employee motivation and training and traditional human resource management practice. Although they concluded that there can be no doubt that 'the internal marketing concept has a major role to play in making employees customer conscious', they felt that the concept of treating 'employee as customer' was problematic for two reasons:

1. The 'products' being sold to employees (their job specifications) generally *have to* be bought by service workers.

Although employees may enter into discussion about the precise nature and form of the role the employer presents them with, ultimately they have no real choice but to accept. The alternative would be to lose the job altogether.

In normal marketing situations customers not only have a range of products to choose from but also can decide not to buy at all, without serious consequences.

2.   The idea that all customers (internal and external) are equally important in a service organisation appears to stand 'on its head one most fundamental axiom of marketing, that the external customer has primacy'.

At its extreme, if employees were to behave as if they were the most important customers in the organisation, they might place demands on the organisation that would lead to a commercially untenable situation.

In practice

The case of EasyJet

EasyJet, the passenger airline, is known to have fully embraced the internal marketing concept. The company was established in 1995 by Stelios Haji-Ioannou who, together with Marketing Director, Tony Anderson, developed a successful airline business, founded on no-nonsense values, and a strong low-price positioning to customers. The down-to-earth culture is reflected in the organisational structure which focuses on eliminating as much bureaucracy and internal hierarchy as possible. All documents are scanned and placed on a central computer system, so that everyone in the company can access them. They include mail, internal memos, press cuttings, business plans and sales data. Everyone knows what everyone else is doing, and a clear effort is made to ensure that all employees can have a say in the development of the marketing strategy. In 'easy land', the company's headquarters at Luton airport, employees are instructed to dress casually and maintain paperless offices like the company owner. This has created a system of working which has been described as 'brutally transparent in the way that information is shared between employees in all departments'.[15]

So, what might be the problems associated with such a full-scale adoption of internal marketing practices?

First, there is a problem of information overload. The internal customers may have to process vast amounts of information that can waste time. Second, staff can feel that they need constantly to be informed about what other parts of the organisation are doing, just in case they are asked to contribute ideas. Third, it can lead to a 'semi-chaotic culture', where, because everyone has a voice, it is difficult for staff to be recognised personally for what they have contributed.[16]

Employees as 'partial' customers

A perhaps less extreme way of treating employees is to view them as 'partial' customers. Bowen[17] presents this as one of the strategies that service organisations should follow when trying to 'create a favourable climate for service'. At its simplest level, this would involve giving employees the same courteous treatment that the management would want the organisation's customers to receive; for instance, giving them a clear understanding of what they can expect from the service experience and help and support from various parts of the organisation. The rationale for giving employees the same treatment as customers stems from the fact that the on-site participation of customers tends to blur the distinction between the two roles. 'Employee and customer perceptions and behaviours' therefore become shaped by the same set of organisational practices and 'become strongly intertwined with each other'.

Value and practice of internal marketing

Rafiq and Ahmed critically appraise the value of using marketing techniques to motivate service employees. They conclude that the most valuable contribution comes from applying promotional and market research techniques internally with employees. Whilst recognising that traditional human resource management practices already include some of these, they acknowledge that marketing techniques can 'add to that array'.

Helman and Payne[18] carried out a pilot study that looked at the nature and extent of 'internal marketing' programmes in a sample of UK companies. Respondents were asked a series of questions in semi-structured interviews which related to the internal marketing programmes taking place in their organisations. Overall, internal marketing in all its forms was recognised as an important activity in developing a customer focused organisation. Specifically, however, the research highlighted a number of other important contributions made by the approach.

- The important role internal marketing can play in reducing conflict between the functional areas of business.

For example, the customer orientation approach adopted within some retail organisations is helping to improve the traditionally antagonistic relationship between the head office functions and stores.

- The importance of effective communication in successful internal marketing.

There is a need for clear communication of the organisation's mission statement.

- The contribution internal marketing can make towards facilitating a spirit of innovation within the organisation.
- The fact that internal marketing is most successful where there is commitment at the highest level, where all employees cooperate, and an open management style exists.
- The role internal marketing approach can play in giving the organisation a competitive advantage.

Additionally, the internal marketing concept is believed to have the potential to greatly reduce the overall gap between what external customers expect from an organisation and what they actually receive.[19]

Increasing job satisfaction of service employees

A basic premise underlying the internal marketing focus is that satisfied employees will lead to satisfied customers. As Bitner *et al.*[20] have noted, and we highlighted in Chapter 4, low job satisfaction has the potential to cause low-quality service encounter performances on the part of the employee. This, in turn, could lead to dissatisfied customers, generating negative word of mouth about the employees and the service firm. Research, focusing on the determinants of job satisfaction for front-line retail customer personnel, looked at the relationship between empathy, role conflict and role clarity and job tension on the job satisfaction of service workers.[21]

The findings highlighted five 'policy concerns' for service managers striving to enhance employee job satisfaction.

1. Service employees with high customer contact need to have a very clear understanding of their role within the organisation.

Job descriptions need to be communicated to them in detail, including an indication as to what actions they can and cannot take. Increasing role clarity in this way was found to reduce the amount of conflict each employee had with others in the organisation and reduce tension generally.

2. Service managers are advised to hire individuals who are highly empathetic (that is, able to take the viewpoint of another, either customers or fellow employees).

This is based on the contention that as employees communicate feelings of empathy to the customer, job tension is reduced and job satisfaction is increased. Although empathy is a quality that service providers can test for at the recruitment stage, it can also be developed in the work situation. J. Sainsbury's, the UK food and grocery retailer, for example, hold customer evenings at their stores where staff sit down with a group of customers and listen to their comments about the store, products and service. This enables staff to understand how customers perceive their offer, and consequently communicate feelings of empathy to the consumer.

3. Employees need to be fully trained in how to deal with customers.

Front-line employees are frequently faced with disgruntled customers who want solutions to problems caused by company policy and procedures. Although individual employees may not be responsible for the problem, they are expected by each customer to find an immediate solution to their problem. As the intensity and quantity of such conflicts increases, job tension rises for employees. As job tension rises, job satisfaction declines. Apart from developing employees' empathetic skills, service providers can use scenario-building to alert employees to potential conflict situations and give them detailed advice about how to resolve issues.

4. Clear lines of command need to be drawn up and communicated between management and employees.

When employees do not know who to consult in order to help resolve a difficult service situation, job tension increases and job satisfaction declines.

5. Employees must be empowered by management to do whatever it takes to satisfy the customer.

Employee empowerment is considered to be a very effective strategy available to service organisations to help improve the relationship between employee and customer, and has received considerable attention in the services marketing literature. Although there are a number of different definitions of the concept, it essentially involves releasing control to the service employee at the crucial moment of contact with the customer, giving them autonomy to make decisions flexibly in response to the customers' demands as and when they occur. Workers are encouraged to think creatively about solutions to problems presented to them by customers rather than being driven by a standard functional 'script'.

Empowerment

Bowen and Lawler[22] provide a more comprehensive definition of the term 'empowerment'. They define it as sharing four organisational ingredients with front-line employees:

1. Information about the organisation's performance.
2. Rewards based on the organisation's performance.
3. Knowledge that enables employees to understand and contribute to organisational performance.
4. Power to make decisions that influence organisational direction and performance.

Research in service organisations has highlighted significant advantages in using this method to manage employees, the advantages relating primarily to increased customer satisfaction with the critical service encounter. Customers frequently recall their most satisfying service encounters as those when employees appear to have 'broken the rules' (in the customers' eyes) and responded quickly and flexibly to their particular service needs. For example, when ordering a banquet for eight people at a Chinese restaurant, the waiter takes into account the individual preferences of the party by balancing the fish and meat dishes in the banquet. This action appears to contradict restaurant policy that promotes a set menu for each group size, but greatly increases the satisfaction of the party with their experience. The customers are surprised and delighted with the waiter's flexible approach.

Bowen and Lawler[23] feel that not only do customers benefit from this approach, but employees clearly feel better about their work. They value having a sense of control and are also more willing to give service management their view on how things should be organised to improve service performance. In this way, empowered employees become a great source of service ideas.

Although there are clearly advantages to empowering service employees, there are also costs that need to be considered. Because of the level of responsibility devolved to service workers, companies tend to spend more time and money on recruitment and training. There can also be a risk of inconsistent delivery, with one service employee responding to a customer complaint in a different way from another. On some occasions this could lead directly to highly dissatisfied customers.

Research has also shown that empowerment as a strategy can be more effective in some service organisations than others. Empowerment appears to be the best approach where service delivery involves managing a relationship, as opposed to simply performing a transaction. This is clearly the situation with many of the cases described in the book. The small business orientation places the emphasis on service providers and employees establishing long-term relationships with their customers. The organisations rely on long-term clients to bring in new business and actively involve them in communication strategy and generating ideas for service development. The promotional material used by Waymark Holidays (Case Study 5), for example, includes comments from customers about their holidays, while the colour consultant (Case Study 3) relies on her loyal clients to identify the new services they would like her to provide. As Bowen and Lawler note, the 'more enduring the relationship (between customer and service organisation), and the more important it is in the service package, the stronger the case for empowerment'.

The success of empowerment also appears to depend on the type of environment in which the business operates. For instance, it can be a very effective approach if the service is heavily influenced by uncontrollable external variables. The leaders used by Waymark Holidays (Case Study 5) are encouraged to take independent decisions about how to handle many situations, as very few problems could be anticipated in advance by the centre. While walking in the Greek mountains one party was attacked by a swarm of bees. The tour guide had to react swiftly without consultation with the centre, and arrange for two group members to get to hospital as well as rearrange the walking schedule for the rest of the group.

SUMMARY

Successful internal marketing is based on the dual tenets that every employee in a service organisation should recognise that they have their own customers to serve, and that all employees should be convinced of the quality of the service provided. The former ensures a customer orientation throughout the support services, as well as for front-line employees. The latter requires the company mission to be 'marketed' to internal customers (the employees) with effective two-way communication systems.

The internal marketing approach has been found to have some flaws from an academic and practical perspective. In organisations that practise internal marketing, better communication, reduced internal conflict and a spirit of innovation are seen as some of the benefits of the approach. The advocates of internal marketing will look to increasing the job satisfaction of service employees in the belief that it will eventually lead to satisfied customers.

Employee job satisfaction may result from role clarification, encouragement of empathetic approaches, effective training, clear lines of command and, in particular, employee empowerment. In appropriate service environments, empowerment is seen as a strategy for increasing both customer specification and employee enjoyment.

LEARNING OUTCOMES

Having read this chapter, you should be able to

● explain the concept of internal marketing

● appreciate the potential benefits of applying traditional marketing techniques with employees

● critically assess the advantages and disadvantages of an internal marketing perspective

● understand the issues facing service organisations that are striving to increase employee job satisfaction

● evaluate employee empowerment as a strategic initiative for service organisations.

DISCUSSION QUESTIONS AND EXERCISES

1. How might 'moments of truth' influence customer (dis)satisfaction?

2. Summarise the ways in which traditional marketing tools for external customers can be implemented with internal customers.

3. To what extent do you believe that satisfied employees lead to satisfied customers?

4. Explain fully the term 'employee empowerment'.

5. Why might role clarification increase the job satisfaction of a service employee?

Notes and references

1. Morves (1984), as quoted in Sargeant, A. and Asif, S., 'The Strategic Application of Internal Marketing – An Investigation of UK Banking', *International Journal of Bank Marketing*, vol. 16, no. 1, 1998, pp. 66–79.
2. Heskett, J. L., Jones, T. O., Loveman, G. W., Earl-Sasser Jr, W. and Schlesinger, L. A., 'Putting the Service Profit–Chain to Work', *Harvard Business Review*, March–April 1994, pp. 164–74.
3. Ibid.
4. Hogg, G., Carter, S. and Dunne, A., 'Investing in People: Internal Marketing and Corporate Culture', *Journal of Marketing Management*, vol. 14, 1998, pp. 879–95.

5. Narver, J. C. and Slater, S. F., 'The Effect of a Marketing Orientation on Business Profitability', *Journal of Marketing*, vol. 54, October 1990, pp. 20–35.
6. Berry, L. L., 'The Employee as Customer', *Journal of Banking*, 3 March 1981, pp. 25–8.
7. Ibid.
8. Berry, 'The Employee as Customer'.
9. Sargeant, A. and Asif, S., 'The Strategic Application of Internal Marketing – An Investigation of UK Banking'.
10. Berry, L. L., 'The Employee as Customer', in C. Lovelock, *Services Marketing*, Kent Publishing, Boston, Mass., 1984, pp. 271–8.
11. Berry, L. L. and Parasuraman, A., *Marketing Services: Competing through Quality*, The Free Press, New York, 1991.
12. Berry, 'The Employee as Customer' (1981).
13. Mangold, W. Glynn, Miller, F., Brockway, G. R. 'Word-of-Mouth Communication in the Service Marketplace', *Journal of Services Marketing*, vol. 13, issue 1. 1999, pp. 73–89.
14. Rafiq, M. and Ahmed, P. K., 'The Scope of Internal Marketing: Defining the Boundary between Marketing and Human Resource Management', *Journal of Marketing Management*, vol. 9, 1993, pp. 219–32.
15. Curtis, J., 'No-frills Airline, No-frills Culture', *Marketing*, 9 July, 1998, pp. 24–5.
16. Ibid.
17. Bowen, D. E., 'Customers as Human Resources in Service Organisations', *Human Resource Management*, vol. 25, no. 3, Fall 1986, pp. 371–83.
18. Helman, D. and Payne, A., 'Internal Marketing: Myth versus Reality', Cranfield School of Management Working Paper, Cranfield SWP 5/92, 1992.
19. Piercy, N. and Morgan, N. (1989), as quoted in Sargeant A. and Asid S., 'The Strategic Application of Internal Marketing – An Investigation of UK Banking'.
20. Bitner, M. J., Booms, B. H. and Tetreault, M. S., 'The Service Encounter: Diagnosing Favourable and Unfavourable Incidents', *Journal of Marketing*, vol. 54, January 1990, pp. 71–84.
21. Rogers, J. D., Clow, K. E. and Kash, T. J., 'Increasing Job Satisfaction of Service Personnel', *Journal of Services Marketing*, vol. 8, no. 1, 1994, pp. 14–26.
22. Bowen, D. E. and Lawler, E. E., 'The Empowerment of Service Workers: What, Why, How and When', *Sloan Management Review*, Spring 1992, pp. 31–9.
23. Ibid.

Service quality and customer satisfaction

Learning Objectives

Overall aim of the chapter:
To present the theory and practical implications relating to the concepts of perceived service quality and customer satisfaction in services.
  In particular, the *chapter objectives* are

- to provide an evaluation of the similarities and differences between the concepts of service quality and customer satisfaction

- to present results showing the determinants and dimensions of perceived service quality

- to evaluate the Gaps model of service quality and the potential causes of the Gaps

- to introduce and critically assess the SERVQUAL instrument

- to introduce and evaluate different perspectives of customer satisfaction

- to summarise the debates on service quality versus customer satisfaction.

Introduction

Service quality has been identified as the 'single most researched area in services marketing to date',[1] and it is maintained that, for service-based companies, 'quality is the lifeblood that brings increased patronage, competitive advantage and long term profitability'.[2] The word 'satisfaction' has been 'fundamental to the marketing concept for over three decades', and the number of academic articles on consumer satisfaction had topped 15 000 by 1992.[3] The topics of service quality and customer/consumer satisfaction have attracted the attention of both academics and practitioners who increasingly consider actions aimed at improving service quality/customer satisfaction to be an integral part of an organisation's long-term strategy.

Research on perceived service quality has emanated largely from the services marketing literature, whereas much of the research on customer satisfaction is to be found within the consumer behaviour literature, where the focus is on satisfaction with physical goods as well as with services. There is often some confusion regarding the similarities and differences between service quality and customer/consumer satisfaction, and this may be attributed to the different origins. Take, for example, some often quoted definitions of the two concepts.

- Perceived service quality: 'the degree and direction of the gap between consumers' perceptions and expectations (of a service)'.[4]

- Consumer satisfaction: 'a function of the similarities between the consumer's expectations and the perceived performance of the purchase'.[5]

Both definitions seem to refer to a comparison between consumers' expectations and perceptions of a service.

In this chapter, we examine, in separate sections, the concepts of service quality and customer satisfaction taking account of their different origins. In the final section, the ideas and issues are brought together to encompass current debates, areas of practical applications, and links to the following two chapters.

Perceived service quality

As we highlighted at the very beginning of this book, defining and monitoring the quality of a service is very different from defining and monitoring the quality of a tangible product. From an internal perspective, a manufacturer can grade pieces of fruit received from a supplier according to certain objective quality criteria; for example, weight, size, colour, texture, and so on. Similarly, from an external perspective, that is, a consumer's viewpoint, a quality assessment of the fruit can be made in the supermarket prior to purchase, by touching or feeling the merchandise, albeit at a more subjective level. In both cases, the quality assessment relates clearly to the finished product. With services, in contrast, customers make judgements about the quality *of the service delivery process, as well as on the final outcome.* The independent businessman, for instance, might assess the quality of the accountant's work not only on the appearance of the final set of accounts, but also on the telephone manner of the accountant's employees and the speed with which the work is carried out.

Because a service is usually made up of both tangible and intangible components, many attempts at defining service quality have made the distinction between objective measures of quality and those which are based on the more subjective perceptions of customers. According to Gronroos,[6] for example, a service can be broken down into two quality dimensions:

1.   technical quality;
2.   functional quality.

Both dimensions are important to the customer. Technical quality refers to the relatively quantifiable aspects of the service; that is, *what* is being done. Functional quality refers to *how* the technical quality is being delivered to customers.

For example, with the service offered by the car mechanic, a customer might look at the machinery being used to fix the cars, and the skills and expertise of the mechanic, to make an assessment of the technical quality of the service. The general attitude and appearance of employees, in contrast, which cannot be measured as accurately as the elements of technical quality, would be components of the functional quality of the service.

However service quality is defined, most researchers agree that it has to be *defined by consumers*. In this case, as each consumer is different, we usually refer to *perceived* service quality.

How consumers assess service quality

Although it may be difficult, service organisations need to take steps to monitor and improve the quality of the service that they provide. According to Lewis and Booms,[7] service quality is 'a measure of how well the service level delivered matches customer expectations. Delivering quality service means conforming to customers' expectations on a consistent basis.' Using this definition of service quality, one of the first steps before implementing a quality improvement programme involves establishing precisely which components of the service influence the consumer's perception of quality. Service quality from the consumer's perspective is examined with reference to the pioneering work carried out by Parasuraman, Zeithaml and Berry.[8,9,10,11] Their research initially identified a set of determinants used by consumers to judge the quality of the service they receive. Using this, and subsequent research, they produced a conceptual framework (a Gaps model) and a measurement instrument SERVQUAL that has been widely used by companies to assess service quality.

Determinants of service quality

Supporting the view of Lewis and Booms, Parasuraman, Zeithaml and Berry (PZB) feel that 'the only criteria that count in evaluating service quality are those defined by the customer'. In their early research, PZB identified ten criteria that customers use to judge the quality of the service that they receive. The first five relate to the quality of the final outcome, while the remainder refer mainly to the quality of the process of service delivery.

1. *Reliability*: This relates to the ability of the service provider to perform the promised service dependably and accurately. The sort of question that a client might ask of the accountant to assess dependability, for example, might relate to whether all the information deadlines specified by the Inland Revenue and the relevant legislation have been met.

2. *Access*: Is the service accessible and delivered with little waiting. For example, do the hairdresser's clients have to wait months before getting an appointment to have their hair cut?

3. *Security*: Is the service free from danger, risk or doubt? For example, how safe does the customer feel using the bank's automatic teller machine?

4. *Credibility*: How trustworthy and honest does the service provider appear to be? If the double-glazing company tells the customer that they will deliver within the week, how likely is that to happen?

5. *Understanding the customer*: How much effort does the organisation make to get to know its customers and understand their needs? A colour consultant, for example, would score highly here, giving individual consultations to clients which involve questioning them on aspects of their lifestyle.

6. *Responsiveness*: How willing are service employees to help customers, and to deal with their specific problems? Is the accountant available to talk over a specific problem whenever the client rings up?

7. *Competence*: To what extent do employees possess the required skills and knowledge to perform the service? Often here, when using a service provider for the first time the customer uses the existence of professional qualifications or membership of certain trade associations to assess this. Accountants, for example, must be members of the Institute of Chartered Accountants in England and Wales to prepare limited company accounts.

8. *Courtesy*: Are staff polite and considerate to consumers? Are the Waymark holiday telephone operators polite and helpful to each customer who makes an inquiry about a booking? (Case Study 5).

9. *Tangibles*: What assessments can be made of the appearance of the physical facilities, equipment, personnel and communication materials? Do all the waiters in the restaurant wear clean uniforms and appear to be concerned about their personal hygiene as well as the cleanliness of the food that they are presenting?

10. *Communication*: How good is the organisation at communicating effectively what is provided in the service and what role customers are expected to play? Specifically, perhaps, are customers kept informed about reasons for possible breakdowns in the delivery system?

PZB point out that the ten determinants are not necessarily independent of each other; that is, there could be some overlap between the categories.

They feel that the determinants are appropriate for assessing quality across a broad variety of services. As they note, 'even though the specific evaluative criteria may vary from service to service, the general dimensions underlying those criteria are captured by our set of ten'.[12]

Dimensions of service quality

After further research into the measurement of service quality, PZB advocated that the ten determinants could be collapsed into five dimensions of quality. They are:

1. Tangibles: including the physical components of the service, e.g. seating, lighting, and so on;

2. Reliability: dependability of service provider and accuracy of performance;

3. Responsiveness: promptness and helpfulness;

4. Assurance: knowledge and courtesy of employees and their ability to inspire trust and confidence;

5. Empathy: caring, individualised attention the firm gives its customers.

The dimensions of tangibles, reliability and responsiveness remain unchanged. 'Assurance' encompasses competence, courtesy, credibility and security, and 'empathy' includes access, communication and understanding the customer. Virtually all subsequent research, by PZB and others, involves use of the five dimensions of quality, rather than the original ten determinants.

Potential causes of service quality shortfalls: the 'Gaps model'

In parallel with their identification of the dimensions of service quality, PZB postulated the major causes of the perceived service quality 'gap'; that is, the gap between consumer expectations and perceptions. They specified four potential causes of this gap, which they labelled as Gap 5:

● First, service providers need to ensure that management appreciate exactly what service attributes are valued by their customers and in what order. A restaurant manager, for example, may believe that customers' evaluation of the quality of the service is influenced primarily by the decor in the restaurant, and that the quality of the food and the attitude of employees towards staff are of little significance. If this is incorrect, decisions could be made about service design and delivery which could significantly affect the customers' evaluation about the quality being provided. This gap they labelled as Gap 1; that is, *the gap between customers' expectations and management perception of customers' expectations.*

● Even if management fully appreciate the attributes valued by customers, they are often unwilling, unable or simply do not care enough to put resources into solving the problem. For example, even though operators of theme parks recognise that the consumers' evaluation of the quality of their experience at the theme park is negatively influenced by the length of time they are forced to spend waiting in a queue for a ride, little has been done by the operators to alleviate the situation. This gap they labelled as Gap 2; that is, *the gap between management perception of customers' expectations and service quality specifications.*

- The research also highlighted a problem that related specifically to service delivery. Even if quality standards are correctly set in accordance with an accurate reading of customer expectations, service quality could still be substandard because of deficiencies that relate to the attitude and manner of contact employees. Employees, for example, may not have been given adequate training and support to carry out the tasks required, or they may not be aware of exactly what they are expected to do. This gap they labelled as Gap 3; that is, *the gap between service quality specifications and actual service delivery.*

- Another problem occurs when organisations promise that they will deliver one level or type of service but in reality deliver something different. This has been termed the 'promises' gap and can easily occur if an actual service experience, at say a retail store, does not reflect the implicit or explicit promises conveyed by a television advertisement. This gap they labelled as Gap 4; that is, *the gap between service delivery and external communications to the customer.*

For many service organisations, one way of closing Gap 4 is to try to develop a strong service brand. As with product branding, the strength of a service brand depends on the extent to which the brand conveys a consistent, positive and clear message to consumers about what is being offered. This is clearly a more difficult task for service organisations given the primarily intangible nature of the offer and the reliance on variable employee interactions to convey brand messages. In theory, a clear brand should help to differentiate the service offered from the competition. As McDonald et al.[13] note, however, different sectors of the service industry have varied in their ability to achieve differentiation with their brands. They contrast the success of service branding in the airline industry where 'if travellers were asked to evaluate Virgin, Lufthansa or Singapore airlines according to punctuality, in-flight entertainment and attentive cabin staff, they would be very likely to talk about differences without hesitation', to the financial and insurance sectors, where very few brands have managed to differentiate themselves. The key to successful service branding involves, first, making the brands 'tangible' by manipulating the physical components associated with the service and second, ensuring that the brand values are understood and effectively communicated to customers by all contact employees.

In essence, Gaps 1, 2, 3 and 4 contribute to the essential gap, Gap 5, the gap between consumer expectations and perceptions; the measure of perceived service quality. The Gaps model has, therefore, understandably resulted in 'follow up' research into the understanding of the antecedents of consumer expectations, and into methods of reducing Gaps 1 to 4.

Antecedents of consumer expectations

PZB identified four key factors that might influence a customer's expectations.

1. *Word of mouth communications*; for example, what your friends think about the hairdresser that you are planning to use.

2. *Personal needs and preferences*; for example, whether you personally think that it is important that sales staff wear the same uniform.

3. *Past experiences*; for example, if you are a regular user of a particular restaurant and have always been given a rose at the end of your meal you would come to expect this treatment. However, if you had never been there before, the rose would not form part of your service expectations.

4. *External communications*; for example, advertising. An advertisement in the newspaper advising you to book three months in advance for a table at a restaurant at Christmas might lead some customers to make inferences about the quality of the food they might receive on the day.

To take a specific example, one of the authors was visiting Australia for the first time, and was booked into the Hotel Ibis Darling Harbour in Sydney. Word of mouth from an Australian colleague indicated that the venue was excellent. The hotel would appear to satisfy hygiene needs, with an added advantage of having a swimming pool. The person concerned had stayed in an Ibis hotel in Luton, England, and had also frequently passed the Manchester Ibis hotel with its very prominent promotion of rooms for only £39.50 per night. The website for the Hotel Ibis Darling Harbour was well developed and informative, with pictures, maps, and so on. All of these sources culminate in building an expectation of the likely service experience of a week's stay in the hotel.

Methods of reducing Gaps 1 to 4

Table 8.1 (overleaf) summarises some of the probable causes of Gaps 1 to 4. Where the causes are relevant to a particular service, management can develop cures to reduce the gap.

It is worth noting that amended versions of Gaps 1 to 4 can be used to measure and monitor *internal* service quality as part of an internal marketing policy.[15]

The main volume of research, undertaken by both academics and practitioners, however, has centred on Gap 5. This is because it is the 'essential' gap, but it is also the only gap that can be examined solely on data from the consumers.[16] Much of the work has applied the research instrument known as SERVQUAL.

SERVQUAL: the research instrument

In 1988, building on their early research, PZB published a multiple-item scale for measuring consumer perceptions of service quality, named SERVQUAL.[17] This was revised in 1991.[18] Based on extended exploratory and empirical

Table 8.1 Causes of the service quality gaps

Service quality gap	Possible causes of the gap
Gap 1: the gap between customers' expectations and management perception of customers' expectations	<ul><li>Lack of marketing research (inaccurate information, inadequate use of the findings)</li><li>Poor upward communication from contact personnel</li><li>Too many management or organisational layers</li></ul>
Gap 2: the gap between management perception of customers' expectations and service quality specifications	<ul><li>Lack of clarity of goal setting, inadequate task standardisation</li><li>Lack of management commitment</li><li>Poor management of planning and planning procedures</li></ul>
Gap 3: the gap between service quality specifications and actual service delivery	<ul><li>Rigid or complicated specifications</li><li>Poor internal marketing</li><li>Employee role ambiguity and/or conflict</li><li>Break-down in technology or systems support</li></ul>
Gap 4: the gap between service delivery and external communications to the customer	<ul><li>Propensity to over-promise and exaggerate</li><li>Marketing communication not integrated between operations and the advertising, sales and human resource functions</li><li>Differences in procedures across the organisation</li></ul>

Source: Adapted from Gronroos.[14]

research, they identified 22 quality related items spread among the five quality dimensions as providing a reliable and valid measure of service quality. SERVQUAL became a major research instrument used by many others.[19,20]

PZB themselves admit that, although 'SERVQUAL is a useful starting point, it is not the final answer for assessing and improving service quality'.[21] It does, however, enable an organisation to compare customer expectations and perceptions over time. For example, a theme park operator may have established during one season that the negative attitude of employees had a detrimental influence on the customers' perception of the quality of the service provided throughout the theme park. Consequently, the owner may embark on an intensive recruitment campaign to employ more highly motivated workers for the next season. The impact of the change can be monitored by a repeat survey.

The organisation can also compare the SERVQUAL score with the competitors. The results can also be used to categorise a company's customers into perceived quality segments on the basis of their individual SERVQUAL scores. Thus, the organisation may find that customers who have been with them for the longest period of time, or are all within a certain age category, assess quality on different service dimensions, and they can take managerial decisions accordingly. Finally, SERVQUAL can be used to assess the quality perceptions of internal customers; that is, different departments may want to know about the quality of service that they provide to others in the organisation.

Conceptual and methodological problems with the SERVQUAL scale

The SERVQUAL research instrument was placed in the public domain by PZB and, not surprisingly, it has been used by many researchers since its publication. These researchers, through attempting to measure service quality in a variety of service sectors, have identified some conceptual and methodological problems with the SERVQUAL scale. Indeed, criticism of SERVQUAL is becoming an academic industry in its own right. Three issues are mentioned here. The chapter's bibliographical references at the end of the chapter allow the interested reader to become up to date with SERVQUAL strengths and weaknesses:

- It is claimed[22] that SERVQUAL dimensions are not generic; that is, the applicability of the SERVQUAL scale to different service settings is questioned. In, for example, office equipment businesses, carrier services, and retailing, it was found to be difficult to apply SERVQUAL meaningfully.

- The timing of expectation measurements is of crucial importance. To use SERVQUAL implies that respondents must rate their expectations (on a scale of 1 = strongly disagree to 7 = strongly agree) and also their perceptions of a particular service, on the same scale, for each of 22 statements. Perhaps, in an ideal world, the bank customer, for example, could be interviewed before taking out an account with the bank (to assess expectations) and interviewed again three months later (to assess perceptions of the actual service). In practice this may be impossible. For very good practical reasons, respondents are often interviewed only once (after the service experience) and asked to rate both their expectations and their perceptions on that one occasion. However, Clow and Vorhies[23] have shown that 'measurement of consumer expectations after the consumption of service are biased by the experience of the customer'.

- If the gap between perceptions (P) and expectations (E) is used literally, that is, P–E, then Teas (taking expectations to be equivalent to an ideal standard) claims that increasing P–E scores do not reflect continually increasing levels of perceived quality.[24] That is, a higher P–E score does not necessarily imply higher quality. Take, for example, the situation where an ideal standard corresponded to a score of six, and a customer rated E and P each at six. The P–E score is nil. If, for pragmatic or pessimistic reasons, a customer gives an E rating of one, and then a P rating of two to a service in the same sector, the P–E score is one. Is the latter of higher perceived service quality than the former?

By 1995, these and other conceptual and methodological reservations with SERVQUAL had been well documented.[25,26] Nevertheless, SERVQUAL-based studies have dominated the empirical services quality research into the twenty-first century, and there is little doubt that the instrument gives a convenient 'kick-start' to practitioners and academics seeking to measure and monitor perceived service quality.

Customer satisfaction

In the introduction to this chapter, the importance of customer satisfaction within the field of marketing was emphasised. We now examine the concept through from three perspectives – the academics', the practitioners', and the customers'. References will be made to the service experiences of the Townsends in the story in Chapter 1 to illustrate the ideas.

The academic perspective

The origin of much of our understanding of customer satisfaction is in the field of consumer behaviour. 'Customer behaviour scholars have proposed that satisfaction depends not on the absolute levels of performance on various attributes, but rather on how the actual performance compares with the *expected* performance.'[27] Following from this approach, satisfaction or dissatisfaction will result if the performance confirms or disconfirms expectations, respectively. Thus, John or Jack Townsend would be satisfied or dissatisfied with their flight to Singapore according to whether or not the actual flight confirmed their expectations of it. Here, satisfaction is seen as a *process*. The theory, known as the expectation–disconfirmation paradigm,[28] underpinned much of the customer/consumer satisfaction research on services in the last quarter of the twentieth century.

However, in parallel, the nature of the *outcome* of customer satisfaction has also received attention.[29] Satisfaction may be regarded as

- *an emotion*: an affective response to a specific service experience

  It would relate to the extent to which John Townsend was happy or excited with the flight experience.

- *a fulfilment*: the achievement of relevant goals

  It would relate to the extent to which Jack Townsend had conquered his fear of flying

- *a state*: the level of reinforcement or arousal

  It would relate to whether the particular flight to Singapore reinforced the Townsends' views of flight travel, or whether it provided a positive or negative 'surprise'.

Measurement of customer satisfaction is appealing to both academics and practitioners. However, reservations have been expressed regarding the use of customer satisfaction surveys. They normally emphasise that the achievement of customer satisfaction should not be an end in itself. 'It's not that satisfaction doesn't matter; it matters a great deal. It's the manner, context and priority of satisfaction measurement that has become a problem. And the problem is that if we fail to link satisfaction scores to customer loyalty and profits, they all too easily become an end in themselves.'[30] There is also evidence of a 'halo effect' in measurements from customer satisfaction surveys, which may render resulting interpretations and actions unreliable.[31] Where a survey measures customer satisfaction on an attribute-by-attribute basis (such as a post-flight satisfaction survey that examines flight food, cabin crew service, in-flight entertainment, and so on), there is evidence that a high/low rating on the dominant attribute will result in positive/negative halo effects on the other attributes. For example, Jack Townsend's delight with the in-flight entertainment may have coloured his views of all the other attributes. As such, customer satisfaction ratings on specific attributes can be misleading.

The practitioner perspective

As customers, we have all had the opportunity to fill in customer satisfaction questionnaires from service providers in the leisure, restaurant, banking, car rental, hotel, retail, airline and other service industries. It has been observed that 'firms spend millions of dollars on tracking customer satisfaction'.[32]

To take an example, J. Sainsbury, the UK multiple food and grocery retailer, conduct a shoppers' customer service survey – which they specify is 'part of a continual programme to ensure that supermarket shoppers receive the very best service'. The major component of the survey consists of 58 statements (on attributes associated with products and service in a supermarket) that respondents have to rate, on an 11-point scale with regard to:

● how important each statement is when shopping at ANY supermarket, and

● how satisfied or dissatisfied they are with the store's performance in relation to each statement.

In the former case, the scale is anchored by 0 = completely unimportant, and 10 = extremely important. In the latter case, the scale is anchored by 0 = completely dissatisfied and 10 = completely satisfied. The statements are grouped into seven categories:

1. *Checkouts*: Example statements are 'helpers at checkouts', 'enough time to pack shopping at checkouts'.

2. *Bags/trolleys/baskets*: Example statements are 'free strong carrier bags', 'trolleys that are easy to steer and push'.

3. *Products*: Example statements are 'wide range of branded products', 'high quality fresh fruit and vegetables'.

4. *Staffed food counters*: Example statements are 'quick service at the staffed delicatessen counter', 'high quality fish from the staffed counter'.

5. *Staff*: Example statements are 'always having staff available on the shop floor', 'polite and friendly staff'.

6. *Prices/offers/promotions*: Example statements are 'clearly marked on-shelf prices', 'the loyalty card scheme'.

7.   *Miscellaneous*: Example statements are 'uncrowded aisles', 'the baby-changing facilities'.

Obviously, the content and length of a customer satisfaction survey will vary according to context, and to the resources required to support the data-gathering exercise. Some customer satisfaction surveys, for instance in a small restaurant, may have as few as five or six questions/statements, relating directly to the quality of the food and the service. The example above is at the other extreme, and is no doubt very costly to administer and support, and it can be seen that the section on customer satisfaction relates to performance only and not to expectations.[33]

Firms need to assess the potential benefits from the survey data against the costs of carrying out the survey. Where firms have many outlets, such as J. Sainsbury, the benefits may include the opportunity to feed back, on a regular basis to the management of each outlet, the customer ratings on the range of attributes. The responses to relatively poor ratings, and to subsequent customer ratings, can then be monitored, with a view to increasing customer satisfaction at each outlet. The effectiveness of this benefit may depend on the level of communication within the organisation, and on the potential halo effects, and respondent fatigue, associated with the attribute-by-attribute measurement.

Most companies, however, would look for benefits associated with increased profits. Here, there is an implicit assumption that increased customer satisfaction will result in increased profit, and so the goal of increased customer satisfaction, supported by (often costly) customer satisfaction surveys is to be pursued. The links between customer satisfaction, customer retention and profitability are discussed in detail in Chapters 10 and 11. For now, it is useful to draw attention to Reichheld's 'satisfaction trap' that companies may fall into if they 'forget that there is no necessary connection between satisfaction scores and cash flow',[34] and to Piercy's reminder that customer satisfaction should not be confused with customer loyalty.[35] While firms would like to view satisfied customers as loyal customers, many customers exist who are satisfied, but not loyal ('name', such as those with three or more supermarket loyalty cards), and who are not satisfied, but loyal ('hostages', such as those who find costs of switching banks too high).

It is not only the service providers themselves that undertake customer satisfaction surveys. The results of formal independent customer satisfaction surveys are often publicised widely. For example, in the USA, changes in the annual Customer Satisfaction Index provide opportunities for journalists to comment on customer service and attribute blame when the index falls. According to the index, since 1994, customer satisfaction has fallen by 5 per cent in the airline sector, 7 per cent in retailing, and even more in the telecommunications sector.[36] This has been attributed to the lack of ability of American companies to keep pace with the volume of demand for goods and services since 1994, and to the replacement of the 'human face and a helping hand' by virtual service using new technologies.[37] Even informal customer satisfaction surveys can be newsworthy, such as when customers were asked for their views on the initiative by London Underground to increase customer satisfaction by introducing perfumed fragrances into the stations.[38]

The customer perspective

What do customers understand by the term 'satisfaction', when responding to surveys by academics or service providers?

Research by Parker and Mathews,[39] that was undertaken specifically to address this question, found that there was considerable variation in the way their sample of consumers had categorised their own recent satisfactory consumption experiences with goods or services. When provided, by the authors, with possible categories, the respondents had categorised satisfaction as follows:

- 'pleasure' (14 per cent of the responses)
- 'an evaluation against what was expected' (13 per cent)
- 'contentment' (13 per cent)
- 'making the right purchase decision' (13 per cent)
- 'a feeling about the consumption experience' (11 per cent)
- 'needs being fulfilled' (11 per cent)
- 'delight' (9 per cent)
- 'relief' (7 per cent)
- 'being suitably rewarded for efforts' (5 per cent)
- 'comparing the situation with those of other people' (4 per cent).

When given an opportunity to offer their own definitions of satisfaction, eight further definitions were forthcoming, with the most popular ones relating to 'cost' (28 per cent), 'quality' (22 per cent), 'absence of dissatisfiers' (14 per cent) and 'convenience' (14%).

Satisfaction clearly means different things to different people in different contexts, and there is a real concern that customer satisfaction surveys may be asking consumers to rate their level of satisfaction on scales where the constructs have no shared meaning. The scale anchors used in the J. Sainsbury example above, that is, 'completely satisfied' and 'completely dissatisfied', are open to many interpretations. Consumers being completely satisfied with, for example, baby-changing facilities, may be expressing a view on the quality of the facility, convenience, a sense of relief, or an absence of dissatisfiers. Each interpretation could lead to a different management response.

Service quality versus satisfaction

Given their different origins, what is the relationship between service quality and satisfaction? 'While service satisfaction and service quality are clearly related, researchers do not share common definitions of the terms, nor is there clear understanding expressed in the literature of how the two relate.'[40]

Service quality as an overall attitude

One explanation of the difference between service quality and customer satisfaction is highlighted by Bateson.[41] 'Quality is generally conceptualised as an attitude, the customer's comprehensive evaluation of a service offering. It is built up from a series of evaluated experiences and hence is less dynamic than satisfaction. Satisfaction is the outcome of the evaluation a consumer makes of any specific transaction.'

For example, imagine a customer taking a car in for a routine service. The customer's level of satisfaction with that particular transaction will relate to the level of disconfirmation between the prior expectation of the service and the actual outcome. If the disconfirmation was relatively small, or if the outcome exceeded expectations (for example, the job was completed quickly enough for the customer to avoid the expense of alternative travel for a day), then he/she will be satisfied (or even delighted). Otherwise, dissatisfaction may be the result. The same customer, however, may judge the overall service quality of the car mechanic on a longer-term basis, and include comparisons with other car service providers in forming expectation of what can, and should, be done by the specific service provider. The service quality rating would not result from a single transaction.

PZB are quite clear about the fact that the SERVQUAL instrument, in its present form, is intended to ascertain customers' global perceptions of a firm's service quality. However, they do suggest that 'modifying SERVQUAL to assess transaction specific service quality is a useful direction for further research'.[42]

Expectations and perceptions

Other researchers[43,44] have suggested that the difference between service quality and customer satisfaction lies in the way disconfirmation is operationalised. In particular, it may depend on how expectations are defined.

They state that in measuring perceived service quality the level of comparison (that is, expectation) is what a consumer *should* expect, whereas in measures of satisfaction the appropriate comparison is what a consumer *would* expect.[45] An expectation about what a customer should expect, say in a particular four-star hotel, will be based not just on experiences with that specific hotel group, but will include best practice of all similar graded hotels. Conversely, an expectation about what a customer would expect of the hotel is more of a prediction based on the appearance of the hotel and previous experiences with, or word-of-mouth communications about, that particular hotel group.

The debate about different types of expectations and the difference between customer satisfaction and service quality continues. Even academics acknowledge some confusion,[46] and for customers completing SERVQUAL-related questionnaires, and service practitioners, the subtle differences may well not be appreciated. If this is the case, just what is SERVQUAL measuring?

PZB[47] still maintain that customer satisfaction is distinct from service quality. Satisfaction is thought to result from the comparison between predicted service and perceived service, whereas service quality refers to the comparison between desired service and perceived service. However, they make the point, in the current state of the debate, that 'both service quality and customer satisfaction can be examined meaningfully from both trans-actions – specific as well as global perspectives'.[48]

Cumulative customer satisfaction

Anderson et al.,[49] as a means of distinguishing between customer satis-faction and service quality, introduce two conceptualisations of customer satisfaction:

1. transaction-specific;
2. cumulative.

We have already considered the transaction-specific conceptualisation in the previous section. The cumulative customer satisfaction is seen to be based on 'the total purchase and consumption experience with a good or service over time', and, as such, is a more fundamental indicator of the firm's past, current and future performance. If perceived service quality is seen as a global judgement of a provider's service offering, then (cumulative) customer satisfaction and perceived service quality can be viewed as distinct because:

- customers require experience with a service to determine satisfaction, whereas quality can be perceived without any actual experience
- customer satisfaction depends on value, where value is a combination of price and quality. Thus satisfaction (and not quality) is dependent on price
- quality relates only to current perceptions, while satisfaction is based on past and future anticipated experiences.

Which is the antecedent?

There is the possibility that practitioners may pose the question 'So what?' to much of the debate on service quality and customer satisfaction, particu-larly in view of the attention given to which precedes the other. Does customer satisfaction lead to service quality, or is it the other way round? Cronin and Taylor[50] suggest that service quality is an antecedent of customer satisfaction and that customer purchase intentions are related more closely to levels of satisfaction than to perceptions of service quality. Thus, other elements of customer satisfaction – price, or availability – may require greater management attention than a striving for even higher quality. Authors concerned with service profitability and the relationships between profitability, quality and satisfaction[51,52] also view service quality as the antecedent of customer satisfaction. Their mathematical equations, con-clusions, and managerial actions and implications depend on the assump-tion that service quality precedes customer satisfaction. For many years, the conventional wisdom, based on PZB's work, supported the opposite view; that is, that transaction-specific satisfaction assessments preceded global perceptions of service quality.

SUMMARY

Issues of service quality and customer satisfaction lie at the heart of services marketing and management. Both are seen as desirable outputs of any service strategy.

Much of the qualitative work on understanding service quality, which produced the determinants, and then the five dimensions, of service quality, has informed academics and practitioners alike. Similarly, the 'Gaps model', which provides the basis for measurement of service quality has been of value as an academic framework, and as a justification for the SERVQUAL format. SERVQUAL and the operationalisation of expectation measurements have been subjects of concern for researchers into service quality, but the methodology is still extensively employed.

Customer satisfaction has its roots in the 'disconfirmation paradigm'; that is, is judged in terms of the level of disconfirmation between the expectation and subsequent experience of a service. As such, there are many similarities between the 'gap' in service quality measurement and the 'disconfirmation' in customer satisfaction measurement. This has led to some confusion over the difference between service quality and customer satisfaction, and to a greater need for an understanding of expectations.

The majority view at the beginning of the twenty-first century, however, is that service quality should be regarded as an antecedent to customer satisfaction,[53] and most of the material in the next two chapters is developed from this view.

LEARNING OUTCOMES

Having read this chapter, you should be able to

- know the distinction between technical and functional service quality and the dimensions of perceived service quality
- critically assess SERVQUAL as a generic instrument for measuring service quality
- know the most likely antecedents of customer expectations and the role of expectations in service quality and customer satisfaction theory
- understand the implications of regarding satisfaction as a process or as an outcome
- appreciate the strengths and limitations of customer satisfaction surveys
- make informed judgements on the academic debates about service quality versus customer satisfaction.

DISCUSSION QUESTIONS AND EXERCISES

1. Describe recent occasions when, in a service context, (i) expectations exceeded perceptions and (ii) perceptions exceeded expectations. Explain the main reasons in each case.

2. Outline the main feature of the 'Gap model' of service quality. How might management seek to reduce Gaps 1 to 4?

3. What are the differences between perceived service quality and customer satisfaction?

4. Are customer satisfaction surveys value for money?

5. What is the 'disconfirmation paradigm'?

Notes and references

1. Fisk, R., Brown, S. and Bitner, M. J., 'Tracking the Evolution of the Services Marketing Literature', *Journal of Retailing*, vol. 69, no. 1, Spring 1993.
2. Clow, K. E. and Vorhies, D. W., 'Building a Competitive Advantage for Service Firms', *Journal of Services Marketing*, vol. 7, 1993, pp. 22–32.
3. Parker, C. and Mathews, B. P., 'Customer Satisfaction: Contrasting Academic and Consumers' Interpretations', *Marketing Intelligence and Planning*, vol. 19, no. 1, 2001, pp. 38–44.
4. Parasuraman, A., Zeithaml, V. A. and Berry, L. L., 'SERVQUAL: A Multiple-Item Scale for Measuring Consumer Perceptions of Service Quality', *Journal of Retailing*, vol. 64, spring 1988, pp. 12–40.
5. Oliver, R. L., 'Measurement and Evaluation of Satisfaction Process in Retail Setting', *Journal of Retailing*, vol. 57, 1981, pp. 25–48.
6. Gronroos, C., 'Innovative Marketing Strategies and Organizational Structures for Service Firms', in L. L. Berry, G. L. Shostack and G. D. Upah (eds), *Emerging Perspectives on Services Marketing*, American Marketing Association, Chicago, 1983, pp. 9–21.
7. Lewis, R. C. and Booms, B. H., 'The Marketing Aspects of Service Quality', in L. L. Berry, G. L. Shostack and G. D. Upah (eds), *Emerging Perspectives on Services Marketing*, American Marketing Association, Chicago, 1983, pp. 99–107.
8. Parasuraman, A., Zeithaml, V. A. and Berry, L. L., 'A Conceptual Model of Service Quality and its Implications for Future Research', *Journal of Marketing*, vol. 49, 1985, pp. 41–50.
9. Parasuraman, Zeithaml and Berry, 'SERVQUAL: A Multiple-Item Scale for Measuring Consumer Perceptions of Service Quality'.
10. Parasuraman, A., Berry, L. L. and Zeithaml, V. A., 'Refinement and Reassessment of the SERVQUAL Scale', *Journal of Retailing*, vol. 67, Winter 1991, pp. 420–50.
11. Zeithaml, V. A., Berry, L. L. and Parasuraman, A., 'The Nature and Determinants of Customer Expectations of Service', *Journal of the Academy of Marketing Science*, vol. 21, 1993, pp. 1–12.
12. Parasuraman, Zeithaml and Berry, 'A Conceptual Model of Service Quality'.
13. McDonald, M. H. B., de Chernatony, L. and Harris, F., 'Corporate Marketing and Service Brands – Moving Beyond the Fast-Moving Consumer Goods Model', *European Journal of Marketing*, vol. 35, no. 3–4, pp. 335–52.

14. Gronroos, C., *Service Management and Marketing*, John Wiley & Sons, Chichester, UK, 2000.

15. Auty, S. and Long, G., '"Tribal Warfare" and Gaps Affecting Internal Service Quality', *International Journal of Service Industry Management*, vol. 10, no. 1, 1999, pp. 7–22.

16. Sultan, F. and Simpson Jr, M. C., 'International Service Variants: Airline Passenger Expectations and Perceptions of Service Quality', *Journal of Services Marketing*, vol. 14, no. 3, 2000, pp 188–216.

17. Parasuraman, Zeithaml and Berry, 'SERVQUAL: A Multiple-Item Scale for Measuring Consumer Perceptions of Service Quality'.

18. Parasuraman, Berry and Zeithaml, 'Refinement and Reassessment of the SERVQUAL Scale'.

19. Carman, J. A., 'Consumer Perceptions of Service Quality: An Assessment of the SERVQUAL Dimensions', *Journal of Retailing*, vol. 66, Spring 1990, pp. 33–55.

20. Cronin, J. J. and Taylor, S. A., 'Measuring Service Quality: A Re-examination and Extension', *Journal of Marketing*, vol. 56, 1992, pp. 55–68.

21. Parasuraman, Berry and Zeithaml, 'Refinement and Reassessment of the SERVQUAL Scale'.

22. Vandamme, R. and Leunin, J., 'Measuring Service Quality in the Retail Sector: An Assessment and Extension of SERVQUAL', Proceedings of the 7th International Conference on Research in Distributive Trades, Stirling, UK, 1993, pp. 364–73.

23. Clow and Vorhies, 'Building a Competitive Advantage for Service Firms'.

24. Teas, R. K., 'Expectations, Performance Evaluation and Consumers' Perceptions of Quality', *Journal of Marketing*, vol. 57, October 1993, pp. 18–34.

25. Smith, A. M., 'Measuring Service Quality: Is SERVQUAL Now Redundant?', *Journal of Marketing Management*, vol. 11, 1995, pp 257–76.

26. Buttle, F., 'SERVQUAL: Review, Critique, Research Agenda', *European Journal of Marketing*, vol. 30, no. 1, 1996, pp. 8–32.

27. Sheth, J. N., Mittal, B. and Newman, B. I., *Customer Behavior: Consumer Behavior and Beyond*, The Dryden Press, Orlando, Fla., 1999.

28. Oliver, R. L., 'Effects of Expectation and Disconfirmation on Post-Exposure Product Evaluations: An Alternative Interpretation', *Journal of Applied Psychology*, vol. 62, no. 4, 1977, pp. 480–6.

29. Parker and Mathews, 'Customer Satisfaction: Contrasting Academic and Consumers' Interpretations'.

30. Reichheld, F. F., *The Loyalty Effect*, HBS Press, Boston Mass., 1996.

31. Wirtz, J., 'Improving the Measurement of Customer Satisfaction: A Test of Three Methods to Reduce Halo', *Managing Service Quality*, vol. 11, no. 2, 2001, pp. 99–111.

32. Ibid.

33. Expectations could have been considered, for example, by anchoring the scales as 0 = fell below expectations, 5 = met expectations, 10 = exceeded expectations.

34. Reichheld, *The Loyalty Effect*.

35. 'Customer satisfaction and customer loyalty are not the same thing; and you cannot buy real loyalty that easily' (p. 40) *Market-led Strategic Change*, Nigel Piercy, 2nd edn., Butterworth Heinemann, Oxford, 1998.

36. Jones, A., 'Have a Nice Day? No Such Luck in Corporate America', *The Times*, London, 12 April 2001.

37. Schulze, H., 'Since When Did I Ask to Help Myself?', *New York Times*, New York, 27 August 2000.

38. Wendlandt, A., 'It's Sure to Get up Travellers' Noses', *Financial Times*, London, 24 April 2001.

39. Parker and Mathews, 'Customer Satisfaction: Contrasting Academic and Consumers' Interpretations'.

40. Fisk, Brown and Bitner, 'Tracking the Evolution of the Services Marketing Literature'.

41. Bateson, J. E. G., *Managing Services Marketing: Text and Readings*, 2nd edn, Dryden Press, London, 1992.

42. Parasuraman, A., Zeithaml, V. A. and Berry, L. L., 'Reassessment of Expectations as a Comparison Standard in Measuring Service Quality: Implications for Further Research', *Journal of Marketing*, vol. 58, January 1994, pp. 111–24.

43. Cronin and Taylor, 'Measuring Service Quality'.

44. Anderson, E. W., Fornell, C. and Lehmann, D. R., 'Customer Satisfaction, Market Share and Profitability: Findings from Sweden', *Journal of Marketing*, vol. 58, July 1994, pp. 53–66.

45. Ibid.

46. Ibid.

47. Zeithaml, Berry and Parasuraman, 'The Nature and Determinants of Customer Expectations of Service'.

48. Parasuraman, Zeithaml and Berry, 'Reassessment of Expectations as a Comparison Standard in Measuring Service Quality'.

49. Anderson, Fornell and Lehmann, 'Customer Satisfaction, Market Share and Profitability'.

50. Cronin and Taylor, 'Measuring Service Quality'.

51. Anderson, Fornell and Lehmann, 'Customer Satisfaction, Market Share and Profitability'.

52. Rust, R. T. and Oliver, R. L., *Service Quality: New Directions in Theory and Practice*, Sage, London, 1994.

53. Sivadas, E. and Baker-Prewitt, J. L., 'An Examination of the Relationship Between Service Quality, Customer Satisfaction and Store Loyalty', *International Journal of Retail and Distribution Management*, vol. 28, no. 2, 2000, pp. 73–82.

Relationship marketing

LEARNING OBJECTIVES

Overall aim of the chapter:
To define the relationship marketing approach and outline the implications of a concentration on customer loyalty and retention.
  In particular, the *chapter objectives* are

- to compare the transaction and relationship marketing approaches

- to explore and contrast the many definitions of relationship marketing from academic and organisational perspectives

- to introduce the concept of market-based relationship marketing, and its advantages and disadvantages for customers and the service organisation

- to demonstrate the internal and external relationships that constitute network-based relationship marketing

- to explore the practical implications of two customer loyalty strategies.

Introduction

A relationship marketing approach draws attention to *the importance of retaining as well as attracting customers* with the emphasis being placed on the development of long-term relationships with existing customers. The approach is not exclusive to the marketing of services. It is, however, at the heart of many service businesses, and something many of them do particularly well. As the Waymark Holidays cross-country skiing literature points out (Case Study 5), 'much of our success over the past two decades has been due to the loyalty of our regular customers, many of whom travel with us every year – in some cases, twice or even three times per season'. The hairdresser (Case Study 1) estimates that about 90 per cent of all customers have been to the salon at least five times. These organisations have been able not only to attract customers to their service in the first instance, but also to develop and maintain a series of long-term relationships with many clients that have helped to secure the survival of their business. Many of their loyal customers act as an important referral source for new business, recommending their service to new clients.

Why is customer loyalty and retention of particular interest and importance to *service* businesses?

One reason is that it is relatively easy to copy many services (as in the travel company and hairdresser examples above), and consequently easy for customers to switch loyalties. It may take only one bad 'moment of truth' in a service encounter to persuade a customer to go to a competitor. Therefore, service businesses incur high switching costs if they do not recognise the importance of customer loyalty and retention. The development of a closer, long-term relationship with customers is particularly important in certain types of service operation: namely, when the service cannot be provided completely on one occasion, for instance, certain treatments at the dentist which require several visits, or a problem with a car which requires more than one visit to the mechanic. Similarly, if the service itself is highly intangible, the existence of a stronger relationship can be an important influence on a customer's decision to pay for the services of one provider in preference to another. If there is little tangible evidence available to assess the quality of the service on offer, customers frequently turn to the provider they have used before, whom they feel they can trust.

Another reason is that, as we have seen, there is a significant *people* element in the *services* marketing mix, and, according to Zineldin:[1] 'Relationship marketing views marketing as an integrative activity involving personnel ... personal relationships, interactions and social exchange are the most important core elements of relationship marketing.' So, one would expect that an approach which has interpersonal interactions at its heart would be of particular relevance to service businesses.

Arguably, many service and other businesses have intuitively adopted such business practices without being aware that their marketing activities are being labelled as 'relationship marketing'. If so, they have adopted a marketing approach, focus and strategy which is different from that which concentrates on single sales or transactions (known as 'transaction marketing').

Relationship marketing is said to differ from transaction marketing in the following ways.

- Transaction marketing is about *attracting* customers using *offensive strategies* (encouraging brand switching and/or recruiting competitors' dissatisfied clients).

- Relationship marketing is about *retaining* customers using *defensive strategies* (minimising customer turnover and maximising customer retention).[2]

In this chapter, we examine relationship marketing (RM) in the service sector. First we set the scene by exploring some of the definitions and features of relationship marketing from both an academic and an organisational perspective. Two themes of relationship marketing – market-based RM and network-based RM – are then explained and evaluated. Finally, strategies that have been embraced by practitioners as a means of maintaining customer loyalty – effective service recovery, and service guarantees – are considered in detail.

Definitions and features of relationship marketing

The academic perspective

Some prominent academics refer to relationship marketing as 'the new paradigm for marketing'.[3,4] There is little doubt that relationship marketing has become a fruitful area for academic research, especially since the early 1990s. There have been many attempts to define what is meant by relationship marketing, and to outline its main features. The sheer volume of academic literature on this area can be daunting, so we have picked out below some key definitions and features of relationship marketing, and provided a summary of relationship marketing (RM) indicators.

1. RM is about 'attracting, maintaining and enhancing customer relationships'[5] and 'the development and enhancement of internal and other external relationships'.[6]

This definition draws attention to the importance of retaining as well as attracting customers with the emphasis being placed on the development of long-term relationships with existing customers. It involves changing the focus of marketing from a transactional to a relationship focus, with the emphasis on customer retention, high customer service and commitment, and quality being a concern for all. It also emphasises that RM is not only about bettering relationships with customer markets, but also about the relationships with supplier, recruitment, referral and influence markets, as well as the internal market (Chapter 7).

2. RM is about 'turning new customers into regular purchasers ... to strong supporters...to active vocal advocates of the company'.[7]

Underlying this definition is the belief that the identification and retention of loyal customers can result in significant financial benefits for the organisation, and that loyalty retention measures should be integral to strategy.[8] Reichheld believes that potentially loyal customers need to be targeted by the company right from the beginning from an analysis of the characteristics of existing users.[9]

3. RM is about 'bringing marketing, customer service and quality together'.[10]

Here, it is argued that relationship marketing orientation involves a closer alignment between three crucial areas; marketing, customer service and quality. They are three components of strategy which may have traditionally been 'treated as separate and unrelated'. In order to be a truly 'customer-focused' service organisation, these three elements need to be integrated together within the organisation. Christopher *et al.*[11] argue that although companies have made efforts to measure and monitor quality within the organisation, their actions have largely been taken from an operations perspective (that is, conformance to set requirements; for example BS5750) rather than from the customer perceived quality perspective. They also argue that measures aimed at improving customer service levels have often been taken in isolation from these quality initiatives. A true relationship marketing orientation would require all three areas to be linked together.

4. RM is about 'developing mutual trust',[12,13] and 'commitment'.[14]

Trust and commitment are features of a relationship marketing approach that have been identified by many researchers. In particular, relationships have been found between customers' trust in the service provider, and commitment to the relationship, and their levels of customer satisfaction and loyalty.[15] In certain service offers, there are opportunities for customer commitment to be mutually beneficial. For example, the personal trainer would like a customer to sign on for a 10-week training programme, ensuring customer retention over the period. From the customer's perspective a commitment to a 10-week programme can enhance the health benefits, which relate to levels of satisfaction not associated with a single training session.

5. RM is about 'the development of database marketing, interactive marketing and network marketing'.[16]

In this context, relationship marketing is about recognising that the organisation's existing customer base is its most important asset and about working to protect it at all costs. One of the major reasons why relationship marketing is attractive to service business managers is because of advances in information technology and specifically the generation of customer databases. These clearly make it easier for service organisations to identify loyal customers. Both small and large service operators use databases in this way. A video retailer, for example, holds membership details of all customers on a database and sends regular users a birthday card with a complimentary voucher for a free video.

For managers of service organisations who are adopting, or who are considering the adoption of a relationship marketing approach, the definitions and features outlined above may help. In addition, Pressey and Mathews[17] provide a very useful summary of the key indicators of a relationship marketing approach. They are:

- a high level of trust between both parties
- a high level of commitment between both parties
- a long time horizon
- open communication channels between both parties with information exchanged between both parties
- having the customer's best interest at heart
- a commitment to quality from both parties
- an attempt to favourably lock-in or retain the customer.

The organisational perspective

Many organisations adopt RM within a function headed 'Customer Relationship Management'. From their perspective, customer loyalty and retention is best addressed through the integration of Marketing Customer Service, and IT.

Customer Relationship Management (CRM), therefore, often involves

- *Precision Marketing*. CRM is believed to be at the heart of customer communications, and is felt to be the future for direct marketing agencies. According to the Chief Executive of IBM's CRM unit, 'Most companies are now competing with more commoditised products, so the only differentiation is the customer relationship'.[18]
- *The use and operation of 'call centres'*. Call centres are central to many CRM projects. The growth in call centres is illustrated by the Datamonitor forecast that the global call centre software market will reach $8.5 billion by 2003. Call centres are being integrated with internet on-line offers. Sometimes, however, CRM may be interpreted as 'customer care' and seen as a cost to the organisation.
- *The development of customer databases*. This is in line with definition five above. A problem, in practice, in the development of effective databases, may be the failure of connection between IT specialists and marketers.

Based on the perspectives above, we now provide a more detailed evaluation of two complementary elements of relationship marketing:[19]

1. *Market-based RM*: Here the focus is on customer retention;
2. *Network-based RM*: Here the focus is on enhancing internal and external relationships.

Market-based relationship marketing

The focus of market-based RM is on keeping existing customers rather than going out to get new ones. Customer retention is the key. Ideally, the organisation would like to treat large numbers of customers individually (and profitably). Therefore the organisation's development and management of a customer database is central to the process.

First, however, we look at the factors that may influence a customer to stay with a service organisation, rather than defect to a competitor.

● 'Exit costs' may be too high.

Customers are retained by some service companies simply because it is too much trouble for the customer to switch to a competitor. Maybe, it is the amount of time required that dissuades customers from defecting, even if they are not particularly satisfied with their existing service. For many years, this was given as a principal reason why customers stayed with a particular bank, even if more favourable interest rates or a wider range of services was being offered elsewhere. In the mobile phone industry, for example, switching costs associated with changing a network service may include costs in time and effort on seeking information about different providers, filling out forms to instigate the switch, and informing relevant people of the new telephone number. Sometimes, however, it is a perception of risk that prevents a customer from switching. They may feel, for example, that other companies are not as reliable as 'British Gas', even though these companies are, according to advertisements, supplying the same gas through the same pipes at a cheaper price.

● The service provider has a detailed understanding of the customer's needs.

Customers may be retained by a service provider because the provider has demonstrated the ability to do a good job for the customer, based on a thorough understanding of the needs of the customer. Such an understanding may not be easily replicated. Personal services, such as those provided by hairdressers, chiropodists, manicurists or chiropractors, may fall into this category, where customers choose their favourite employee to carry out the service, and possibly build up a strong interpersonal relationship. With professional services, such as counselling, accounting and legal services, clients, having disclosed personal details to a person whose confidences they trust and who they feel is empathetic, are likely to remain with the service. Customers are likely to return to restaurants or hotels which cater to particular customer needs for, say, children's menus, special diets, or speedy service. A hotel in Zurich, for example, has opened exclusively for women.[20] The high likelihood of repatronage for female executives is due not just to the physical features (bigger and better-lit bathrooms, for example) but also to a reduction of anxiety (not feeling intimidated by dining alone in a hotel restaurant).

● Customer choice is restricted.

Often customers are tied into a service, because they have little or no choice. Commuters may have to travel by train or bus, simply because there may be no feasible alternative mode of transport to travel to work. Guarantees, which accompany the purchases of goods ranging from cars to washing machines to satellite television, involve the employment of contracted maintenance services, over which the purchaser has no choice. Even if the service levels in these situations are extremely poor, customers cannot defect to a preferred service provider.

Service organisations have responded to these factors by attempting to know their customers better through the development and management of customer databases, developing personal relationships with customers through their employees and tying in customers to the organisation with guarantees or through long-term commitments. In banks, for example, loyal and profitable customers (identified through the database) may be offered a personal bank manager whose role is to build a personal relationship with the customer, making switching more 'costly', and increasing long-term commitments through favourable loan packages covering several years. However, other banks, looking at attracting new customers, may view the high exit costs as something to challenge. For example, the Abbey National, one of the new UK banks, produced a national advertising campaign which focused on how easy it is for a customer to transfer their accounts from any bank to the Abbey National – just a signature is needed.

Market-based RM aims for customer retention and long-term relationships. However, it is not always appropriate for the two parties; that is, the customer and the organisation. From the many research projects on RM, it is clear that there are both advantages and disadvantages of market-based RM for each party. We summarise the findings below.

Advantages of market-based relationship marketing

For the customer

- Market-based RM can contribute to a sense of well-being, stability and quality of life.

The relationship with the organisation (or employee(s) representing the organisation) is something that the customer can rely on. For the elderly customer, the fortnightly visit by the mobile gardener not only results in an improvement in the look of the garden, but also provide opportunities for gardening-related conversations. For the business person, the favourite restaurant and waiter provides a safe venue for the client lunch.

- Market-based RM can make it unnecessary for the customer to incur high switching costs.

It is becoming easier for customers to switch service providers, even those, such as banks or insurance companies, where there has been a long historical commitment. Nevertheless, customers may still find it difficult, inconvenient and, in some cases, stressful to make the switch. If, through market-based RM, the existing service providers are responding to the customer's needs, the customer avoids the potential anxieties and costs associated with switching.

- Market-based RM can be part of a customer's social support system.

By encouraging and supporting 'regulars', service providers are providing the physical space for customer social interactions (as shown in the section on customer-to-customer interactions in Chapter 4). The obvious examples are pubs, bistros and coffee shops, but other service settings, such as hairdressers, launderettes, betting shops, adult learning centres, retail outlets and leisure clubs become the meeting places for social groups.

For the service organisation

- Market-based RM can result in customers spending more.

Reichheld and Sasser[21] showed that customers, across a variety of services, spend more each year they are with an organisation. For example, if the car mechanic or dealership retains customers, the customers may pay more each year for regular 'car services' as they upgrade their cars. Similarly, wine club members will pay more as their tastes for fine wines develop. They calculated that a 5 per cent increase in customer loyalty can produce profit increases from 25 per cent to 85 per cent.

- Market-based RM can result in lower marketing costs.

Recruiting new clients or customers is costly. For example, many leisure clubs permanently employ a person whose sole task is to recruit new members, while, according to the UK Advertising Association, businesses in the holiday travel and transport industries spend over £250 million per year on advertising to solicit new customers. In contrast, it is widely believed that the cost of retaining customers can be as little as one sixth of that of recruiting new customers.

- Market-based RM can result in free positive word-of-mouth recommendation.

Services, because of their intangible nature, rely a lot on word-of-mouth (WOM) to reassure potential customers to make a purchase. For example, specialist holiday companies build strong relationships with segments of their customers, such as retired people, or families with very young children, knowing that recommendations from their existing customers, through positive WOM, will be perceived as credible by others from within those segments.

- Market-based RM can increase *employee* retention.

It is believed that employees feel happier in long-term relationships with customers. Face-to-face service encounters which occur on a regular basis with loyal customers, such as those experienced by hairdressers, aerobics teachers, pre-school playgroups and residential care assistants, often result in enjoyable conversation and repartee between the employees and customers. This, in turn, can make the employee's job more enjoyable or rewarding, or, at the very least, reduce potential boredom, resulting in a reduction of employee turnover costs.

Disadvantages of market-based relationship marketing

For the customer

- Market-based RM can be irritating.

Not every customer wants a 'relationship' with representatives of each and every service provider. If customers feel that they are being forced into such a relationship, the organisation's market-based RM moves may be counter-productive. The customer's irritation with an overly friendly service employee can be increased if the friendliness is perceived as being false, and an act.

- Market-based RM can be intrusive.

Organisations will understandably wish to use their customer databases to target loyal customers with offers designed to meet their needs. Careless use of market-based RM and customer databases, however, can result in customer feelings of intrusion. RM can raise privacy issues and may bring accusations of exploitation when the relationship is one-sided in favour of the organisation.

To counter this, some service organisations segment their customers according to the relationship the customers may want with the organisation, and then handle the segments differently. One such segmentation in a retailing context is shown in Table 9.1. There is the recognition, for example, of the segment of customers who wish to remain anonymous. An organisational respect for customer anonymity can pay dividends. For example, Boots, a UK multiple retailer, respects that shoppers want to be anonymous. With their 'Advantage' Loyalty Card Scheme, they do not undertake any personalised analyses of associated databases, partly because the sensitive nature of purchases of health care products. Any abuse of the sensitivities could have deterred shoppers from going to their shops. As a result, sales rose significantly in parallel with the establishment of the loyalty scheme.

Table 9.1 An example of customer relationship segmentation

Segment	Features
● Purely anonymous customers	Do not wish to provide name or personal information or participate in any of the company's individualised services.
● Anonymous customers	Are prepared to use personalised shopping services very occasionally.
● Customers who choose to access and provide information	Are happy to provide lots of personal information in the belief that they will get better deals.
● Customers who seek an individual relationship with the retailer	Cash-rich, time-poor people who are happy to have a personal shopper to advise and get products together for them.

Source: Philippe Lemoine, Galaries Lafayette.[22]

At the other end of the scale, there are customers who are willing to pay for relationship services even more personalised than a retailer's personal shopper. Hilary Clinton is just one of a number of individuals who have paid for the services of a 'life coach' – someone 'at the end of the phone who will cajole, push, bully and beg you to lose weight, find a better job, or just get plain organised'.[23]

For the organisation

● Market-based RM can stifle innovation and employee creativity.

Clients may change advertising agencies precisely because the strong relationships are felt to have resulted in a dearth of new ideas, brought about by a similarity of thinking. Employees having regular, and similar, service encounters with loyal customers may feel frustrated by the lack of variety and opportunity to display different talents. This may apply to the hairdresser who sees the same customers for the same cut every six weeks, or to the driving instructor who has a slow-learning client.

● Market-based RM can raise customer expectations.

In Chapter 8, it was argued that customer satisfaction relates to customer disconfirmation of expectations of the service. Because market-based RM aims to make loyal customers feel they are being treated as individuals, or even as 'special', this may raise their expectations, making customer satisfaction progressively more difficult to achieve.

● The benefits of market-based RM 'loyalty schemes' do not always outweigh the costs.

In the UK, there has been some high profile strategy changes, especially in the grocery retail sector, regarding the use of loyalty cards. While the leading UK grocery retailer, Tesco, achieved a high penetration of loyalty card holders (over 18 per cent of UK households in 1998), two other grocery retailers, Asda and Safeway, abandoned their loyalty card schemes, with Safeway claiming that there were too many loyalty schemes in the market for them to work any more. There are problems too with the use of the customer databases, with 'data overload' preventing organisations targeting individuals successfully with tailor-made offers.[24]

Network-based relationship marketing

The focus on network-based RM is on enhancing networks of internal and external relationships.

Relationships with suppliers

As far as relationships with suppliers are concerned, there is clear evidence that organisations are moving away from a traditionally adversarial relationship to one based on mutual support and cooperation. There is increasing awareness of the benefits to be gained by working together to meet the needs of the final consumer. Waymark Holidays (Case Study 5), for example, recognises that, as nearly all their holidays use scheduled flights, strong relationships with airlines are crucial to success. The company feels that their dealings with airlines are built on 'confidence and trust' which it has taken 20 years to build up.

Many retail organisations in the UK are making a deliberate effort to reduce the number of suppliers that they deal with in order to develop stronger, more mutually beneficial relationships with the remaining few. By employing 'category management' and 'efficient consumer response' systems, both the retailers and their suppliers can develop a customer focus. The supermarket retailer can work with a limited number of suppliers to provide the 'Saturday night in' experience for its customers by selling popcorn, drinks, chocolates, and a 'take-away meal for two' to go with a film video. The retail buyer recognises the fact that suppliers are very much a part of the final product, and that working together with suppliers can increase the benefits to both parties. Benefits in this context have been found to include shorter delivery lead times, lower stock levels, fewer quality problems and faster implementation of design changes.

Relationships with recruitment markets

Network-based RM also involves having a closer relationship with those who supply human resources to the organisation; that is, recruitment markets. We have already highlighted, in Chapter 7, the important role played by employees in generating customer loyalty. Service organisations need to cultivate long-term relationships with the suppliers of such employees to ensure that they receive both the right quantity and quality of employees.

Some companies, for example, work closely with university departments who have sizeable numbers of undergraduates and postgraduates in business and management related courses. The companies may provide student placement opportunities for the undergraduates, guest speakers on the course units, and real-world student projects, with an aim to assess potentially suitable service-oriented employees. Such initiatives provide mutual benefits for the relationship partners.

Relationships with internal markets

Internal marketing is highlighted as being a crucial element in network-based RM approach. Employees need to feel that they have formed a long-term relationship with the service provider and have a shared understanding of the mission of the organisation. Human resource strategies need to focus on internal markets and specifically on employee retention.

It is important, however, that such strategies are fully thought through. For instance, some companies provide support for their managers to obtain higher qualifications, such as the MBA, as a means of showing their commitment to the manager's future, and to generate a reciprocal commitment from the manager to stay longer with the company. This is in the belief that 'the longer employees stay with the company, the more familiar they become with the business, the more they learn, and the more valuable they can be'.[25] However, managers attaining new skills and knowledge through their qualification course can become frustrated (and leave the organisation) if company structures do not allow them to implement the skills and knowledge.

Relationships with referral markets

Relationships need to be developed with referral markets. Specific strategies need to be devised to reward the referral sources that generate the most business. Although, traditionally, satisfied customers are the key referral source for service organisations, other sources might include suppliers, other agencies dealing with the company, for instance, banks, and in some cases even competitors. The wedding photographer can have mutually beneficial referral relationships with the suit hire shop, the wedding-dress shop and the specialist cake maker, or the accountant may recommend that a customer should approach another firm for expert advice on insolvency if they cannot provide this element of the service in house.

Relationships with influence markets

Influence markets can also affect the strength of the relationship the organisation has with its customers. Here, Christopher *et. al.*[26] refer to legislatory bodies, political groups, and trade and consumer associations. Professional organisations, such as accountants, holiday tour operators and funeral services all feel that it is important to develop and maintain strong links with the relevant trade associations. This not only enables them to keep up to date with developments in the industry, but also gives a signal to their customers that they are serious about the relationship they have developed with them. Organisations benefit from building up relationships with their local newspapers. A running club, for example, can gain extensive editorial coverage showing the achievements of their members, which, in turn, can ensure a regular set of enquiries from potential new members.

Strategies for maintaining customer loyalty

Practitioners have sought strategies for maintaining and enhancing customer loyalty. Two of the more popular ones relate to effective service recovery and service guarantees.

Effective service recovery

Research on the nature and characteristics of customer complaints in service organisations has revealed that those consumers who bother to complain about the service that they receive tend to be the loyal users. Although these 'complainers' may represent only a small percentage of dissatisfied customers, the service provider is usually able to identify them and, more importantly, take some action to maintain their loyalty. As we have noted already, relationship marketing is all about retaining loyal customers, not just attracting new ones. A number of researchers have offered advice to service organisations setting up service recovery strategies. Some have suggested that, as breakdowns usually occur as a result of inbuilt faults in the delivery system, organisations need to focus on service design to reduce complaints.[27] Zemke and Bell[28] highlighted the fact that different customers will have different views about how they want their problems to be dealt with, that is, different recovery expectations. The way to respond, in this case, is to design a recovery strategy that will meet the needs and expectations of each customer. Empowered employees are the best vehicle to carry out these recovery processes as they can respond flexibly as, and when, a problem arises. The study of service encounters carried out by Bitner *et al.*,[29] and referred to in Chapter 4, highlighted the positive impact that employee verbal responses to service failures could have on customer perceptions of the service. They noted that 'even service delivery system failures can be remembered as highly satisfactory if handled properly'. In their study, for example, when an employee compensated a customer for a long wait in a restaurant with a free drink, or upgraded a guest's room because the original booking was not available, customers registered the incident as very satisfying even though the problem was caused by a system failure in the first instance.

A more recent study by Johnston,[30] based on an analysis of 224 anecdotes from customers in a wide range of service organisations, looked specifically at the issue of service recovery. One of the objectives of the study was to identify more clearly what constituted service failure in the minds of the consumers. The findings drew attention to some interesting concerns for service management. The situations that customers described as failures all related to something that had gone wrong during the service experience. Although the responsibility for many of the problems could be traced back to the service provider (for example, a doctor's surgery which was running late), at least 25 per cent of failure incidents were caused by customer mistakes. This clearly presents certain managerial problems for the service provider attempting to set in place a planned service recovery strategy. Although it may be possible to identify the sorts of failure situations that might occur for one's own service, and therefore design appropriate procedures, it would be impossible to identify all the problems that the customers might themselves cause. Johnston suggests that 'the response to such a wide range of situations may lead organisations away from more prescriptive procedures to a greater reliance on the training and empowerment of individual contact staff'.

The impact that empowered employees, with finely tuned interpersonal skills, can have on the service recovery process was highlighted in the study. Johnston found that those employees who listened attentively to the customer's problem, and showed concern and sympathy for the situation, could go a long way towards placating a disgruntled customer. However, the response was most effective when the employee had the power to react flexibly to every different situation, perhaps doing something extra or totally unexpected for the customer to make amends. Research in this area emphasises yet again the crucial role played by employees in the service organisation.

In general, research suggests that effective service recovery strategies must include

- an understanding of how customers want the service organisation to handle complaints
- priority given to improving customers' waiting experience.

An understanding of customers' evaluations of complaint handling

When evaluating a company's attempts at service recovery or complaint handling, it is felt that customers may weigh up their own inputs (for example, time, money, emotion, energy) against the outputs associated with the recovery tactic (for example, apology, cash compensation, replacement), and then make a judgement as to whether the recovery tactic was fair or just. Customers are looking for *justice*. Perceived justice may take three forms:[31]

1. *Distributive justice*: relates to the *outcomes* of the service recovery efforts. A problem here is that companies may assume they know what customers regard as a fair and just outcome without finding out from customers themselves. This may even lead to companies overestimating the rewards customers would accept as fair to compensate for a service failure. For example, a pizza company offered delivery within 30 minutes or a free pizza, but changed the policy to delivery within 30 minutes or $3 off the pizza, because customers regarded the former as too generous!

2. *Procedural justice*: relates to the *processes or procedures* that take place to achieve the outcome. Very often customers will engage in very negative word-of-mouth about a service organisation if they perceive that they have been treated poorly during the recovery process – if they feel that they have been passed from one service employee to another, or have not had their telephone call returned, or never been given the opportunity to speak to a particular employee.

3. *Interactional justice*: deals with 'interpersonal behaviour in the enactment of procedures and the delivery of outcomes'.[32] This relates to the *people* element of the services marketing mix. How did the customer judge the people who handled the complaint? Customers who perceive that the employees did not seem to care, nor understand the importance to them of the service failure, will be judging interactional justice in a negative way.

The extent to which the three types of perceived justice are likely to affect customers' evaluations of the effectiveness of the service recovery may depend on factors such as the duration of the encounter, the degree of customisation, or the extent of the switching costs.[33]

Giving priority to improving customers' waiting experience

Because of the difficulties in always having the supply to match the demand for services, and the 'real time' nature of service delivery, customers frequently spend time waiting for services. Delays are often not only inevitable, but also are a major source of dissatisfaction for customers. How companies are perceived to be handling customers' waiting experiences as part of service recovery can be critical in maintaining customer loyalty. The management of service waits can focus on reducing *actual* waiting times, reducing *perceptions* of waiting times or managing the *impact* of the delay:[34]

1. *Reducing actual waiting times.* To attempt to reduce actual waiting times, companies would look to techniques for forecasting customer demand, and employ employee resource allocation techniques to deal with the variations in hourly, daily and weekly demand.[35] Alternatively, they may invest in technology that will speed up customer throughput. The potential success of these operational approaches will depend on the accuracy of the forecasts (which for many services is very difficult to achieve), the availability of part-time and full-time staff to work at short notice, and the available funds for investment.

2. *Reducing perceptions of waiting times.* There is some evidence that when customers are entertained or distracted during a wait, they perceive that they have waited for less time. This was mentioned in the section on impression management in Chapter 2. However, there may be a limit to the effectiveness of such devices.

3. *Managing the impact of delay.* Despite the attention given to the two approaches above, delays still occur in the majority of services and so any sustainable and effective service recovery system must also be able to deal with the impact of the delay on the customer. The organisation will need to manage how waits are interpreted by customers and the way that they respond. Two aspects are very important here. First, employee efforts during a delay may well determine customer reactions.

Where employees are perceived to be showing genuine empathy, customers may forgive the company for the delay. However, if employees are perceived as uncaring, through, for example, carrying on other tasks which have no effect on the reduction of the waiting times, then this converts a delay into a service failure. Second, apologies for the wait, made by employees, are known to affect customer demeanour. A sincere apology is expected and welcomed by most customers. Conversely, a scripted and seemingly insincere apology, such as the standard scripts adopted by rail and airline employees, can be counterproductive and generate angry customer responses.[36]

Service guarantees

In addition to devising an effective service recovery strategy to maintain customer loyalty, the service provider may also decide to offer customers a service guarantee. The basic function of the guarantee is to reduce the risk to consumers associated with the purchase decision, both before and after the event. Slimming clubs, for example, often promise to return clients' membership fee within a given time period if participants do not experience some weight loss. Faced with this promise, and with no other way of assessing the quality of the service they are paying for beforehand, customers feel much happier about parting with the comparatively high joining fee.

Many service providers argue that it is impossible to offer a guarantee for something that cannot be totally controlled by the operator; for example, where different customers get involved in the delivery system and make unpredictable contributions to the service. Thus, it would be difficult to give a 100 per cent guarantee that customers will have the 'holiday of a lifetime' when they book with a certain tour operator, when so many of the elements that could ruin the experience could be to do with the personality of the individual, rather than the arrangements made by the firm.

However, guarantees can be given for many of the more tangible components of the service and are often used not only to reassure customers about the quality of the service they are likely to receive, but also to differentiate the service provided by one operator from another. A double-glazing company, for example, might guarantee to customers that all windows provided will be made from the best available materials and will be installed in less than a week from the time the order is placed. Clearly, these are both elements of the service that can be carefully controlled by the company.

Conditions for effective guarantees

Hart[37] states that the chances of gaining a powerful impact from a service guarantee will be highest when one or more of the following conditions exist:

- *The price of the service is high or perceived to be high by customers*. For example, when customers are paying to have all their house windows double glazed.

- *The customer's personal reputation could be affected if the service goes wrong*. For example, when a customer pays to have make-up put on only to have someone tell her/him that it looks terrible.

- *The customer does not really understand whether the service has been carried out properly or not*. That is, they do not have the relevant expertise to make a judgement. For example, many customers who go to the car mechanic do not know whether he has done a good job.

- *The negative consequences of service failure are high*. This relates to personal reputation, but might occur, for example, if a customer has ordered some documents to be photocopied for an important meeting and on the morning of the event turns up to collect them and the job has not been completed.

- *The success of the company depends on frequent customer repurchases*. As Hart notes, 'The smaller the size of the potential market of new triers, the more attention management should pay to increasing the loyalty and repurchase of existing customers – objectives that a good service guarantee will serve.'

- *The company's business is affected deeply by word of mouth.* Almost all the cases in this book share this characteristic. The majority of new business is generated from referrals from the existing group of satisfied customers. Where customer satisfaction can be increased by the provision of service guarantees, this will clearly have a knock-on effect on new customers.

Qualities of the ideal guarantee

Heskett, Sasser and Hart[38] have also identified a number of qualities which characterise the ideal guarantee.

- Guarantees should be easy to understand and communicate.

A simple and concise message is important so that customers and service employees know exactly what is being provided. Some hospitals, for example, guarantee that everyone waiting to see a doctor will be seen within 30 minutes of their original appointment time. If they have not been seen by that time, patients are requested to see the receptionist. This information is displayed prominently in the patients' waiting room.

- Guarantees should be focused on customer needs.

There is no point guaranteeing customers in a restaurant the fastest service in town if they have come to you in the hope of enjoying a relaxing meal with friends whom they have not seen for some time.

- Guarantees should be meaningful with real penalties or payouts.

For example, an 18-month guarantee on all repairs and replacement parts needed to mend a television set is clearly meaningful to a customer as it could substantially reduce the risk associated with buying a new set. It might be the factor that causes them to buy rather than rent the set. It becomes less meaningful however, if a clause in the guarantee states that the customer has to pay extra if the television screen is broken during that period.

- Guarantees should be easy to invoke.

Many guarantees are rendered ineffective because customers have to go to so much trouble finally to receive the payout promised. Customers in retail clothing outlets who are told, before purchase, that they can have their money back on merchandise if it doesn't fit often have trouble getting retailers to comply with such a guarantee. The customer can expect to queue up in several different parts of the store and be asked to explain the reason for the returned merchandise to several different company employees before finally getting any money back. Not only does this prevent customers from trying to get their money back (and suffering their dissatisfaction in silence), but such obstacles can deter many from shopping there in the first place.

● Service guarantees should be unconditional.

Any conditional clauses can considerably reduce the potential impact of the guarantee. In the example above, stores frequently state that customers can have their money back on merchandise provided that the goods have been bought in the last month, or the customer provides the receipt of purchase and/or the material the goods were originally wrapped in. A lengthy list of conditions can ruin the impact of the guarantee.

SUMMARY

The interest in relationship marketing, especially in relation to service businesses, has been on the increase throughout the 1990s and the early part of the twenty-first century. There are many definitions of relationship marketing, but also a consensus on the two strands – market-based RM and network-based RM. The initial enthusiasm for relationship marketing has been tempered by the recognition that there are both positive and negative consequences for customers and organisations. Strategies for maintaining customer loyalty include effective service recovery systems and the use of service guarantees.

LEARNING OUTCOMES

Having read this chapter, you should be able to

● define relationship marketing from academic and organisational perspectives

● outline and evaluate the features of a relationship marketing approach

● understand the focus of market-based relationship marketing, and appreciate its potential advantages and disadvantages for both customers and the service organisation

● summarise the internal and external relationships that make up network-based relationship marketing, and apply these ideas to specific service companies

● discuss and evaluate the customer loyalty strategies associated with service recovery and service guarantees.

DISCUSSION QUESTIONS AND EXERCISES

1. Are the definitions of relationship marketing by academics and practitioner markedly different?

2. What is the difference between Market-based RM and Network-based RM?

3. Outline the main strategies that service companies can employ in order to maintain customer loyalty.

4. What do you understand by the terms 'distributive justice', 'procedural justice' and 'interactional justice'?

5. With which service organisations do you feel that you have a relationship? Why is it the case?

Notes and references

1. Zineldin, M., 'Beyond Relationship Marketing: Technologicalship Marketing', *Marketing Intelligence and Planning*, vol. 18, no. 2, 2000, pp. 9–23.

2. Fornell, C. and Wenerfelt, B., 'Defensive Marketing Strategy by Consumer complaint management: A theoretical analysis', *Journal of Marketing Research* 1987, vol. 24, pp. 337–46.

3. Sheth, J. N. and Kellstadt, C. H., 'Relationship Marketing: An Emerging School of Marketing Thought', Paper presented at the American Marketing Association, 13th Faculty Consortium in Services Marketing, Arizona, USA, 1993.

4. Gronroos, C., 'From Marketing Mix to Relationship Marketing: Towards a Paradigm Shift in Marketing', *Management Decision*, vol. 32, no. 2, pp. 4–20.

5. Ibid.

6. Christopher, M., Payne, A. and Ballantyne, D., *Relationship Marketing: Bringing Quality, Customer Service and Marketing Together*, Butterworth Heinemann, Oxford, 1991.

7. Ibid.

8. Reichheld, F. F. and Sasser Jr, W. E., 'Zero Defections: Quality Comes to Services', *Harvard Business Review*, September-October 1990, pp. 105–11.

9. Reichheld, F. F., 'Loyalty-Based Management', *Harvard Business Review*, March-April 1993, pp. 64–73.

10. Christopher, Payne and Ballantyne, *Relationship Marketing*.

11. Ibid.

12. Crosby, L. A. and Stephens, N., 'Effects of Relationship Marketing on Satisfactory Retention and Prices in the Life Insurance Industry', *Journal of Marketing Research*, vol. 24, November 1987, pp. 404–11.

13. Morgan, R. M. and Hunt, S. D., 'The Commitment–Trust Theory of Relationship Marketing', *Journal of Marketing*, vol. 58, pp. 20–38.

14. Beaton, M. and Beaton, C., 'Marrying Service Providers and Their Clients: A Relationship Approach to Service Management', *Journal of Marketing Management*, vol. 11, pp. 55–70.

15. Crosby and Stephens, 'Effects of Relationship Marketing'.

16. Brodie, J., Coviello, N., Brookes, R. and Little, V., 'Towards a paradigm shift in marketing? An examination of current marketing practices', *Journal of Marketing Management* 1997, vol. 13, pp. 383–406.

17. Pressey, A. D. and Mathews, B. P., 'Barriers to Relationship Marketing in Consumer Retailing', *Journal of Services Marketing*, vol. 14, no. 3, 2000, pp. 272–85.

18. Special issue of *Financial Times* on 'Understanding CRM', Spring 2000, www.ft.com/crm

19. Moller, K. and Halinen, A., 'Consumer versus Interorganisational Relationship Marketing: A Metatheoretical Analysis', in J. Sheth and A. Menon (eds), *New Frontiers in Relationship Marketing Theory and Practice*, Emory University, Atlanta, Ga, 1998.

20. Follain, J., 'Swiss Women Book into Man-Free Hotel', *Sunday Times*, London, 18 February 2001.

21. Reichheld and Sasser Jr, 'Zero Defections'.

22. Special issue of *Financial Times* on 'Understanding CRM', Spring 2000, p. 8, www.ft.com/crm

23. Taylor, H. K., 'Call the Doctor', *Sunday Times Magazine*, London, 3 December, 2000.

24. O'Malley, L. and Tynan, C., 'Relationship Marketing in Consumer Markets – Rhetoric or Reality?', *European Journal of Marketing*, vol. 34, no. 7, 2000, pp. 797–815.

25. Reichheld and Sasser Jr, 'Zero Defections'.

26. Christopher, Payne and Ballantyne, *Relationship Marketing*.

27. Schlesinger, L. A. and Heskett, J. L., 'The Service Driven Service Company', *Harvard Business Review*, September-October 1991, pp. 71–81.

28. Zemke, R. and Bell, C. R., *Service Wisdom: Creating and Maintaining the Customer Service Edge*, Lakewood Books, Minneapolis, 1989.

29. Bitner, M. J., Booms, B. H. and Tetreault, M. S., 'The Service Encounter: Diagnosing Favourable and Unfavourable Incidents', *Journal of Marketing*, vol. 54, 1990, pp. 71–84.

30. Johnston, R., 'Service Recovery: An Empirical Study', Proceedings of the 3rd International Research Seminar in Service Management, La-Londe-les-Maures, France, May 1994.

31. Hoffman, K. D. and Kelley, S. W., 'Perceived Justice Needs and Recovery Evaluation: A Contingency Approach', *European Journal of Marketing*, vol. 34, no. 3–4, 2000, pp. 418–32.

32. Tax, S. S., Brown, S. W. and Chandrashekaran, M., 'Customer Evaluations of Service Complaint Experiences: Implications for Relationship Marketing', *Journal of Marketing*, vol. 62, April 1998, pp. 60–76.

33. Johnston, 'Service Recovery'.

34. Sarel, D. and Marmorstein, H., 'Managing the Delayed Service Encounter: The Role of Employee Action and Customer Prior Experience', *Journal of Services Marketing*, vol. 12, no. 3, 1998, pp. 195–208.

35. Slack, N., Chambers, S., Howland, C., Harrison, A. and Johnston, R. *'Operations Management'*, Financial Times Pitman Publishing, London UK (2nd edn) 1998.

36. Sarel and Marmorstein, 'Managing the Delayed Service Encounter'.

37. Hart, C. W. L., 'The Power of Unconditional Service Guarantees', Harvard *Business Review*, July-August 1988, pp. 54-62.

38. Heskett, J. L., Sasser Jr, W. E. and Hart, C. W. L., *Service Breakthroughs – Changing the Rules of the Game*, The Free Press, New York, 1989.

chapter 10

Service profitability

LEARNING OBJECTIVES

Overall aim of the chapter:
To summarise academic and practitioner research on the drivers of service profitability.
   In particular, the *chapter objectives* are

- to highlight the relationships between service profitability and services marketing variables – quality, satisfaction, loyalty, productivity

- to explore macro-level links between service quality and service profitability

- to explore the trade-offs between productivity and quality in relation to service profitability

- to comprehend the models linking customer (and employee) loyalty to profitability

- to appreciate the statistical approaches to service profitability measurement and their applications to customer satisfaction indices.

Introduction

In an International Research Seminar in Service Management in the mid-1990s,[1] discussion at the final session focused on the relative lack of work on profitability of services. It was pointed out that only six of the 37 papers presented at the seminar made any reference at all to profitability and that the seminar was, in this respect, representative of research activity in Services Marketing and Management at the time. However, it was also recognised that the subject of profitability of services was becoming increasingly important, in the light of reports of companies, described by some commentators as 'excellent', experiencing severe financial difficulties.

Managers of service and other organisations were beginning to ask more questions, and seek further understanding, of the relationships between profitability and variables such as service quality, customer satisfaction, customer loyalty and productivity. Questions were being asked such as:

- Are there economic benefits to improving customer satisfaction?[2]
- What is the impact of quality on the bottom line?[3]
- What impact do customer defections have on the bottom line?[4]
- Do productivity improvements cause profits?[5]

In this chapter we will examine, in broad terms, the findings of the groups of researchers and practitioners who have brought service profitability to the fore. The chapter is in four sections. We start with a look at the work that has taken a macro-level view on the links between quality and business results. This will be followed by a description and discussion of the Q, P and P (Quality, Productivity and Profitability) programme being undertaken by Gummesson and colleagues in Sweden.[6,7] We then further examine the work on the relationship between customer loyalty, employee loyalty and profitability, and the related 'Service–Profit Chain', and review some of the recent work that tests the propositions regarding the links of the chain. Finally, the results and applications of some of the quantitative studies that explore the relationship between profitability and customer satisfaction, at the company and national level, are presented.

Macro-level links between quality and business results

Results from the PIMS database

The PIMS database contains measures of quality, profitability and shareholder values over several years for a large number of organisations in many different US industries and markets. The information is held at the level of the business unit for over 2500 business units.[8] Through careful interrogation of the PIMS database it is possible to examine the relationship between measures of quality and those of profitability (or other financial indicators) over a number of years. This, in turn, makes it possible to derive some quantitative indicators of the effect of quality on various financial performance measures.

The early PIMS findings on the relationship between quality and profitability were used to justify a financial investment in, and concentration on, quality improvement methods for service organisations. For example, Zeithaml *et al.*[9] reproduce a graph originally constructed by Buzzell and Gale[10] which showed a positive relationship between relative perceived quality and return on investment. More recent PIMS findings were graphically presented by Gale.[11] In summary, they are:

1. *Superior quality leads to higher selling prices.* In particular, 'businesses that have achieved a superior quality position earn prices eight per cent higher than businesses that have been shoved into an inferior quality position'.

2. *Achieving superior quality does not mean higher cost.* In particular, 'businesses with superior quality positions have relative direct costs that are slightly lower than businesses with inferior perceived quality'.

3. *Superior quality drives profitability.* This is a logical result of 1 and 2 but, in particular, 'businesses with superior quality are three times as profitable as those with inferior quality'.

Gale goes on to examine the relationships between quality and other financial measures such as cash flow, shareholder value and market value of businesses. The interested reader is urged to consult the original article.

The results are convincing and intuitively appealing. However, caution needs to be exercised regarding interpretation and applicability because:

● The measurement of quality is extremely difficult.

The PIMS database uses one particular measure, the market perceived quality ratio that relies on identifying appropriate quality attributes for a business and assigning relative weights to these attributes. This is in addition to obtaining reliable customer ratings of these attributes for a business unit, and its competitors. The market-perceived quality ratio is highly sensitive to the weights assigned to the attributes and the sample of customers surveyed. Once the market-perceived quality ratio has been computed, business units are assigned to one of five categories:

1. inferior quality
2. somewhat worse quality
3. about the same quality
4. somewhat better quality
5. superior quality

for the purpose of further analysis.

● The relationship between quality measures and financial indicators is not necessarily similar for all industries and sectors.

Indeed, Gummesson[12] concludes that there is no general cost–quality relationship, only specific relationships.

- Some of the earlier quality measures in the PIMS database were based on the firm's assessment of what they believe to be their customers' perception of quality, and not on the customers' actual ratings.

- The relationships do not explicitly explore the processes by which quality impacts on profitability.

- The companies in the PIMS database are large organisations and the findings may not apply to the numerous small businesses in the service sector.

Despite these reservations, the PIMS database, and the analysis of the data, will continue to provide useful insights into the relationship between profitability and quality.

Awards for companies investing in quality

A number of national and international government bodies make awards on an annual basis to companies that invest in quality. Many companies enter the competitions for these awards, which are perceived as prestigious, and winning an award is regarded as very important.

One of the pioneering awards was the Malcolm Baldrige National Quality Award (MBNQA), created by the National Institute of Standards and Technology in the USA in 1987. The MBNQA was set up to encourage leadership by the United States in product and process quality, something that was being challenged at the time by foreign (mainly Japanese) competition. There was a belief that poor quality was costing companies as much as 20 per cent of sales revenue.[13] The national quality award was intended to help improve quality and productivity of American companies by:

1. 'helping to stimulate American companies to improve quality and productivity for the pride of recognition while obtaining a competitive edge through increased profits;

2. recognising the achievements of those companies that improve the quality of their goods and services and providing an example to others;

3. establishing guidelines and criteria that can be used by business, industrial, governmental, and other organisations in evaluating their own quality improvement efforts;

4. providing specific guidance for other American organisations that wish to learn how to manage for high quality by making available detailed information on how winning organisations were able to challenge their cultures and achieve eminence'.[14]

This was an award for quality of both goods and services. There is a link between investment in quality and company profitability (in 1 above), but it is not presented as starkly as in the PIMS literature where superior quality is said to drive profitability.

The examiners for the MBNQA rate the applicants according to seven criteria: leadership, strategic planning, customer and market focus, information and analysis, human resource focus, process management and business results. Los Alamos National Bank, an independent community bank with 167 employees, won the MBNQA for small businesses in 2000. Its quality and business achievements included high percentages of customers who were very satisfied with the service they received, and a high level of customer loyalty (with a third of the customers having five or more banking relationships), very high employee satisfaction results and correspondingly low employee turnover, high productivity levels, and a commitment to the community.[15] Most of the criteria have been addressed in earlier chapters. It is interesting that the criterion of social responsibility (and its association with successful service businesses) is now being recognised explicitly.[16]

In Europe, the European Foundation for Quality Management has been responsible for the European Quality Award (EQA) since 1992.[17] The criteria, based on a business excellence model, are very similar to those used for the MBNQA. Applicants are scored on leadership (10 per cent), people management (9 per cent), policy and strategy (8 per cent), resources (9 per cent), processes (14 per cent), people satisfaction (9 per cent), customer satisfaction (20 per cent), impact on society (6 per cent) and business results (15 per cent). Foxdenton School and Integrated Nursery from Oldham UK, who won a prize in the public sector category in 2000, is a school that caters primarily for children with special educational needs. They attribute their winning formula to 'high expectations to raise achievements in pupils, learning from the people we serve, a premium on staff development, upbeat communications, involvement of all our stakeholders, promoting partnerships, and an emphasis on structuring success and building self esteem for all members of the community' – a mix of 'customer' focus, internal marketing, network relationship marketing and social responsibility.[18] Having a category for the public sector acknowledges that the business excellence model criteria can be applicable to not-for-profit organisations.

But are the private companies that meet the awards criteria those that are more profitable?

There were some doubts, initially, when one of the early MBNQA winners had to file for bankruptcy. However, there have been some recent studies which have compared stock performances of MBNQA award winners with those of the Standard and Poor's (S&P) 500 companies. The returns on the MBNQA stocks consistently out-performed the S&P 500 index, both before and after the award, and more so after the award.[19] Moreover, some of the criteria for the awards, information management, HRM and customer focus, have been found to have a significant effect on customer satisfaction and business results.[20]

Quality, productivity and profitability programme

The Q, P and P programme, that examines the interactions between quality, productivity and profitability in service operations, has been advocated by Gummesson and colleagues in Sweden. The programme, which was set up in 1993, regards quality, productivity and profitability as 'triplets' with the implication that 'separating one from the others creates an unhappy family'.[21] Unimpressed by current measures of productivity in particular, the group have sought, through actual company case studies, to better understand the interactions between quality, productivity and profitability before attempting to quantify what is not yet fully understood.

A simple framework (Figure 10.1) shows the basic relationship, in financial terms, between the triplets:

1. A concentration, by a service company, on productivity means that the company will look towards an effective use of resources and towards producing more for less.

2. A concentration, by the company, on service quality means that it will look towards satisfying customers and, through customer retention and loyalty, increasing revenue.

3. A concentration on profitability means that the company will address the combined effect of cost reduction and revenue generation. This should involve an active interest in both productivity and quality.

According to the framework, all three elements of the triplets are pulling in the same direction. In practice, even within a single service organisation, the interactions between the elements may be affected by a tribal culture,[22] where the different tribes – the productivity tribe, the quality tribe, and the profitability tribe – have different mindsets and do not necessarily understand one another or work together to a common aim. Expanding on Gummesson's arguments it is suggested that

● The productivity tribe are concerned primarily with issues of definition of productivity and the various mathematical formulae to 'measure'

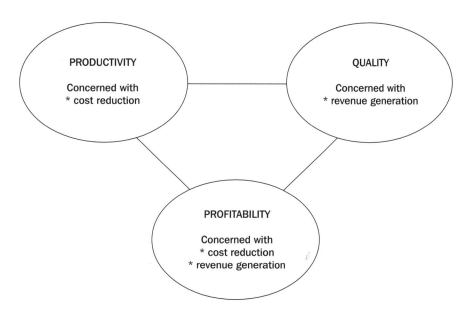

Figure 10.1 Interaction between productivity, quality and profitability

productivity. Their concern is with, for example, the number of patients seen per hour in the surgery, or the average service time per supermarket customer.

● The quality tribe are concerned primarily with customer expectations, perceptions and levels of satisfaction. Their concern is with the quality of the service encounter and with arguments regarding customisation versus standardisation of service.

● The profitability tribe, normally educated in accounting practice, are concerned primarily with the balance sheet and profit and loss statements, and on relatively short-term financial results.

Perhaps these tribal differences are less obvious in the operation of a small service business. In the case study of the dental practice (Case Study 10), for example, the father and son agreed on a course of action which reflected a quality, rather than productivity, approach. They have tried to ensure, for many of their patients, that time is made available for talk and explanation and a more relaxing appointment, rather than attempt to increase the number of patients per hour. Their concern for productivity is in the service support area, particularly through the use of computer systems.

However, in many larger organisations, the tribes exist and can be identified. The whole issue is further complicated by the fact that many organisations do not conform to the traditional hierarchical structure with clearly defined boundaries. Networks of communications and relationships make organisational boundaries more fluid and add to the problem of understanding the interactions between quality, productivity and profitability.

In effect, research on the Q, P and P programme has caused the group to question their original findings that gave qualified support to the notions that

1. productivity improvements lead to increased profits;
2. quality improvements lead to increased productivity;
3. quality improvements lead to increased profits.

The early conclusions were based on what the group now acknowledge as 'deceptively clear' definitions of the three triplets. They argue strongly that a premature move to quantifying relationships between the triplets will fail to address the many tribal and interpersonal contributions to an organisation's operation. This may result in measuring the wrong things, or only looking at variables that are of relevance or importance to members of a particular tribe.

If many companies are regarded as networks, then quality issues are said to affect all members of a network and not just the provider and customer. Relationships in the networks take on an even greater prominence that is not reflected in the assets of a company, nor in company performance. The Q, P and P group observes that the accounting tribe do not measure the profitability of *relationships*. The group therefore raises the notion of a *return on relationships*, based on a recognition of the *intellectual* capital of an organisation, as a way of assessing financial outcomes. It poses the question 'How should we measure the return on relationships and how should we evaluate the contributions to profits from the various actors in a network?'[23]

Loyalty and profitability

During the 1990s a series of articles in the *Harvard Business Review* drew attention to the issues of customer, and employee, loyalty, and their likely effects on a firm's profits. Many of the conclusions are derived from studies of businesses operating primarily within the service sector of the US economy. These same businesses have provided the examples of sales and profit figures per customer which are used in the articles.

Customer defections

In late 1990, Reichheld and Sasser[24] provided results of studies of customer defections over a range of service companies: including auto-services, credit cards, banking, insurance, industrial distribution, office building, and software. They concluded that customer defections 'have a surprisingly powerful impact on the bottom line'. The results demonstrated

● how much profit a (loyal) customer generates over time.

For example, a new credit-card customer represents a loss to the credit card company of $51 in the first year, but the typical loyal customer generates a profit of $55 during the fifth year. The profit per customer of an auto-servicing business increases from $25 in year one to $88 in the fifth year.

● that a reduction in customer defections of five per cent can boost profits by 25 per cent to 85 per cent.

Based on net present value calculations of average customers, a five per cent reduction in customer defections would, for example, increase profits in the credit card company by 75 per cent and those in the auto-servicing company by 30 per cent.

Some of the reasons given as to why customers can become more profitable over time are:

● a reduction in operating costs per customer.

First-time customers incur a number of one-off costs; for example, checking credit-rating, adding to database. As a service organisation gets to know its customers, service can be dealt with more efficiently. This is illustrated well in the Waymark Holiday case (Case Study 5), where telephone discussions with repeat customers can more easily deal with customer requirements, without first having to establish customer walking or skiing capabilities.

● a 'trading-up' of customers over time.

Customers may wish to 'trade-up' or be willing to pay a price premium for a service they know or trust. A good experience with a financial advisor, for example, may result in customers looking to increase the investment through a person or company that they trust, or a decision to purchase more financial products.

● the free advertising they provide.

Positive word of mouth can result in much further business for a service organisation. It is a major factor for all the small businesses in our case studies.

An implication of these findings is that companies should go all out for customer loyalty and devise a defections management policy within a relationship marketing framework (see Chapter 9).

Employee loyalty

Schlesinger and Heskett[25] support the attention given to the economics of customer loyalty, but in addition present a critical look at the economics of employee loyalty and turnover in service organisations. To attempt to put some figures on employee costs, turnover, revenues and profits, they quoted results from company studies. Examples are:

● The US retailer Sears found, from a regular customer survey carried out in 1989, that employee turnover and customer satisfaction were negatively correlated. Stores with high customer service scores experienced lower annual employee turnover rates.

● Findings at two divisions of the Marriott Corporation suggest that a 10 per cent reduction in employee turnover would raise revenues by $50 million to $150 million (by reducing customer defections).

● At Merck & Co. it was estimated that the transactional, disruption and administrative costs associated with placing staff on and off the payroll raised the total costs of employee turnover to 1.5 times an employee's salary.

While such examples may indicate the direction of further studies, Schlesinger and Heskett concluded that 'the economics of employee loyalty are still largely unexplored'. They warn against what they call the 'cycle-of-failure', where companies, for short-term cost reductions, may increase employee turnover. This in turn can result in fewer, less knowledgeable contact personnel, and customers becoming dissatisfied and expressing their negative feelings. The resulting demotivating effect on staff may lead to further employee turnover, and the cycle continues.

Loyalty-based system chain

Reichheld, in a follow-up article in the spring of 1993[26], sets out a logical framework which encapsulates the concepts of customer and employee loyalty and links them to a service company's competitive position. The chain is triggered by a will to pay employees well. It is summarised in Figure 10.2.

Figure 10.2 Loyalty-based system chain

The chain has an intuitive appeal, but it must be stressed that the causality links required further testing and verification over a range of firms and industries and were regarded as hypotheses at that stage of research. Reichheld himself doubted that many executives would agree to a 25 per cent pay increase to employees in order to reduce employee turnover by five per cent and increase customer retention, even though the resultant reduction in customer defections to the competition can increase profits considerably.

The service–profit chain

The postulated relationship between loyalty (both customer and employee) and profitability was visualised with reference to the 'service–profit chain', constructed by Heskett and his colleagues in 1994.[27] The service–profit chain showed the proposed relationships between profitability, customer loyalty, and employee satisfaction, loyalty and productivity. It is reproduced here as Figure 10.3.

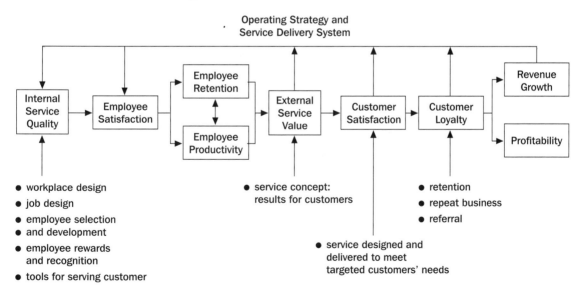

Source: Heskett, J. L., Jones, T. O., Loveman, G. W., Sasser Jr, W. E. and Schlesinger, L. A., 'Putting the Service–Profit Chain to Work', *Harvard Business Review*, March–April 1994.

Figure 10.3 The links in the service–profit chain

Figure 10.3 is an expanded version of Figure 10.2, with profitability and revenue growth explicitly included. As with the loyalty-based chain, the links in the service–profit chain should, as the authors themselves emphasise, be regarded as propositions. They provide evidence to support each proposition and further suggest how a service company can conduct a service-audit on the elements in the chain.

The service–profit chain provided, probably for the first time, an intuitively feasible and simply visible set of links between the internal marketing and management of an organisation, the external focus on the customer and business performance. As such it has been embraced by some companies as part of their philosophy. A C Nielsen, a global market research company, states on its Australian website that 'We live and breathe the service–profit chain, understanding our customers are fundamental to our success – satisfied employees make satisfied clients, make happy shareholders'.[28] Maritz Limited, a marketing service company, claim, on their UK website, to 'optimise our client's route to market, from production to consumption. We use the "service–profit chain" to define and measure each link of the chain.'[29]

Testing the propositions in the service–profit chain

Subsequent published research that has investigated the propositions within the service–profit chain has resulted in some contradictory findings, and has highlighted potential differences in the relationships between employee and customer satisfaction within different service offers. The service–profit chain may, for example, be more applicable to professional and management services, or business-to-business services, than to consumer services, such as retailing. For example, a study of the service–profit chain links in grocery retailing[30] found that

● there were no significant correlations between service value and either employee satisfaction, employee loyalty or internal capability

● there was no relationship between employee satisfaction and customer satisfaction, and furthermore, employee satisfaction was *negatively* correlated with the store's profit margin.

While other factors, such as variation in store size, may explain some of the correlations, there was no obvious explanation as to why employee satisfaction and loyalty did not mirror customer satisfaction and loyalty.

Employee loyalty may relate to either employee commitment or employee tenure.[31] Loveman, in an empirical study of the service–profit chain in the context of a US regional bank, found that

● there were significant positive relationships between employee satisfaction and stated employee commitment, but not with tenure, whereas

● customer satisfaction was positively correlated with employee tenure, but not with stated employee commitment.

In a study entitled 'From People to Profits', carried out by the Institute of Employment Studies in the UK[32], employee commitment to a company was linked to company profitability via three routes:

1. *Directly*. The study estimated that a one-point increase in employee commitment could lead to a monthly increase of up to £200 000 in sales per service outlet.

2. *Via customer satisfaction with the service*. This is the link shown in Figure 10.3, and assumes that customer satisfaction mirrors employee satisfaction.

3. *Through a reduction in staff absence*. This relates to the costs of unwanted staff turnover.

Unsurprisingly, the study concludes that companies should invest in employees and look beyond simple measures of employee satisfaction to measures which increase employee commitment.

Overall, the service–profit chain has certainly succeeded in one of its aims; that is, to provide 'a tool for managers and students of management to use in thinking about how to improve performance of service organisations'.[33] Empirical support for the links of the chain is mixed. For those of you who wish to explore this area in more detail, reviews of the range of empirical findings are summarised by Lau[34] and Payne, Holt and Frow.[35]

Statistical estimations of the relationships between profitability, customer satisfaction and quality

When companies are employing resources with a view to improving service quality or increasing customer satisfaction, the management often feel happier when they have some concrete figures showing the financial justification for such strategies. The same can be said for national or international groups that advocate the goals of customer satisfaction and/or service quality. The figures may be forthcoming if mathematical equations could be constructed which relate profitability to customer satisfaction, quality and other variables. Given that there are many problems with the measurement of quality and satisfaction, and that there are limited databases of company information, the production of equations using statistical estimation techniques presents a great challenge.

On a national and international level, we have seen the development of customer satisfaction indices to measure the economic benefits of customer satisfaction. At the level of the firm, there have been attempts to measure Return on Quality (ROQ) as a means of monitoring the financial accountability of service quality.[36]

Customer satisfaction indices

The first attempt to derive a national index of customer satisfaction was the Swedish Customer Satisfaction Barometer (SCSB).[37] The SCSB provides yearly updates on customer-based measures of performance of Swedish firms in a variety of industries. The measures are of variables such as quality, expectations and customer satisfaction for each firm, and are based on annual customer surveys. The extensive customer generated data and the method of weighting attributes distinguishes SCSB from PIMS. For each firm, standard financial performance data such as market share and return on investment are also readily available. In the spirit of PIMS, quality and satisfaction measures can be linked to financial performance measures.

In addition to estimating correlations between the variables, however, Anderson et al.[38] set out to provide a mathematical model (through a set of equations) which contributes to a greater understanding of the relationships between profitability, satisfaction, quality and expectations. Because of the more detailed availability of customer-based measures of the variables within the SCSB, statistical techniques were employed to estimate the coefficients of the equations.

Using Return on Investment (ROI) as the financial performance measure, their model can be represented by the set of equations below (Anderson et al., p. 60).

$$\text{EXP}_t = a_1 + b_{11} \text{EXP}_{t-1} + b_{12} \text{QUAL}_{t-1} + b_{13} \text{TREND} + e_{1t} \tag{1}$$
$$\text{SAT}_t = a_2 + b_{21} \text{SAT}_{t-1} + b_{22} \text{QUAL}_t + b_{23} \text{EXP}_t + b_{24} \text{TREND} + e_{2t} \tag{2}$$
$$\text{ROI}_t = a_3 + b_{31} \text{ROI}_{t-1} + b_{32} \text{SAT}_t + b_{33} \text{TREND} + e_{3t} \tag{3}$$

where

EXP_t = Expectation at time period t.
QUAL_t = Customer perceived quality at time period t.
SAT_t = Customer satisfaction at time period t.
ROI_t = Return on Investment at time period t.
TREND = Net effect of other variables which change over time

Values a_1, a_2, a_3, a_{11}, b_{12}, b_{13}, b_{21}, b_{22}, b_{23}, b_{24}, b_{31}, b_{32}, b_{33} are coefficients to be estimated, e_{1t}, e_{2t}, e_{3t} are the disturbance times.

In effect, equation (3) postulates that a firm's ROI at any period is a function of return on investment at the previous period, current customer satisfaction, and the trend. Equation (2) postulates that customer satisfaction with a firm at any period is, in turn, a function of satisfaction at the previous period, current customer perceived quality, current customer expectations, and the trend. From equation (1) it is postulated that customer expectations of a firm at any period are, in turn, a function of expectations at the previous period, perceived quality at the previous period, and the trend.

Extensive justifications are given by Anderson et al.[39] for the structures of the equations. The statistical techniques for estimating the a and b coefficients are also described. To obtain a flavour of the implications of the analysis, let us look at equations (2) and (3) once the estimates of the coefficients have been inserted. They are:

$$\text{SAT}_t = -.12 + .44 \text{SAT}_{t-1} + .49 \text{QUAL}_t + .10 \text{EXP}_t - .003 \text{TREND} \tag{2}$$
$$\text{ROI}_t = -1.10 + .75 \text{ROI}_{t-1} + .40 \text{SAT}_t + .002 \text{TREND} \tag{3}$$

From (2), a 1-point increase in quality results in, all other things being equal, a .49 increase in satisfaction (from the estimate of b_{22}). From (3), a 1-point increase in satisfaction results in a .40 increase in ROI (from the estimate of b_{32}). Taken together, the two effects suggest that a 1-point increase in quality results in a $0.49 \times 0.40 = .196$ increase in ROI. This result is consistent with earlier PIMS findings.

The equations can be used in a number of other ways, including a calculation of returns on investment due to a one point increase in satisfaction each year.[40] It should be stressed, however, that, as with any statistical analysis, the structures and strengths of the relationships will inevitably be subjected to further studies, and interpretations may be modified as the result of the further empirical work.

The methodologies for computing the elements of the SCSB were employed to start the American Customer Satisfaction Index (ACSI)[41] in 1994 and the European Customer Satisfaction Index (ECSI)[42] in 1997 (see Figure 10.4).

In turn, as more annual data becomes available on the indices, there will be further research to demonstrate the strength of the relationship between customer satisfaction and financial performance.[43]

Return on quality

The work on 'return on quality' is also concerned with statistical relationships between satisfaction, quality and profitability. However, the focus is different. A return on quality (ROQ) system is being developed to provide decision support to *managers of a particular business*. The aim is for managers to use the ROQ system in order to

● quantify the financial impact of quality

● identify opportunities for quality improvement

● estimate optimal expenditure levels

● reveal opportunities for spending reductions

● conduct 'what if' analyses of potential decision alternatives.[44]

The ROQ system acknowledges that while quality is an investment, it is possible to spend too much on quality (the case of a company that, in order to win an award, spent so much on quality improvements that it went bankrupt is quoted as evidence to support this view). The ROQ system is

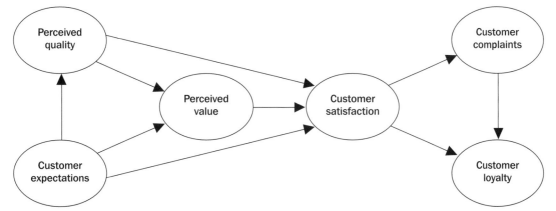

Source: Adapted from ACSI Methodology, University of Michigan Business School.

Figure 10.4 Methodology behind the computation of the SCSB, ACSI and ECSI

Figure 10.5 Return on quality – chain of effects

based on the chain of effects shown in Figure 10.5. This is similar to sections of the service–profit chain shown in Figure 10.3. It must be remembered, however, that for the ROQ decision support system, all the elements of the chain refer to a single company.

Through the use of customer survey data, internal company information and competitor financial data, sets of equations have been derived to represent each link in the chain for two test company cases. Profits can, through a series of equations, be linked to customer satisfaction or quality improvement costs.

One of the key features of the system is that it is not just an overall customer satisfaction measure which is extracted from customer surveys, but also satisfaction measures on various service processes. In one of the test companies for the system, a hotel group, it was possible to measure the impact on profits of several processes – for instance, room service, restaurant, staff, bathroom – and to further identify the impact of various features of each process. It was found that it was bathrooms, and in particular cleanliness of bathrooms, which had the most impact on profits. Further use of the system could establish whether to spend more on ensuring bathroom cleanliness, and if so how much more, and assess the potential effect of the decision on the bottom line. The same system may identify elements of the process where it is better to spend less, without adversely affecting profitability.

Clearly, decision support systems, such as ROQ, are attractive to managers. However, they are still in their infancy. Rust *et al.*[45] reckoned that 'thorough testing of the ROQ decision support system will require several years to complete'. However, the group do state that 'The ROQ approach enables managers to determine where to spend on service quality, how much to spend, and the likely financial impact from service expenditures, in terms of revenues, profits and return on investments in quality improvement ...'[46] This system, like the SCSB-based equations, relies on assumptions, one of which is that quality is an antecedent of satisfaction. Not all services marketers would agree, particularly if satisfaction is seen to be associated with single service encounters and perceived service quality is associated with a longer-term overall judgement (see Chapter 7).

SUMMARY

Although, as was indicated at the beginning of this section, the subject of service profitability has probably not received as much attention as other aspects of services marketing, there are clear signs that research groups and practitioners are increasing understanding, and striving towards appropriate measures of the relationships between satisfaction, quality and profitability.

We have looked very briefly at four approaches to service profitability. The first looks at the macro-level links between *quality* and business results. The PIMS database examines relationships between financial indicators (including profit) and quality measures over time, and bases conclusions on the temporal correlations. The national and international quality awards are based on scoring systems which link quality performance criteria to business results. In turn, the award-winning companies then provide a focus for comparisons in terms of quality. The second examines the relationships between the triplets of quality, productivity and profitability, and is using a mainly case-study-based approach to reach a greater understanding of the triplet relationships, and the value of network relationships. The third, in the form of a service–profit chain, focuses on the effects of loyalty (both customer and employee) on profitability and utilises customer retention and defection figures from a range of service industries. The fourth uses statistical techniques to provide series of equations which quantify the relationship between profitability and customer satisfaction at either the national/international or business level.

There are many aspects of all four approaches which have been omitted in this brief summary. The original sources can be found in the references for this chapter at the end of chapter.

A recurring theme has been a frustration with the inability of most accounting systems to measure such variables as costs of customer–employee turnover or profit margins generated by repeat custom. As Gummesson[47] bemoans, 'An essential conclusion is that service organisations cannot be correctly assessed by studying the traditional information in the balance sheet and the cost and revenue statements of the annual report.'

LEARNING OUTCOMES

Having read this chapter, you should be able to

● summarise the results and evaluate the implications arising from work associated with the PIMS database

● outline the criteria used in awarding companies that invest in quality

- appreciate the perspectives of the quality, productivity and profitability 'tribes', and the difficulties in recognising the contribution of relationships to profitability

- demonstrate knowledge of the propositions presented in the service–profit chain, and of the work undertaken to test the propositions

- appreciate the models and methodology behind the computations of national satisfaction indices, and company specific measures of return on quality.

DISCUSSION QUESTIONS AND EXERCISES

1. Does investment in quality lead to increased profits?

2. Is quality compatible with productivity?

3. Find examples and counter-examples to the propositions represented by the links in the service–profit chain.

4. Explain the methodology behind the computations of national customer satisfaction indices.

5. Why might the concept of 'Return on Quality' be attractive to managers?

Notes and references

1. 3rd International Research Seminar in Service Management, La-Londe-les-Maures, France, May 1994.
2. Ibid.
3. Anderson, E. W., Fornell, C. and Lehmann, D. R., 'Customer Satisfaction, Market Share and Profitability: Findings from Sweden', *Journal of Marketing*, vol. 58, July 1994, pp. 53–66.
4 Rust, R. T. and Varki, S., 'Making Service Quality Financially Accountable', Proceedings of 3rd International Research Seminar in Service Management, La-Londe-les-Maures, France, May 1994, pp. 645–58.
5. Reichheld, F. F. and Sasser Jr, W. E., 'Zero Defections: Quality Comes to Services', *Harvard Business Review*, September-October 1990, pp. 105–11.
6. Gummesson, E., 'Service Productivity: A Blasphemous Approach', Proceedings of 2nd International Research Seminar in Service Management, La-Londe-les-Maures, France, June 1992.
7. Gummesson, E., 'Productivity, Quality and Relationship Marketing in Service Operations', *International Journal of Contemporary Hospitality Management*, vol. 10, issue 1, 1998, pp. 4–15.
8. Gale, B. T., 'Customer Satisfaction – Relative to Competitors – Is Where It's At (strong evidence that superior quality drives the bottom line and shareholder value)', *Marketing and Research Today*, February 1994.

9. Zeithaml, V. A., Parasuraman, A. and Berry, L. L., *Delivering Quality Service: Balancing Customer Perceptions and Expectations*, The Free Press, New York, 1990.

10. Buzzell, R. and Gale, B. T., *The PIMS Principles: Linking Strategy to Performance*, The Free Press, New York, 1987.

11. Gale, 'Customer Satisfaction'.

12. Gummesson, 'Service Productivity'.

13. http://www.quality.nist.gov/law.htm

14. Ibid.

15. http://www.nist.gov/public-affairs/baldrige00/LosAlamos.htm

16. Baron, S., Harris, K. and Parker, C., 'Understanding the Consumer Experience: It's "Good to Talk" ', *Journal of Marketing Management*, vol. 16, issues 1–3, 2000, pp. 111–27.

17. http://www.efqm.org/award/PressRelease.htm

18. http://www.foxdenton.oldham.sch.uk

19. Soteriou, A. C. and Zenios, S. A., 'On the Impact of Quality on Performance: First Empirical Evidence from the Financial Industry', Proceedings of the Fifth Conference of the Association of Asian-Pacific Operations Research Societies, Singapore, July 2000.

20. Pannirselvam, G. P. and Ferguson, L. A., 'A Study of the Relationships Between the Baldrige Categories', *International Journal of Quality and Reliability Management*, vol. 18, no. 1, 2001, pp. 14–37.

21. Bylund, E. and Lepidoth Jr, J., 'Service Quality and Productivity: A Post-Industrial Approach', Proceedings of 3rd International Research Seminar in Service Management, La-Londe-les-Maures, France, May 1994.

22. Gummesson, 'Service Productivity'.

23. Gummesson, 'Productivity, Quality and Relationship Marketing'.

24. Reichheld and Sasser Jr, 'Zero Defections'.

25. Schlesinger, L. A. and Heskett, J. L., 'The Service-Driven Service Company', *Harvard Business Review*, September-October 1991, pp. 71–81.

26. Reichheld, F. F., 'Loyalty-Based Management', *Harvard Business Review*, March-April 1993, pp. 64–73.

27. Heskett, J. L., Jones, T. O., Loveman, G. W., Sasser Jr, W. E. and Schlesinger, L. A., 'Putting the Service–Profit Chain to Work', *Harvard Business Review*, March-April 1994, pp. 164–74.

28. http://www.acnielsen.com.au/jobs.asp

29. http://www.maritz.com/UK/OurApproach/OurApproach.htm

30. Silvestro, R. and Cross, S., 'Applying the Service–Profit Chain in a Retail Environment', *International Journal of Service Industry Management*, vol. 11, no. 3, 2000, pp. 244–68.

31. Loveman, G. W., 'Employee Satisfaction, Customer Loyalty and Financial Performance', *Journal of Service Research*, vol. 1, no. 1, 1998, pp. 18–31.

32. Barber, L., Hayday, S. and Bevan, S., ' From People to Profits', *IES Report* 355, 1999, ISBN I-85184-284-5.

33. Loveman, 'Employee Satisfaction'.

34. Lau, R. S. M., 'Quality of Work Life and Performance – An ad hoc Investigation of Two Key Elements in the Service–Profit Chain Model', *International Journal of Service Industry Management*, vol. 11, no. 5, 2000, pp. 422–37.

35. Payne, A., Holt, S. and Frow, P., 'Integrating Employee, Customer and Shareholder Value Through an Enterprise Performance Model: An Opportunity for Financial Services', *The International Journal of Bank Marketing*, vol. 18, no. 6, 2000, pp. 258–73.

36. Rust, R. T. and Oliver, R. L., *Service Quality: New Directions in Theory and Practice*, Sage, London, 1994.

37. Fornell, C., 'A National Customer Satisfaction Barometer: The Swedish Experience', *Journal of Marketing*, vol. 55, 1992, pp. 1–21.

38. Anderson, Fornell and Lehmann, 'Customer Satisfaction, Market Share and Profitability'.

39. Ibid.

40. Ibid.

41. See wysiwyg://2/http://www.bus.umich.edu/research/nqrc/acsi.html

42. http://www.eoq.org/ECSI.html

43. Yeung, M. C. H. and Ennew, C. T., 'From Customer Satisfaction to Profitability', *Journal of Strategic Marketing*, vol. 8, no. 4, 2000, pp. 313–26.

44. Rust and Oliver, *Service Quality*.

45. Ibid.

46. Rust, R. T., Zahorik, A. J. and Keiningham, T. L., 'Return on Quality (ROQ): Making Service Quality Financially Accountable', *Journal of Marketing*, vol. 59, April 1995, pp. 58–70.

47. Gummesson, E., 'Service Quality and Productivity in the Imaginary Organization', Proceedings of 3rd International Seminar in Service Management, La-Londe-les-Maures, France, May 1994.

Future research issues

LEARNING OBJECTIVES

Overall aim of chapter:
To outline some of the potentially fruitful areas of research for service marketers at the beginning of the twenty-first century.
  In particular, the *chapter objectives* are

- to present an overview of service marketing issues that are engaging academics and practitioners at the beginning of the twenty-first century

- to identify areas and issues within the services marketing discipline where further understanding is needed.

Introduction

Our principal aim when writing this book was to present you with a concise summary of the issues, models and theories currently recognised as representing the sub-discipline of services marketing. We have included a bank of special small business case studies to give the reader the opportunity to explore how these issues, models and theories can be applied to a realistic business situation. The topics selected for inclusion in the book broadly reflect the areas of study which have been engaging the attention of academics and practitioners from the beginning of the 1990s. However, we are conscious of the fact that in the previous ten chapters we have not been able to cover every topic in as much detail as we would have liked, and that certain of the more traditional marketing topics have not been covered explicitly at all. For example, chapters have not been devoted to discussion of some of the components of the services marketing mix, such as promoting, pricing and distributing services.

This final chapter is mainly for those of you who have been sufficiently encouraged and excited by the field of services marketing that you want to keep abreast with some of the key research issues of the twenty-first century. It is presented in two sections. The first section outlines the issues that are already engaging academics and practitioners. The second section represents the authors' views as to where and how research could be meaningfully employed to increase the understanding of important fundamentals of services marketing theory and practice.

Issues engaging academics and practitioners

We describe here three areas of services marketing research on which academics and practitioners are currently working together. They are:

- the total customer experience
- customer equity
- the emergence of service/solutions providers.

We then examine the case of the creation of the 'breakplace' convenience store format, by US petroleum retailer Conoco, that brings together the three areas.

The total customer experience

The first plenary session and discussion at the 10th Annual Frontiers in Services Conference in October 2001 was on 'the total customer experience' – a demonstration of its importance to practitioners. So what do we understand by this expression?

It is said that the total customer experience

includes every contact that a customer has with your organization, across all channels of communication, including the call center, Internet, sales and marketing.[1]

It is regarded as a strategic initiative to be supported by Customer Relationship Management (CRM):

CRM should be about managing (and improving) the customer's total experience with the organisation:

- *Across all touchpoints (call center, Web, kiosks, service technicians, etc.)*
- *Across all company divisions or departments*
- *Across all experiential elements (pre-sales activity, product/service experience, post sales support, etc.).[2]*

It is embedded within 'experience marketing' and has applications in business-to-business marketing as well as in consumer marketing (as seen in Chapter 5). One of the advocates of experience marketing is 'Experience Engineering', a company that

tries to integrate and manage all the experiences a customer or client might have with a business, from the person who answers the phone to the carpeting on the floor.[3]

The underpinning principle that is common to the statements above is that the experience of the customer/client/consumer with the organisation is made up of many separate incidents, and that the organisation must take a holistic view of the incidents through the eyes of the customer. The total customer experience perspective, therefore, draws on ideas from service encounters and the notion of multiple points of contact (Chapter 4), relationship marketing (Chapter 9), customer satisfaction and loyalty (Chapters 8 and 9), and service blueprinting (Chapter 6). Experience Engineering, for example, will spend considerable time tracing customers' many contacts with, say, a hospital in order to gain a feel for the customers' total experience with the hospital.

We walked the pathway that a car would take and walked into the emergency room from the parking lot ... we just knew the emergency room was the third door on the left. But if you went in the first door, you were in shipping and receiving, and the second door was the exit ...[4]

This is, in fact, no different from the customer trail that produces the visible part of a service blueprint.

While many of the ideas behind the total customer experience may not be original, the ideas for implementation can be radical. Hewlett Packard, for example, completely reorganised their distribution channels and organisational structure in order to embrace fully the philosophy of creating the total customer experience. A distribution structure based entirely around product lines was changed to consist of three customer-facing organisations and three product-generating organisations, and also, two senior executives were placed in charge of 'owning' the total customer experience, on the consumer and enterprise sides of the business, respectively.

The importance, for practitioners, of understanding and managing the total customer experience is clear. It is claimed that the total customer experience is formed by four elements – technology choices that a company makes, services offered and problem resolution, relationship building/retention programmes and measurements used.[5] The other chapters of the book have addressed these elements, and so maybe the future lies in co-ordinating them, within an innovative organisation structure. The different perspectives that customers, academics and companies have on the meaning of 'experience' (Chapter 5) are also worth revisiting in this context.

Customer equity

In the previous chapter, we introduced Gummesson's notion that there are intangible assets of a company that relate to its network of relationships, and his plea that measures of these assets should be reported in company accounts. Recent work on customer equity represents attempts to measure outcomes related to company expenditures on, for example, CRM or service quality. According to the Arthur Andersen Consultancy:

> there are value-creating assets within organizations that are not listed on any balance sheet. These "intangible" assets do, however, contribute to shareholders equity and are recognised in public markets.[6]

Customer equity is defined as 'the net present value of all the business a firm expects to receive from its customers',[7] or 'the total discounted lifetime values of all of its customers'.[8]

Both definitions are essentially the same. Two features are inherent in these definitions.

1.   There is a focus on *customer profitability* as opposed to product profitability.

2.   There is a focus on *the future* as well as the present.

The importance of the concept of customer equity is reflected in the publication of two academic textbooks on the issue that received high acclaim by practitioners. Blattberg *et al.*[9] refer to customer equity as depending on the company's efficiency and effectiveness in carrying out three customer-related activities: acquisition, retention and add-on selling. Rust et *al.*[10] identify three drivers of customer equity – value equity, brand equity and retention equity – and advise managers how they can base their strategies around these drivers.

The Rust *et al.* approach is intuitively appealing to managers as it includes a 'metric' for calculating the outcomes (in terms of improvement in customer equity) of marketing interventions, such as investments on direct mail programmes to improve customer retention, or on quality improvement programmes. The customer equity concept incorporates their 'return on quality' ideas (Chapter 10) into a wider and more flexible arena. The customer equity philosophy would be difficult, if not impossible, to operationalise under many current organisational structures, especially those based on a product-centred approach. So, once again, we see arguments put forward for organisational restructuring, this time with a Customer Equity Executive as the intermediary between the CEO and four officers – Value Equity Officer, Retention Equity Officer, Brand Equity Officer and a Chief Information Officer.

There is clearly scope to build on, and even contest, the current approaches to customer equity. Equally clearly, practitioners are demanding a clearer picture of the desired outcomes of CRM programmes through measures 'that reflect the value of their customer relationships and the contribution it makes to future growth prospects'.[11] The research is very much on-going.

The emergence of service/solutions providers

Steven Brown, Director of the Center for Services Marketing and Management at Arizona State University, in a keynote address to the American Marketing Association Services Marketing Special Interest Group in May 2001, identified *former product manufacturers* as the principal group of practitioners who are interested in the practice and theory of services marketing and management. Companies that originated in manufacturing, and became known for the physical products that they made and sold, are finding that the more profitable components of their business are the services and solutions that they provide. For example:

- IBM employs 240 000 people in their service/support arm, which makes up 40 per cent of its business
- 60 per cent of General Electric's business is from services (with the CEO having the vision of General Electric being a global service provider that also sells electrical products)
- Pitney Bowes have moved from a concentration on mailroom equipment to a focus on mailroom operations services.

In the business-to-business sector, there is a continuing trend to out-source services which had been traditionally provided in-house, in order to concentrate on core competencies. Specialist consultancy groups, together with the large (former manufacturing) companies with specialist product knowledge and access to networks, are providing the out-sourced services and solutions.

Key Resource Solutions Inc., a New Jersey-based software consultancy firm, claim, for example, to help 'bridge the gap between the conceptual and the actual' by supporting the client company's IT initiatives as managers, enablers, personnel providers, creative consultants and project initiators.[12] They also offer technical expertise on

- project management
- project development
- maintenance support
- management/technical staff augmentation
- application and system development and support
- database administration
- internet, intranet and e-business development.

The range of services and 'solutions' that can be offered by such consultancies is impressively large.

The range of services and solutions offered by the large (former manufacturing) companies can be staggering. On the 'products and services' page of the IBM website[13] is a list of services and solutions offered by the company. Services are in four main groups – Business services, IT services, Training, and Financing. Within each group are sub-groups of services. For example, IT services include Infrastructure, Systems Management, Networking and Connectivity, Outsourcing, and Web Hosting. Each subgroup is further divided into 'service descriptions'. The list below shows the service descriptions within the sub-group 'Outsourcing'.

Business innovation services

- Business intelligence services
- Custom systems integration services
- Customer relationship management services
- Digital branding and marketing
- e-business strategy and design consulting
- e-commerce services
- Enterprise resource planning services
- Knowledge and content management services
- Merger and acquisition services
- Procurement services
- Security and privacy services
- Skills development services for e-business
- Supply chain management services
- Web application development

Integrated technology services

- Business continuity and recovery services
- e-business infrastructure services
- Information technology consulting
- Infrastructure & systems management services
- IT consolidation services
- IT product training
- Midrange express services
- Networking & connectivity services
- Technical support services
- Total systems management services

Strategic outsourcing services

- Application management services
- Data center outsourcing services
- Desktop outsourcing services

- e-business hosting services
- Network outsourcing services

The Solutions are also in four groups – Industry solutions, Cross-industry and alliance solutions, Government and Education. Again, within each group of solutions, there are subgroups of solutions. For example, Education includes Universities and Colleges, and Schools. The solution descriptions for Universities and Colleges are listed below.

Resources
- Search for jobs
- Download software
- Get latest technology and education news
- Collaboration with IBM on research projects

Solutions for higher education
- Build and manage technology infrastructure
- Improve institution's services
- Advance delivery of education

Research
- Access announcements
- Research programmes
- Available product discounts

The company offers hundreds of services/solutions, at the level of the service/solution description, to clients in all sectors of the economy all over the world. IBM claims to be a global service provider, but like many former product-based companies, the change of focus from product to service-based company is difficult. Steven Brown's conference address emphasised the need for research into the management of such changes.

The case of Conoco's new convenience store format – 'breakplace'[14]

In the mid-1990s, Conoco saw profit opportunities in a convenience store format that could differentiate itself from those offered by competitors. They worked on the philosophy that:

> Brands are enhanced or eroded during countless interactions between customer and company. The challenge is to design a customer experience in harmony with the brand, then allocate investment to the areas of greatest potential return.

Ongoing relationships with customers were seen as crucially important.

> This total customer experience, which often extends beyond the purchase of a product or service, is composed of multiple 'moments of truth'. Each of these interactions to varying degrees helps build or destroy a brand's 'equity'.

The process used to anticipate customer requirements was

- identify target customers and the key segment(s)
- understand the priorities of the key customer segments
- determine which interactions (moments of truth) matter most to customers in the key segments
- design from the ground up – create experiences that delight the target customers
- test, execute and assess.

The overall lesson learnt, after opening over 40 'breakplace' stores, was that 'designing a customer experience in harmony with the brand is critical in a service-intensive economy'.

Focus for future research – personal views

This edition is being written at a time when business practice is viewed in relation to the 'new service economy', with near-instant global communications systems giving rise to e-commerce and m-commerce (mobile commerce). The speed of change and access to 'information' makes for exciting times. In some ways, this means that understanding the *people* involved in services (customers and employees) is even more important. 'As consumers are increasingly expected to interface with automation rather than with humans, the importance of those remaining human interactions is magnified.'[15]

Precisely because of the speed of change in the business and technological environment, it is necessary to gain a greater understanding of human behaviour in order to offer services that engender customer and employee satisfaction and loyalty. Let us look at some statements that we have heard that make assumptions about the way people behave.

- 'Text messaging on mobile phones is for teenagers'

The popular image of the text message user is the 10–20-year-old swapping stories, pleasantries, or details of whereabouts with their peers. This undoubtedly happens, but just how much do the over-20s use text messaging and why? Answers to these questions would not only provide useful information to the mobile phone manufacturers, network providers and communications companies, but they would have wider implications for service providers interested in how adults work and play. To our knowledge, such questions remain, as yet, unanswered.

- 'Rail passengers will pay an extra supplement to sit in a carriage with additional facilities, when they are faced with crowding in the economy carriages'

One of the UK rail operators has a premier carriage on trains on some of the busier routes, equipped with, for example, curtains and electrical sockets for laptop computers. After each stop, there is a tannoy announcement that passengers can sit in the premier carriage for an additional payment. In practice, passengers often remain standing in the crowded economy carriage, or feel that it is their right to sit in the premier carriage without any further payment, and may even mock the additional facilities. Before service initiatives are implemented, a rich understanding of passenger behaviour is required, some of which may relate to cultural practices within the context. The same level of understanding is needed in other service contexts where consumers undergo an extended, and often repeated service experience.

● 'All the employees are now on email'

This is the type of statement made about employees within an organisation, with some implicit assumption that they will all work in a homogeneous way with the communication medium. But how do employees use email? How frequently do they use it, and for what reason? How do they manage emails? A study into the use and management of emails, by academics in a section of a university business school, showed enormous variation in email behaviour.[16] For example, some people deleted emails immediately, while others kept them all. The number of files used to store emails varied between 3 and 91. Some used lower case letters in their emails to demonstrate friendliness and lack of formality, while others preferred memo-style. Some replied immediately to emails, while others filed them for later response or replied by telephone. Some read all their emails, while others deleted some emails without reading them, based on the sender and/or the subject details. Some took great care that their message would not upset the recipient, while others chose brief, factual responses with few, if any pleasantries.

Such variations in behaviour have both internal and external marketing implications for a service organisation, and yet the reasons for the variations are not fully understood.

The three examples above are illustrative of the need for service marketing researchers to remain focused on people in services, and on how they behave. Two areas of behaviour seem particularly fruitful for future research.

Behaviour with technology and communication media

In Chapter 4, some of the findings on customer satisfaction and dissatisfaction with technology-based services were summarised.

However, here, we call for more wide-ranging behavioural studies on *how and why* people use the various technological means of communication for work-related and social-related reasons. Both the *variety* of communication media and the *speed* of communications have resulted in behavioural practices that were simply not available, nor envisaged, as recently as the mid-1990s. (Indeed, the *Oxford English Dictionary* only recognised the word 'text' *as a verb* in July 2001.) Research has not had the chance to catch up on the new behavioural practices.

When we wrote the first edition of this book in 1995, the chapters were hand-written and typed, by secretarial staff on a very early version of a word processing package. We both worked for the same institution and most of the communication was face-to-face meetings. Neither emails nor mobile phones were an option. In writing this edition, we are located at different institutions and have both spent time at home (with computer dial-in facilities) and at work, working on the book and other research/teaching. The differences in behavioural practices over a six-year period are enormous. Now, we prepare all our own documents (Word and Powerpoint). We can only meet face-to-face infrequently, and so we use a variety of communication media – fixed telephone, mobile telephone and text messaging (and neither of us is in the 10–20-year age group), email and attachments. Such differences in practice can be seen in many occupations in different sectors of the service economy. Also, surveys show that '40% of Americans are in daily contact with their workplace while on holiday, thanks to e-mail, mobile phones and PCs'.[17] The questions of interest to us are: What combinations of the communication methods do people choose to use, and why? What are the perceived advantages of using one form of communication over another: for example, email, rather than telephone or text message for a simple query?

The speed and mobility of communication, and the widespread global information available on satellite and cable television, can create crises for service businesses. The old adage that bad word-of-mouth (about a service, say) reaches more people than good word-of-mouth is made more telling because of the speed with which any kind of news (good or bad) can travel. Take the unfounded rumour in the UK, based on a 'joke' made by a Welsh DJ, that there was a petrol (gas) crisis, with pumps running out. Within hours, petrol stations all over the UK were empty as a result of panic buying, and delivery services of firms reliant on road transport were affected significantly. Another example was the effect on overseas tourism, of the UK foot-and-mouth epidemic, even in urban areas! The many service businesses that rely on tourism were hit badly at the Easter period, one of their busiest times.

The services marketing literature has, as yet, little to offer on the management of crises that hit service businesses so quickly as a result of the speed and mobility of communications. Even the work on service recovery may be of limited value, as strategies for service recovery imply that service failures are the fault of the service organisation or the customer, which is often not the case in crises. A small hotel in rural England whose management has achieved the highest levels of service practice may become unprofitable because of a crisis. We think that it is timely for some interdisciplinary research that applies crisis management methods to the service industry, underpinned by studies of how and why people communicate with the different technologies.

Behaviour relating to a (sub)culture

The statement relating to rail passengers, above, and the subsequent commentary, demonstrates that there can be a cultural dimension associated with participation in services that affects people's behaviours. The shared beliefs and understandings of a sub-culture, such as rail passengers, can be very subtle, and unlikely to be revealed in conventional customer-survey-based research. Little, for example, is documented about the interactive behaviour between fellow passengers, and yet such interactions, such as reassurances from regular passengers to infrequent passengers, may impact greatly on both persons' perceptions of the journey experience.

It is important to recognise that there may be a cultural dimension to the human behaviours and activities in even the most routine of services, such as rail travel. In situations where the sub-culture is more specifically based around hobby-related activities, if the behaviours of the members are better understood, those providing services to them can benefit from the understanding. Take, for example, the increasing popularity, in the UK, of cycling by women. Retailers of bicycles, by and large, are not providing the types of bicycles that are being demanded by women who want to race or do sustained riding. 'When it comes to bicycles for women ... "ladies'"' models tend to be identical to the equivalent "gentlemen's" models except they lack a crossbar – a design originally intended to make it easier to cycle in the voluminous skirts of the late nineteenth century'.[18] The sub-culture of women competitive cyclists, and their behaviours and motivations, are seemingly little appreciated by retailers (and designers) that support the activity.

When it comes to national cultures, we had argued in the first edition of the book for more cross-cultural studies on consumer behaviour during service encounters. There should be greater opportunities to carry out cross-cultural studies now, precisely because of the more efficient means of communication. Academics, who may not have even met, can systematically carry out comparative research in different countries through email and attachments. In our own experience, this is happening more and more and should lead to some fascinating findings in the near future.

On research methodology

Although it is likely that mainly quantitative research techniques will continue to be used extensively in many areas of investigation, researchers are presently being encouraged to draw on a range of quantitative and qualitative research to provide richer insights into a range of topics: specifically the use of field experiments, participant observation and more laboratory experiments. Researchers are making a deliberate effort to combine different research techniques to investigate some of the more difficult issues. Price, Arnould and Deibler,[19] for example, used both participant observation and consumer diary methodologies to gain new insights into the interpersonal dimensions of service encounters. In the latter, consumers were recruited and trained to record characteristics of their service encounters, along with their own emotional responses. These records were completed immediately after each encounter.

The services marketing academic community seem more open to encourage the application of innovative research methods. It is recognised that survey-based, quantitative studies, which still dominate the published articles in many of the academic journals, can be complemented by more qualitative studies. For example, the editorial in the first edition of the *Journal of Service Research* emphasised that many business disciplines are represented on the editorial board, which 'is also inclusive of quantitative, behavioural and qualitative approaches'.[20] In a more recent editorial in the *Journal of Services Marketing*, the appropriateness of studies that involve 'pilot studies, or "exploratory" research that offer some data to tentatively address relevant research questions, and ... case studies that show the relevance or application of the topic in a specific company setting', in the early stages of a topic's lifestyle, was restated.[21]

Our rally, above, for a greater understanding of how and why people behave the way they do, would require qualitative research based on *extended observations* of the people concerned, and interpretations of their behaviour. Such studies should add richness to the data collected and uncover the subtleties in behaviour that are related to cultures or technologies.

LEARNING OUTCOMES

Having read this chapter, you should be able to

- appreciate the importance, to the academic and practitioner community, of the concepts of 'the total customer experience' and 'customer equity'

- provide examples of the migration of manufacturing companies to service and solution providing companies

- be aware of the importance of understanding 'people' behaviours in the changing service environment at the beginning of the twenty-first century

- appreciate the potential contribution of observational research to an understanding of human behaviour in service contexts.

Notes and references

1. http://www.pyramidupdate.com/newsite, 'Mutual Fund Branding and the Total Customer Experience'.
2. Calhoun, J., 'CRM: Driving Loyalty by Managing the Total Customer Experience, http://www.crmproject.com/wp/calhoun.html
3. Applegate, J., 'Experience Marketing', http://www.entrepreneur.com, 2 February, 2000.
4. Ibid.
5. http://www.pyramidupdate.com/newsite
6. 'New Metrics for a New Millennium: Customer Equity', produced by Arthur Andersen and Trimax, available from www.trimax.com
7. Ibid.
8. Rust, R. T., Zeithaml, V. A. and Lemon, K. N., *Driving Customer Equity*, The Free Press, New York, 2000.
9. Blattberg, R. C., Getz, G. and Thomas, J. S., *Customer Equity*, Harvard Business Press, 18 July 2001.

10. Rust, Zeithaml, and Lemon, *Driving Customer Equity*.
11. Renner, D., 'Focusing on Customer Equity – The Unrealized Asset', http://www.crmproject.com/crm/toc/keynote.html
12. http://www.keyresourcesolutions.com
13. http://www.ibm.com
14. The interested reader can find details of this case in Feakins, K. H. and Zea, M., 'How Conoco Broke the Convenience Store Mold: Building Brand Equity Through Many "Moments of Truth"', http://www.lippincott-margulies.com/publications/journal14/4-Designing.html
15. Martin, C. L., 'Editorial, Technology and Service: Unintended Consequences', *Journal of Services Marketing*, vol. 13, no. 2, 1999, pp. 98–9.
16. Maxwell, K., 'E-mail: Effective Internal Communication Tool in the Business Environment?', Unpublished dissertation, Manchester Metropolitan University.
17. Stelzer, I., 'American Account', *Sunday Times*, London, 18 July, 2001.
18. Rosen, P., 'Up the Velorution: Appropriating the Bicycle and the Politics of Technology', in R. Eglash, J. Bleeker, J. Croissant, R. Fouche and G. Di Chiro, (eds), *Appropriating Technology*, University of Minnesota Press, 2000.
19. Price, L. L., Arnould, E. J. and Deibler, S. L., 'Service Provider influence on consumers' emotional responses to Service encounters', Proceedings of the 3rd International research Seminar on Services Management, La-Londe-Les-Maures, France, May 1994.
20. Rust, R. T., 'Editorial, What Kind of Journal is the Journal of Service Research?', *Journal of Service Research*, vol. 1, no. 1, 1998, pp. 3–4.
21. Martin, C. L., 'Editorial, Completing Your Life with JSM', *Journal of Services Marketing*, Vol. 15, No. 2, 2001, pp. 78–81.

Case study 1
Joe & Co, Hairdressing

History and background of the business

Joe & Co Hairdressing, owned by Anthony Keates, was established in August 1990 in Leek, in the north Midlands of England. Given the 'up-market' position of the salon relative to competitors in the Leek area, Anthony could easily have used his own name for the hairdressing business. He chose instead, however, to adopt the nickname 'Joe' in the title, which was originally given to him by his team mates in his local Sunday morning football team. Although 'Joe & Co' was set up in 1990, Anthony had owned a salon in Leek between 1981 and 1986. He subsequently gave this up to take up a teaching career in hairdressing. While he enjoyed the experience of teaching, and learnt a lot in four years about different types of hairdressing businesses (by visiting trainee students on hairdressing placements), he felt he still had too much to offer as a practising professional hairdresser to stay in teaching full-time. He decided to open up a new business in a different part of Leek. In 1990, despite the four years' absence from full-time hairdressing, Anthony used his knowledge of the community and old contacts to build up a strong customer base for the new salon. He found that 15 per cent of the customers he had dealt with in 1986 appeared on his doorstep as clients for the new business.

The present salon operates with two part-time female stylists, Anthony himself and two junior staff who are learning the profession. Details of the range of services offered are given in Figure CS 1.1. The salon opens five days a week and closes on a Monday. Two stylists work each day. They each have eight clients booked for an appointment every day, working to a target of one client per hour. The restriction on the number of client bookings was a deliberate policy decision by Anthony who feels that only by allowing each client this amount of time can he guarantee that they will receive what he considers to be a 'necessary' level of customer service.

Every customer deserves to be greeted with a cup of coffee, have their coat taken and receive a quality haircut in a professional environment. You cannot do this properly if you are always worrying about finishing one client's hair to get another one through the door!

He does not do any advertising for the business as the client book is always full.

The salon

From the outside, the salon looks professional. The exterior and interior decor has a distinctive black and white theme with a simple but effective painting on the door stating 'Joe & Co Hairdressing'. The window has not been deliberately designed to attract passing trade as all new customers come from recommendations made by existing clients.

Inside, there is a black and white marble floor with black cushioned chairs for customers. The staff wear black trousers and waistcoats and white shirts or blouses, and coffee is served in black and white mugs with the Joe & Co logo on the outside.

Plants are placed strategically around the mirrors in the salon to enhance the perception of a clean, fresh working environment. The physical environment has been deliberately designed to create the professional image that Anthony considers to be such a critical part of good customer service.

The customer profile

The majority of customers are female aged between 30 and 60. According to Anthony, what they all have in common is that they appreciate a good cut! This was confirmed by a regular customer who described the cutting side of the service as the best in the area. Although the salon is technically unisex, only about 10 per cent of customers are male, and very few are teenagers. Anthony attributes this largely to the attitude of these particular client groups towards hairdressing. With only eight appointments per stylist available each day, appointments have to be carefully scheduled and planned by clients in advance. As they leave one appointment, regular clients are encouraged to book their next six-weekly appointment. The system makes it very difficult for anyone just to turn up in the hope of getting an appointment. They can expect to have to wait at least six weeks to get in for a haircut. In Anthony's experience, men and younger fashion-conscious women are rarely prepared to wait that long. The technical 'cut' of their hair is just not that important to them.

Anthony considers each of his clients as 'long-term' prospects. It is important that he establishes a good relationship with them from the very beginning so that he can 'manage' the development of their hair. Although many clients may not feel that they have changed their style very much since they have been visiting the salon, Anthony knows that in comparison to how they looked since first attending, many of them are significantly different. Many clients have been with Joe & Co since the business opened in 1990. Customers who do not stay are usually those who were not prepared to wait for an appointment. As the majority of customers know each other well (having been recruited by personal recommendation), they chat easily while having their hair cut. As Leek is a small rural community where almost everyone is interested and involved in community events, the salon acts as a focal point for debate and 'gossip'. The atmosphere in the salon is consequently very relaxed and informal.

Restrictions on growth

Anthony has been operating the strict 'appointment only' system for over a year. It was originally set up because the stylists were so busy that clients were having to wait too long in the salon itself between appointments. Although the system ensures that all clients receive the full attention of each stylist for at least an hour, and clearly generates strong customer loyalty, there are negative aspects to the policy. As well as the obvious frustration felt by clients who are unable to get extra appointments for special occasions or change appointments at the last minute, Anthony himself feels personally frustrated at times. In one sense he is a victim of his own success. 'Although having such a regular group of customers means that I am always busy, it is difficult to keep interested in the technical side of the job, with familiar clientele.'

He attends hairdressing seminars and keeps up to date with the latest fashion styles by reading magazines and journals, but he feels at times that his creative talents are being stifled by the system. Whilst he has the full range of hairdressing qualifications, as well as a hairdressing teaching qualification, he feels that, for his personal development, it is important to experiment with new styles and deal with new faces on a regular basis. One way to do this would be to move away from Leek and join a number of different salons in a large city. There he feels he would have the opportunity to compare his cutting skills with those of fellow professionals and gain recognition from them, as well as from clients. As a hairdressing professional, Anthony feels that this is an important component of his work. He is not motivated solely by money. As long as he can make enough to live comfortably, it is much more important that he enjoys his job. He is keen to have the opportunity to develop his own professional skills and expertise by working with some of the top hairdressers.

Another development option might be to open a second salon in another area. As Anthony explains, the difficulty here would be finding suitably qualified staff to work for him. He is conscious that his clients keep returning to the salon because of the particular skills and personalities of individual stylists. It is unlikely that they would stay loyal to Joe & Co if Anthony, Bev or Pip left to work in a second shop in a new location. Although the three stylists have very different personalities and strengths, they all have their own group of regular customers who expect their particular 'brand' of hairdressing service. Anthony, for example, attracts clients who are mainly interested in the technical quality of their haircut. He spends most of the time allotted concentrating on the detail of the cut itself. Pip and Bev have more outgoing personalities and allow time within the service to talk to customers, giving them a slightly different service 'experience'.

It appears to be very difficult to attract suitably qualified stylists to work in a salon of this type. Anthony recently advertised for a new stylist to take up a 'chair' in the salon on particular days of the week. For the rest of the time he/she might travel to work in different locations. Anthony felt that this would present an ideal opportunity for a motivated hairdresser to build up a loyal customer base without having to incur the overheads associated with actually generating your own premises.

A third development option might be to act as a representative for one of the leading hairdressing manufacturers, calling on other hairdressers and giving them technical advice on how to get the best out of their products.

Staff development

As well as his personal development, Anthony is conscious of the need to train and develop the junior staff in the salon. He feels that one of the advantages of working for a smaller business, and operating a system that allocates an hour to each client, is that trainees can get hands-on experience in all aspects of the hairdressing business. He has the time to talk to the trainees about each aspect of the haircut as he works on each client. Even though the training may be good, however, he does not expect the young trainees to stay with Joe & Co for very long. Because of the dynamic nature of the hairdressing business, he feels that young people should be travelling around, building up their experience and learning new skills and techniques from professionals all over the world. He sees hairdressing as a very exciting and challenging career for young people who are prepared to dedicate themselves to reaching the top.

Competition

There are a number of other salons in the town of Leek and the surrounding area, but Anthony does not feel that these present serious competition to his business. He has more clients than he can manage at this point in time and feels that he must be doing enough to satisfy them for this to be the case. Although he recognises that the other salons provide a service for males, younger people and passing trade, he does not consider these to be the types of clients who would appreciate his particular offer. He finds it difficult to hide his frustration with customers who don't appreciate the quality of a good haircut. He treats every style like a work of art describing himself as a perfectionist who takes pride in the technical quality of his work.

The future

Anthony is confident about his skills as a hairdresser, but he does not feel that he handles the business side of things as well as he might if his object-ive was to make as much money as possible. Although he sells his own hairdressing products in the salon, with the Joe & Co logo clearly inscribed on the bottles, he does not think that it is fair to 'push' customers into buying them just so that he can make more money. They are the products that they use every day in the salon, and if customers ask for his advice then he recommends them as he feels they are quality products, but it is totally up to the individual client what they buy.

Prices for services are laid out on the pricing card (see Figure CS 1.1). However, Anthony likes to retain a certain amount of flexibility with the prices charged. For example, he explains, 'If I do not feel that a client's hair has taken as long as it should for the price charged and treatment received, I will reduce the price accordingly. I suppose that this would not be considered very good business practice but then ...'

Whilst each client is treated as a long-term prospect, Anthony does not have a clearly defined long-term strategy for the business. He does not feel that he or his staff have the necessary expertise to offer other services to customers as some other hairdressers are beginning to do. These may include, for example, make-up advice, colour consultancy, skin-care treatments including sunbeds and facials. His main problem at the moment is working out how he is going to fit in all his regular clients for a haircut before Christmas!

PRICE LIST
PERMANENT WAVING SERVICES
(not including any other service)

	Joe		Pip/Bev	
	Acid	Alkaline	Acid	Alkaline
Top Perm	£14.00	£10.00	£13.00	£10.00
Three Quarter Perm	£16.50	£14.50	£15.50	£13.50
Full Head Perm	£20.00	£17.50	£18.00	£16.00
Technical Winding	Upon application			
Long Hair	upon application			
Le Coiffeur (exclusive)	£25.00		£23.00	

LADIES

	Joe	Pip/Bev
Restyling (inc. Wash and Dry)	£16.50	£13.50
Cutting (inc. Wash and Dry)	£14.00	£12.00
Trimming (by prior arrangement)	£7.50	£7.00
Blow Drying	£7.00	£6.00
Setting	£7.00	£5.00

GENTS

	Joe	Pip/Bev
Cutting (inc. ash and Dry)	£7.50	£6.50

(Dry cutting by prior agreement with Bev only)

COLOURING SERVICES
(not including any other service)

		Joe	Pip/Bev
Permanent Colour: Full Head		£13.50	£12.00
Roots		£10.50	£10.00
Colourbath		£8.00	£7.50
Semi Permanent Colour		£5.50	£5.00
Highlighting/Lowlighting:			
Cap	Full Head	£13.00	£12.00
	Part Head	£10.00	£10.00
Highlighting/Lowlighting: Essi meche. foils			
Full Head		£20.00	£20.00
Part Head		£14.00	£14.00
Roots		£16.00	£16.00

CONDITIONING SERVICES
Le Coiffeur Conditioning Treatments from £3.00
All prices inclusive of styling products and refreshments

Figure CS 1.1   Ranges of services offered by Joe & Co

Case study 2
George Ball & Son, Funeral Directors

History of the company

In 1870, George Ball was a joiner working in the Heaton Moor area of Stockport, a town six miles south of Manchester in the north-west of England. As part of his trade, he made coffins of solid wood and people came to him for these in particular. In those days it was a basic need to have a coffin as it was normal for the deceased to be kept at home prior to a funeral, rather than be taken to a chapel of rest. George's wife was the local nurse and midwife and it was part of her duties to 'lay out' people who had died; that is, wash the body and prepare it for the funeral. Because of their dual roles, a funeral business evolved. George and his wife began to hire horse-drawn hearses from the Parish Borough Carriage Company.

At the time there were many small funeral directors, even within a couple of streets of each other, but nearly all the funeral services were additional to the main business. As well as joinery/building businesses, furniture shops with skilled cabinetmakers would also make coffins and 'undertake' the services required for burials. George Ball, however, was the first funeral director in Stockport to provide a chapel of rest. George passed the business on to his son, also called George, who in turn passed it on to his son Sidney Ball in 1954. The company is now run by Margaret Arnison, Sidney's daughter, who took over in 1978 when her father retired at 65, and the family business is now in its fourth generation. It operates as a sole trader, not as a limited company. Until three years ago, Margaret's husband was running a building business in conjunction with the funeral business.

The current premises

The business is located, since February 1994, at a former print works which was refurbished by Margaret's husband. It is next door to their previous premises and, in addition to having 'loads of space', is ideal because of the access for vehicles to the back of the building. The business has now got its own fleet of vehicles, complete with GBS personalised number plates, an option which was not available to them (because of lack of access to the rear) at the previous address.

On entering the front door, there is an office to the right and an interview room to the left. Towards the rear of the building are two small chapels of rest separated by a curtain. When the curtain is open the combined space of the two chapels of rest is large enough for a service to be held. Some people prefer a service here to one at a church.

Further back is a garage for the vehicles and a workshop/storeroom. The latter has a stock of coffins, many accessories and an engraving machine. Nowadays it is very rare to have solid wood coffins. Large joinery firms started making coffin sets (that is, sides, base and lids) to various sizes, and moved on to making veneers. George Ball & Son have not made their own coffins for the last twenty-five years. It is economically sensible for them to order coffins rather than make them. Also the regulations to protect the environment, with regard to cremations, are very strict; great care has to be taken to ensure that the correct glues, varnishes and finishes are used.

They own another smaller office in Heaton Norris, three miles away, which they purchased five years ago. This office is not always manned but is always operational with a telephone transfer to the main Heaton Moor office. It contains a small chapel of rest, a facility that is needed in Heaton Norris. A series of takeovers and closures of funeral businesses had left people in the area without a conveniently located chapel of rest.

The staff

There are three full-time staff working for the business: Margaret Arnison herself, another funeral director, Nick Luty and Margaret's 21-year-old son Daniel. Margaret and Nick split the funeral directing between them, supported by a part-time lady who runs the office. Daniel takes on a whole range of duties including office work, driving, and coffin preparation. Margaret's husband, Bill, also helps out with any building work, such as the recent refurbishment, and 'covering' the office when needed.

Staff working in a funeral business do not require any qualifications or registration by law. People can start up a funeral business with no training or experience whatsoever, and some do. This used to cause problems for the image of funeral businesses in general. According to Margaret Arnison, it is not so much of a problem now as anyone proposing to start up a funeral business would require substantial financial backing.

George Ball & Son, with over 120 years of experience in the business, are very aware of the importance of having the right staff, who are fully trained, to work in such a sensitive area. They insist that staff are 'straight as a die, discreet, and aware of the regulations so that they don't overstep the mark in any sense'. There is a qualification available – the Diploma in Funeral Directing – that is run under the auspices of the National Association of Funeral Directors (NAFD). Training and Education in Funeral Services (TEFS), which incorporates NAFD, is currently taking on board the National Vocational Qualification (NVQ) framework for the award. This move introduces a test with a number of practical competencies associated with the job; for example, fitting out a coffin and cleaning the car, which are basic skills, but ones that really matter in the job. The practical competencies support the other tested area; the knowledge of procedures. Knowing the regulations and the appropriate forms to be completed is vitally important. When someone rings in to say a relative has died, there are many standard procedures to go through before the body can be moved to the chapel of rest. Failure to apply the procedures can lead to problems with the coroner if the death was believed to have occurred in suspicious circumstances.

In general, staff need to be ultra flexible (they can be rung up in the middle of the night), good with people (they have to deal with doctors, ministers, families, old people, young people) and be confident on the telephone. If someone rings up, a member of staff must clearly and confidently establish what kind of funeral is required from people who are anxious and distressed.

The service

George Ball & Son deal with approximately 250 funerals a year. In a given week, there can be as many as twelve funerals. Unlike the situation half a century ago, there is now no discernible seasonality in demand. Whilst there are many technical, logistical and procedural elements to the service, they acknowledge that they offer the first line of bereavement counselling. They are 'looking after people at a very vulnerable time; getting them through the first week when they don't want to make any decisions but certain choices have to be made'.

There is much to bereavement counselling and every occasion is different. On the day everything must be right, and it must be right first time. There is no second chance. The funeral director must listen carefully to what has happened – was it a sudden death or long illness? was it a tragedy or a relief? – so that he/she can take the background into account when planning the details of a funeral which takes the form that the bereaved would prefer. In most cases, the longer-term bereavement counselling must be taken on by someone else. People do not always want to keep seeing the funeral director after the funeral itself. On occasions, however, someone who is on their own will call in regularly for help or just a chat, and the staff will always make themselves available even though the main business has finished.

At the time of the first contact with the funeral business, people need to be put at their ease. In particular, they need to know that the first decision, often taken at a time of great stress, need not be final. They can change their mind if they want to. Information about available alternatives needs to be given in a clear and sympathetic way. The funeral director will also need to be able to respond to worries about all the 'red tape' that has to be gone through. The bereaved find probate – the process of officially proving the validity of a will – particularly confusing and an intrusion into their private financial circumstances. To be able to explain the procedure and, often more importantly, why the procedure has to take place, is a further skill required of funeral directors, even though probate is not directly their responsibility.

It is clear that 'no two funerals are ever the same'. Margaret Arnison sums up the company's attitude to bereavement counselling and the provision of a funeral service as follows:

> *It's making the families know and feel that whatever they ask is normal for them, and that it's no trouble for us, even if we have to pull out all the stops to make it happen.*

There are many examples of them carrying out this philosophy. They range from requests to dress the deceased in a particular way – even in thermal underwear to keep out the cold – to making special arrangements for transport and equipment. One lady, for example, requested a white coffin and white limousines. The limousines were hired from a company that has wedding cars. On another occasion, four grey Rolls-Royces were brought in from Huddersfield, fifty miles away, at the request of the widow of a businessman who had always been a 'showman'. The HRH number plate on the Rolls-Royces added to the occasion. The funeral caused quite a stir and the occasion suited and helped the family to remember the deceased in an appropriate way. It was just the right touch.

There have been occasions when George Ball & Son have made arrangements for a body to be flown home quickly, when a relative has died abroad. Although there is a repatriation service available, based in London, it is more costly and does not offer an individual service. Margaret Arnison can recall a situation where, after a phone call on a Saturday from the deceased's mother, the body of the daughter was in Stockport, flown from South Africa, by the following Thursday. To do this involved teamwork and knowing what to do, and making use of networks of contacts who are members of the NAFD.

Teamwork

Teamwork is of paramount importance in providing the service. Not only must individuals in the business work as a team with a common philosophy – all being willing, for example, to pick up relatives and drive them to the registrar or to the chapel of rest – but the business must form a team with other 'players' such as ministers, doctors and grave diggers. Funerals are likened to a jigsaw. On the outside are the fixed elements – the time, the place, the minister – and there is a picture in the middle which makes it right for the particular customer. The elements of the picture may include a special piece of music played at the service or a reading by a long-standing friend.

At one funeral, a reading was given by the schoolfriend of the deceased, who managed it in a very composed manner. However, the minister had a copy of the speech in case the school-friend found the occasion too much. One lady had expected only a few people to attend her father's funeral. However, Margaret Arnison received a phone call from the 'Normandy veterans' to say that the deceased was an ex-member of their association. After many subsequent phone calls between Margaret, the minister, and the veterans, they were able to provide a union flag, poppy wreath (each provided by George Ball & Son), a tape of the last post (provided by the veterans), and a guard of honour at the service. The family were overwhelmed by the simple tribute and the kindness of the veterans.

It is clear that, where such teamwork is essential, an oversight by one of the team can cause a problem with the funeral service. This may happen, for example, if flowers have not been ordered or the wrong hymns are played, or family names are forgotten in the service. Through experience, fail-safes and contingency plans can be devised to prevent such mistakes happening more than once.

A 'popular' image of a funeral service is governed by what is seen by those attending a funeral. Some people perceive the funeral directors as driving up on the day of the funeral, being on hand for an hour or two, and departing. They wonder why it can cost £900. They do not see, or understand, what is happening behind the scenes, and do not take into account that the business is 'open' twenty-four hours a day, 365 days a year with premises to be run, 'bone fide' staff to be employed (for example, coffin bearers), and the responsibility and effort to be applied to getting things right for the customer. It is probably not appreciated by most that there is a considerable amount of expenditure on the premises alone, as refrigeration or cooling systems need to be in place because of the type of building, and hoists need to be installed for the many lifting jobs in compliance with Health and Safety regulations.

Orders have to be made for coffin sets, sometimes in special sizes, and the coffins must be prepared. Handles and other accessories have to be attached at the workshop and engraving applied. All these tasks require training and skills. Virtually all the accessories and the gowns are obtained from a single supplier.

Methods of payment and record keeping

Customers normally do not pay the funeral business directly. Payment is made through the customer's solicitor. George Ball & Son do not accept credit cards and receive payments mainly by cheque and cash. Their bills are made up in two parts: the funeral services and disbursements. Disbursements are the payments made by the funeral business on behalf of the customer to cemeteries, crematoria, ministers, churches, doctors, and so on. At any point in time, George Ball & Son have laid out very large amounts of money on behalf of customers prior to receiving payment. As Margaret Arnison says, 'Disbursements can be horrendous.' Some 50 per cent of the bills are paid within two months, but in some cases it can be as long as two years before the bill is finally settled. Often delays in payment are out of control of the family of the deceased, who can be very embarrassed about them. Some solicitors do not rate funeral payments at the top of their list of priorities. The funeral business is, in effect, offering an interest free money-lending service.

At George Ball & Son, records of orders, invoices, payments and all other details are kept in a manual system. They have contemplated computerisation, and are not averse to it, but currently hold the view that the business can be managed efficiently without computer databases. All the order forms from past funerals are kept in a filing cabinet in the office. It only takes a few minutes to locate a particular file, even one going back many years. This is required when, for example, a family is using the business for a second or subsequent time, and the previous file(s) are consulted as a reminder of the circumstances of the earlier death(s). It is recognised that such a system could be computerised but because the scale of the business is manageable – 250 new files per year – and the investment in time to create a database is considerable, the manual system is being kept. In contrast, the Manchester Crematorium has recently been computerised with over 200 000 funeral records, from 1892 to the present, on their database.

Making contact with customers

Most business comes from recommendations or tradition. Recommendations can be made via some very involved routes – 'the nephew of a person who died worked with the son of the man whose funeral we had just done'. There are also many families who, by tradition, use George Ball & Son for their funerals.

The nature of the funeral business makes it different from most others, from a marketing perspective. A funeral is infrequent (people may only make contact with the business once or twice in a lifetime) and is something that is a necessity, not a choice. Other businesses where customer contact is infrequent, but where the customer exercises a choice, can use mainstream promotional tactics, with special offers. Clearly, such tactics are inappropriate for funeral services. When *Yellow Pages* ring up saying how advertisements will encourage business, Margaret Arnison is not impressed.

They do advertise in the *Yellow Pages* and the *Thompson's Directory*, but believe that people will normally look for their telephone number in there, not use them as a means of making a choice. They always advertise in the local free paper, the *Heaton Guardian*, and have done so for many years. Again, the main purpose is to provide easy access to their telephone number, as people in the district will know it will be in the free paper. They also place advertisements in the various church magazines in the area. Such magazines are funded by the advertising revenue.

George Ball & Son are one of the nominated funeral directors for the largest UK prepayment plan, 'Chosen Heritage' (see next section and appendices). Such plans are now becoming popular and the company will be assured of regular business in the future through this scheme.

In general, people will use either a private family firm or the 'Co-op' for their funerals. The Co-op, or Co-operative Society, operate under their own name, or under the name of groups which they have bought out in the past. In Manchester, for example, there are very few family businesses left. Most funeral businesses are operated by the Co-op in one guise or another. In contrast, in Stockport, local membership of the NAFD is made up almost entirely of local family businesses (approximately 17 in all). Margaret Arnison is secretary/treasurer for the NAFD in Stockport. The Co-op has a presence in Stockport but no longer contributes to the local association of the NAFD. The family businesses can usually offer a lower price than the Co-op, but do not have the brand name or the regional/national catchment area.

'Chosen Heritage' recommended funeral plans

Chosen Heritage Limited, who have operated since 1986, run a pre-arranged scheme where funeral plans can be paid for, in advance, by single payment or by 12, 24 or 60 monthly payments. In conjunction with the charity Age Concern, they offer special discounts for people aged 60 and over. Most of the 70 000 subscribers to the scheme are from the South of England. George Ball & Son is the nominated funeral director for the South Manchester area. This entails a much larger area to service than Stockport alone, and there are about 500 Chosen Heritage members on their list. An extract from the Chosen Heritage brochure, outlining the benefits of such a prepayment plan, is included in Appendix 1.

Three types of plan are offered – The Simplicity Plan, the Traditional Plan and the Heritage Plan. Nominated funeral directors must be capable of offering such plans to the highest standards. Details of the three plans are shown in Appendix 2.

As part of the scheme, Margaret Arnison would like to produce some literature about George Ball & Son. She has been talking to representatives of Age Concern who wish to promote the scheme, and believes that they could work together on this, as well as on an introduction to the company with details on how to find them. There would be more general information on how people can cope with grief and the willingness of the company to listen. By working together on the literature, the local branch of Age Concern and George Ball & Son can jointly provide information of specific relevance to South Manchester members of the scheme.

Service quality

We establish the needs of the bereaved, and then are as flexible as we can be to meet those needs.

Service Quality for the company consists of the successful application of listening skills (to establish needs) and flexibility (to tailor the service, where possible, to meet the needs).

Customers are sometimes very surprised and appreciative of the flexibility. Some funeral directors still tell the customer *when* the funeral is to take place. George Ball & Son, as a matter of course, ask which day would be best, and whether morning, lunchtime or afternoon is preferable. They have found that some people find even this aspect incredible, as they have just been told a date and time in the past. Flexibility such as this may not cost any more to provide. Indeed, the business operates at a charge that is lower than that of most large organisations. What may be different is the ethos. Margaret Arnison insists that 'service is the first order of the day – the lads know that as well – we aim to do whatever the customer wants plus that bit extra'.

Fellow members of the NAFD believe that funeral directors should be client-oriented, providing customer-based services, and Margaret Arnison means to ensure that such a policy is carried out in practice. She has considered the possibility of applying for BS 5750 (ISO 9000) approval, but has doubts whether the business is big enough to warrant an application.

The future

The business will stay as a family business, building on over 120 years of tradition and experience. People's expectations of funeral services are changing and they are responding accordingly. Much of their business is gained through personal recommendations or family loyalty. If the Chosen Heritage scheme really takes off in the north-west of England, the company may need to expand to accommodate the extra business, whilst maintaining the strengths of the personal customer service currently being offered.

Appendix 1

Some of the Benefits of a Chosen Heritage Plan

- ☑ Firm arrangements are made and understood in advance – avoiding future concern and distress for your relatives.
- ☑ A guarantee that, if you join today, the funeral is paid for at today's price. Whenever the funeral is actually required. Whatever the prices are at the time.
- ☑ Total security – your funeral payments are placed in National Funeral Trust, with Barclays Bank PLC as Custodian Trustee.
- ☑ Plans may be paid for by a single payment or in easy instalments. Suitable for those of any age – with no health questions.
- ☑ Available throughout England, Wales and mainland Scotland (also available in Northern Ireland – please ask for separate brochure).

Appendix 2

Burial Option

If you require burial instead of cremation, the Traditional and Heritage plans will cover the funeral director's services as itemised. In addition, because burial fees vary so widely, a contribution equivalent to the value of the cremation service fee prevailing at the time of the funeral will be made towards the burial fees. The current value of the Burial Contribution is shown on the enclosed application form.

Traditional®

The Traditional Plan is designed for those who require the customary features of a traditional funeral, whatever their religion. Either cremation or burial (see Burial Option below) can be selected.

- Confidential and sympathetic advice on the social and legal aspects to be considered when arranging a funeral.

- Helpful information and counselling if required on the religious ceremony and other matters.

- Guidance on the certification and registration of death.

- Removal of the deceased from the place of death within England, Wales and mainland Scotland to the funeral director's premises.

- Preparation and care of the body in accordance with the wishes of the family.

- High quality oak veneered coffin.

- Viewing by the family at the funeral director's chapel of rest or other convenient place.

- Provision of a hearse and limousine to start from the house (calling at a local church for a service if required) and then proceed to a local crematorium or cemetery.

- Funeral director and staff attending as required, before, during and after the service.

- Guidance to the religious and other authorities on the ishes of the deceased and relatives.

- Complimentary 'return thanks' cards and full listing of floral tributes.

- Cremation Service Fee to cover the cost of a service at a local crematorium, the minister's fee and cremation medical certificates (or Burial Option).

Figure CS 2.1 Range of services offered by George Ball & Son

Heritage®

The Heritage Plan provides all the elements of the Traditional Plan, together with the following additional features, to complete the highest quality service

- A coffin of solid hardwood (instead of oak veneer).
- Conveyance of the deceased to a local church the evening before the service, if required
- Provision of two limousines (rather than one).
- An obituary notice, placed by the funeral director in a local weekly newspaper.

SIMPLICITY®

The Simplicity Plan provides an economical option for those who require a very basic cremation funeral, including only the essential features with the minimum of ceremony.

- Guidance on the certification and registration of death.
- Removal of the deceased from the place of death within England, Wales and mainland Scotland to the funeral director's premises.
- Care of the body prior to cremation (facilities for viewing are not included).
- Simplicity coffin.
- Provision of a hearse to meet the family at a local crematorium (the plan does not include a funeral procession from the house, or attendance at a church service).
- All necessary staff for the service.
- Cremation Service Fee to cover the cost of a service at a local crematorium, the minister's fee and cremation medical certificates.

Figure CS 2.1 *cont'd*

Case study 3
Anne Duinkerk, Colour Consultant

The service

Anne Duinkerk is a professional colour consultant. She advises clients about the colour of clothing and make-up that they should wear, based on an analysis of their natural skin tone, eye colour and, more generally, lifestyle. She carries out 'colour analysis' on her clients. The axiom on which colour analysis hinges is that every person has a 'season' of colours, based on their skin tone and eye colour, which they should wear to make the most of their appearance. A summer person for example should wear soft muted shades: soft whites and blue, rose and grey undertones. A winter person, however, can wear bolder, cool colours and is the only 'season' to wear black and white.

Wearing the wrong colour can result in a pale, sallow or muddy complexion, accentuating lines or shadows around the mouth and nose. The right colour, however, can smooth and clarify the complexion. Skin will look naturally healthy and lines with shadows and dark circles round the eyes kept to a minimum. Anne tells her clients:

> As you get older you start to get lines on your face, but the right colours can in fact soften them. Putting the wrong colours on can create all sorts of illusions, such as making you look as if you've got a double chin, which can be what people remember about you.

To establish her clients' season, Anne removes all existing make-up and places the clients' faces in direct sunlight. A white cloth is then draped around the neck to highlight the natural skin-tone. Anne might then hold a piece of warm gold and silver cloth against their face. If it is the wrong colour, the face will look drained; with the right colour, the complexion will glow. This provides the starting point for further analysis.

Background

Anne operates as a sole trader. When she left school, she trained as a hairdresser and a beautician. Her apprenticeship covered every aspect of beauty, including the basics of cosmetics and even wigmaking. She worked part-time in London until she had her children, and then she decided to pursue her interest in colour work in a more systematic manner. She began reading about the subject, attending colour demonstrations and making enquiries about the cost of formal training.

There was the opportunity to open a franchise business with the House of Colour, but Anne rejected this avenue, not only because of the high initial start-up costs, but also because of the constraints that she felt would be imposed on her freedom of operation. Her 'training' in colour work was provided by a lady in the north-west of England, who believed in learning through 'doing' rather than relying heavily on textbooks. She encouraged Anne to learn about colour coordination by visiting material shops in Manchester, collecting her own colour swatches of different coloured materials and matching them together. Nowadays, newcomers to colour consultancy can obtain the colour swatches by simply buying them from the colour houses.

Although there are many other individuals and organisations offering the 'colour consultancy service', particularly in the south of England, Anne feels that her hairdressing/beautician background gives her a distinct competitive advantage. Although her clients may be paying for colour consultancy when they arrive at her house, she can give them advice on hairstyle and colour and make-up, which she feels are all crucial components of the complete 'look'. Colour consultancy was well established in the south of England when Anne first started, but there was little interest from customers around Manchester. Consequently, she had to spend some time communicating to different groups about the benefits of the service. Newspaper advertisements did not seem to be very effective, so Anne began by offering demonstrations to corporate clients who were generally interested in ways of improving the appearance of their front-line employees.

Group demonstrations

Anne still finds company demonstrations very rewarding and challenging even though she now has many individual clients (some of whom were generated by word-of-mouth recommendations from earlier demonstrations). She admits that they require a very different style of delivery from the individual consultations that still make up almost 70 per cent of her workload. She has to be much more 'professional' and have a very well-rehearsed script. She often feels that a group can be much more sceptical about the long-term benefits of colour consultancy. Although they may not be paying for the service themselves there is occasionally some resentment from employees who feel that their boss is trying to tell them what to wear. In these circumstances Anne has to use her full range of interpersonal skills and perhaps more importantly be flexible with her delivery.

In a group situation she tries to build on the experiences of the participants. For example, Anne gets them to talk about clothes that they have in their present wardrobes which they hardly ever wear. Very often such clothes are left untouched because they are the wrong colour for the individual's season, although this was not realised before the demonstration. This simple exercise gets clients to appreciate the difference between buying clothes in colours that they like rather than in colours that actually suit them. Many group sessions take on a life of their own even though participants may be meeting for the first time. Conversations often move on from a discussion of the colours that people wear to the make-up and facial cleansing products that they use. Participants share experiences and opinions about different brands that are available on the market.

When dealing with groups, Anne has a number of set pieces to her demonstration that she uses to reinforce the benefits of good colour coordination. She brings along a very small suitcase, for example, and demonstrates how you can pack six changes of clothing including accessories into the one case in preparation for that unexpected 'weekend away'. All that is needed is a good understanding of the colours and shades in the individual's 'season'.

The group sessions are not always for corporate clients. Some of her most satisfying sessions have been demonstrations given to patients undergoing occupational therapy at nursing homes. Most of the ladies here are aged between 70 and 90 and can really appreciate the difference that wearing the right colours can make to their appearance. They put on make-up and walk about admiring themselves in the mirror. For many of them the new look can make them appear about twenty years younger. Another group who seem to get a lot from the sessions is young mothers who have spent the last nine months wearing large garments and are trying hard to regain their previous appearance and shape. Although colour advice does not help them physically shed the extra weight, it can make them feel more confident about their appearance, getting them to make the most of what they have.

Anne feels that although she is called a Colour Consultant she is really in the business of 'confidence building'. What all her clients have in common is their desire to feel better about themselves and improve their self-image. It is often the case that the most 'hostile clients', the ones who tell her at the beginning of a session that they already 'know exactly what suits them', are the ones who need most help and who lack the most confidence.

As Anne's business cards stress, 'Complete Image will show you how to look good, to feel good and to improve your image.'

Building long-term relationships

With her individual clients, Anne believes that the key to success is developing long-term relationships with them. She keeps record cards of all her clients, detailing the service she has provided and information about how they came to contact her in the first place. Many of her regular clients have been customers for many years. Although they initially received the colour advice, they have subsequently received help with make-up and wardrobe planning. The latter service means that Anne needs to have a detailed understanding of the individual's lifestyle as well as the contents of their wardrobe! She accompanies many of her regular clients on shopping expeditions, particularly if they are buying an outfit for a special occasion and are prepared to spend more money than usual. Often when shopping alone Anne might see an outfit that she knows would suit a certain client. She will ring them up and suggest that they look at it. These clients rely heavily on Anne's expert judgement.

Anne offers a special service for weddings. Not only does she give advice on the outfits for the bride and bridesmaids, but she also coordinates the total colour theme for the special day, advising on the best colours for the groom, best man and parents of the couple. In order that the flowers form an important part of the total 'look' on the big day, Anne works closely with the florist. As a qualified hairdresser, Anne can look after the full range of beauty treatments for the bride including hair colouring and make-up.

Forecasting demand

One of the major problems with the colour consultancy work is that demand can fluctuate considerably from one month to the next. Anne may find herself inundated with requests for wedding consultancies during the spring and summer months, and special occasion work around Christmas, but have periods in between which are relatively quiet. She overcomes this problem to some extent by working part-time at a local hair and beauty salon in order to keep up to date with developments in the hairdressing world.

It is also difficult for her to gauge how much business has been generated from group demonstrations, as individual clients may not come to her until almost a year after they have taken part in a group session. Anne feels that this can be explained by the fact that many people perceive her service as a 'treat', a once in a lifetime service they can only afford if they have that extra little bit of money. In contrast, in America, and some parts of mainland Europe, wardrobe consultancy is viewed as an integral part of a woman's weekly or monthly beauty regime. It is very difficult to convince people about the benefits of a service like colour consultancy when they may not fully appreciate the benefits themselves until long after the session. For some it may take weeks, months or even years before they realise how much better they look or how much money they can save by following the simple guidelines.

Pricing

It is partly because of the way that people perceive the service that Anne has to be fairly flexible with her pricing structure. People are generally reluctant to pay very much money up-front before they have had a chance to experience the benefits of colour consultancy. Although she always tries to make sure that she charges less than the price charged by the franchised colour houses for individual colour consultations, she finds that she can spend almost two hours with customers who visit for the first time, giving them advice, not only on colour but also on make-up. She charges only £40 for such a session. A make-up lesson is £17 and bridal make-up is usually £30. She does not have a set price for the range of other services that she offers, for example, wardrobe consultancy and shopping visits, but will tailor the price to the needs of the individual client.

Creating the ambience

Anne is able to keep the business costs fairly low by doing most of the work from home. She has a room in the house which she uses exclusively for the colour sessions, and has designed it specifically to create the right impression on her clients. The furnishings are carefully colour coordinated and the seats are arranged to make maximum use of daylight. Natural light is important for establishing the client's correct 'season'.

When people first come to the house Anne is aware that they look closely both at the appearance of the house and, more importantly, at her own appearance to help them decide whether she is qualified to advise them. Many of them, however, will have already formed some expectation about what to expect from the friends who recommended her service in the first instance. Anne believes that first impressions are very important and can contribute greatly to the success of the session. All the clients receive a wallet of colour swatches to take away with them at the end of their session. This reminds them, when they go shopping, which colours to select and which to avoid. However, Anne encourages all her clients to 'pop back' to the house at any time to get her advice if they are unsure about any purchase.

Although she buys her make-up and the colour wallets ready prepared from one supplier, she gives them the personal touch by adding extra colours which might suit a particular individual, and she includes her personal card. With any make-up that clients may buy from her, Anne always gives them the opportunity to return items if they are not satisfied. She simply uses any unwanted items in her demonstration pack. She does not proactively sell the make-up items during the demonstrations, but finds that many clients like to buy a little something to take away as a memento of the occasion. Often they also want to be able to recreate the exact 'look' that Anne has created during the session.

Many of Anne's clients contact her after their session to tell her how the colour coordination is working out. For Anne this feedback is one of the most satisfying parts of the work. For example, one elderly client arrived for an individual session and explained that she wanted to know how to improve her appearance. Anne gave her a full colour and make-up analysis and asked her to keep in contact to tell her what a difference it had made to her life. The following day the client telephoned Anne in a very emotional state to thank her for her advice. She said that on the previous evening, when she had returned home after the session, she was sitting in the lounge knitting under a lampshade when her husband walked in, looked at her and said, 'You look very beautiful tonight dear'. The lady was absolutely astounded. She informed Anne on the telephone that he had never told her that she looked beautiful in all the years they had been married.

The future

Anne feels there are many more people who could benefit from the colour consultancy service. She is also aware of the growing number of consultants entering the market all offering a very similar package. She continues to rely on word-of-mouth to generate more clients but wonders whether she should start advertising again in the local paper to stimulate more interest. She may have as many clients as she can handle at the moment but realises that it is important to plan for the future.

Case study 4
Durham High School for Girls

History and background[1]

Durham High School for Girls is an independent day school, founded in 1884 by the Church Schools' Company. In 1911, the management of the school was vested in a local governing body, and a year later, as a result of the need to accommodate boarding pupils, it was located at Leazes House in Durham in the north of England, where it remained for more than 50 years. In 1961, the governors decided to discontinue the provision of boarding education. A proposed major road development within Durham City threatened to encroach on the grounds and playing fields, and to secure its future the school moved to its present location at Farewell Hall in 1968. It is situated on a 'greenfield' site of 10 acres on the southern outskirts of Durham, surrounded by open countryside, and with good access by road from most directions.

The school retains its Christian ethos, and this is evidenced by a strong ecclesiastical representation amongst the governors. Since concentrating once again on day education, it has built a reputation for academic excellence that is reflected in outstanding examination results at GCSE and A Level.[2] Between the years of 1997 and 2001, pupils achieved a 100 per cent pass rate at GCSE (with 65 per cent of the grades being A/A*), and a 99 per cent pass rate at A Level (with 63 per cent of the grades being at A/B). The school can attract pupils from a wide catchment area, with school transport being made available from a number of locations in the area. In the school prospectus, the Headmistress, Mrs Ann Templeman, says:

> We believe that there is more to a first-class education than acquisition of knowledge and skills. Our school is firmly based on Christian principles and we regard each individual as fundamentally important. During her time here, we hope that each girl will find the spiritual and moral resources she needs to give her integrity and direction in our modern world.

Mrs Templeman is a member of the Girls School Association, an institution that represents quality amongst independent girls' schools.

The school year runs from September to July, over three terms, and new pupils normally join in September at ages of 3, 4, 7, 9, 10, 11, or 16. Prospective parents are required to formally register their children before they can be considered for places. A non-refundable registration fee of £50 is payable at this time and a deposit fee of £100 is payable once a place is accepted. (This is set off against the final term's fees.) The two fees are not significant to the school's finances, but assist in ascertaining the true intentions of prospective parents who may register their children with a number of schools. Schools can be particularly vulnerable to 'no shows' as their income is generally determined at the start of a school year and there is little opportunity to influence it during the course of the school year. The tuition fees for the school year 2001–2 were from £1360 per term for the Nursery (3-year-olds) to £2045 per term for the 11–18-year-olds in the 'Senior House'. These are relatively high in comparison to the competition in the region. All girls are expected to eat school lunches which cost a further £115 per term.

The organisation of the school

The school is structured according to two 'Houses', the Junior House and the Senior House. The Junior House accommodates girls who are aged 3–10 years at the start of a school year, and the Senior House accommodates those aged 11–17 years at the start of a school year. Within each House, the cohorts of students are in 'forms' according to their ages. As with nearly all schools in the UK, the GCSE examinations are sat in Year 11, and the A Level examinations are sat in the 'Upper Sixth'. The table below outlines the school structure in relation to the national examinations and tests taken by the pupils.

House	Form (age)	National examinations
Junior	Nursery (3–4)	
Junior	Reception (4–5)	
Junior	Year 1 (5–6)	
Junior	Year 2 (6–7)	SAT (Key Stage 1)[3]
Junior	Year 3 (7–8)	
Junior	Year 4 (8–9)	
Junior	Year 5 (9–10)	
Junior	Year 6 (10–11)	SAT (Key Stage 2)
Senior	Year 7 (11–12)	
Senior	Year 8 (12–13)	
Senior	Year 9 (13–14)	SAT (Key Stage 3)
Senior	Year 10 (14–15)	GCSE
Senior	Year 11 (15–16)	GCSE
Senior	Lower VI (16–17)	A Level
Senior	Upper VI (17–18)	A Level

In the UK, compulsory education ends at 16 years, so girls can leave school after Year 11. Most of the girls do, however, continue through to the sixth form, although some may change school at the end of Year 11 – a feature that is not unique to this particular school.

According to the Durham High School for Girls prospectus:

The Nursery is a secure, warm place that we see as an extension to home. We look after the needs of each individual in our care – we know that if a child is happy and settled, she will learn quickly and achieve success. The children play, discover, learn and talk with adults and other children and they learn to share and show concern for others ...

Junior House provides a stimulating caring environment in which girls develop enthusiasm for learning and grow in confidence. There is a balance of academic work (including French), sport, music and many extra-curricular activities, supplemented by regular outings to the theatre, museums and places of educational interest ...

We welcome into Senior House girls who join us from a wide range of state and independent schools. Our teaching staff are highly-qualified, subject specialists, who are committed to helping each girl to make the most of her own gifts ... Girls in the first three years of the Senior House follow all the subjects of the National Curriculum, with the addition of German, as a second modern language, and Latin. We place great emphasis on the importance of an all-round education, with a balance of Arts, Sciences, practical and creative subjects.

Facilities and finance

Since moving to Farewell Hall, the school has extended its facilities by adding a sports hall, computer and audio suites, tennis courts, a new building that provides eight classrooms for the Junior House, and the Nursery. There is a purpose-built sixth form centre with a large common-room and quiet study-room. Further improvements are planned to include a science block and a library and resource centre. There are good car-parking facilities, although the influx of parents at the beginning and end of each day causes serious congestion on occasions. The single entry/exit carriageway at the front of the school becomes blocked, resulting in vehicles that are waiting to enter the school blocking the public road. The reception/lobby to the school is small and relatively unimpressive in comparison with other facilities, and in need of development. There are no seats for visitors (prospective parents) waiting for appointments and there is a lack of informative signage.

The school is totally dependent upon fee income for its operations. It has no endowments, and does not receive any public funds or grants. The normal arrangement is for fees to be paid in advance at the start of each term, and the school is now offering parents the option of spreading payments over 9 months for a fee of 3 per cent. The gross fee income is over £2.5 million per year, of which about £40 000 is available for scholarships and over £200 000 for bursaries. The former, currently worth up to 50 per cent of fees, are awarded on academic merit alone. The latter are awarded on the basis of financial need and assessed annually in the light of personal circumstances. They are awarded a percentage of fees, usually up to 50 per cent.

The people

Pupils

In the year 2001, there are 550 pupils in total at the school. To become pupils at the school, girls must go through an admissions process. Admission to the Nursery is based on an informal assessment of the child, by the school, through play. Admission to other years in the Junior House is by 'assessment, appropriate to age'. Admission to the Senior House (up to Year 11) is based on an examination, an interview and a school report. Admission to the Sixth Form is based on an interview, school report and GCSE results. Girls are unlikely to be admitted at this stage with fewer than 5 GCSE passes at Grades A–C.

In general, the pupils at the school recognise its strong academic standards, examination successes and religious education, and appreciate the pastoral care, and the opportunities for cultural activities that are offered. They often refer to the school and its staff as caring and friendly. The Sixth Form pupils do not have to wear school uniform. Nevertheless, some of the older pupils would like to have a greater freedom of choice of dress, enjoy a more liberal regime over school bounds, and have boys at the school!

They have mixed views about some of the school facilities. The ICT facilities are being upgraded, but for some pupils they are not considered as 'state-of-the-art' – lack of access to the internet being regarded as a drawback. Most of the sporting facilities are regarded as good, but the lack of a school swimming pool and of an all-weather (Astroturf) outdoor surface lead to common grumbles. Pupils are aware of the school's aim to 'promote fitness and good health through a lasting interest in sport ... and to provide something which will appeal to everyone'. Regarding sport, some pupils feel that excellence is being rewarded as part of an ethos that does not recognise effort in the same way. The majority of the pupils voice a concern about, and even a dislike of the school lunch provision. The concerns span issues such as quality, choice, quantity, presentation and catering hygiene.

The governors and staff

There are 12 members of a board of governors that oversees the strategic management of the school. The school is also a registered charity, and so the Governors have obligations as charity trustees under the 1992 and 1993 Charities Acts.

The day-to-day management of the school is delegated to the Headmistress, supported by a 'senior management team' consisting of the Deputy Headmistress, Mrs Dunsford, the Head of the Junior House, Mrs Stone, and the Bursar, Mrs Ruskin.

The teaching staff are highly qualified. In the Senior House, there are 35 teachers (31 female, 4 male). All except one have first degrees, several have Masters degrees, and two teachers have PhDs. Many graduated at the Universities of Durham or Newcastle, demonstrating a strong local connection. In the Junior House, there are 12 teachers (11 female, 1 male), all with degrees or certificates in education, supported by 4 further staff with nursery nursing qualifications. Visiting teachers provide tuition in specialist areas such as practical music and speech and drama. The pupil/ staff ratio is relatively low at 10:1. The non-teaching staff consist of a Headmistress's Secretary, Deputy Bursar, Financial Assistant, Database Manager, Senior Technician, ICT Technician, Technician, Librarian, Catering Manager, Laboratory Assistant, Head Caretaker, Assistant Caretaker, and two Receptionists.

The parents

The parents, in general, appreciate the high academic standards, the quality of teaching and very good examination results, as well as the pastoral care, religious education, and cultural activities being offered. They also see benefits from a single-sex school, and the relatively small class sizes. Half the parents had chosen to send their daughters to the school on the advice of existing parents. Groups of parents meet regularly at 'drop off' and 'pick up' times each day, and often discuss school-related matters, offering honest opinions of issues affecting the whole range of school activities. There is an active Parents' Association that has the twin aims of organising social activities and fund-raising. They are not involved in the day-to-day running of the school.

Prospective parents receive a glossy school prospectus, with 'inserts' that provide information on admissions and fees, the school staff, recent GCSE and A Level results and the university places taken up by recent school-leavers. (The school proclaims that the Sixth Form courses are 'aimed mainly at entry to Higher Education'.) A website, developed recently, also provides similar information (http://www.dhsfg.org.uk).

And finally...

The 'Welcome' in the school prospectus states:

> At Durham High School we provide a lively, friendly and caring community for girls throughout their school career, from three to 18. We encourage each one to strive for academic excellence and acquire a genuine love of learning. We also expect every girl to seek the highest standards in all areas of personal development: in art, in music, in drama, in community service and in leadership.

Notes

1. This case study was written by Tom Reay, Franke Burke, Colin McDougall and Edith Newrick, and adapted by the authors.
2. GCSE = General Certificate in Education, with a highest possible grade of A/A*. A Level = Advanced Level, with highest possible grade of A.
3. The National Curriculum for Education in the UK identifies three Key Stages. At each Key Stage, Standard Assessment Tasks (SATs) are taken by all children and are graded by school staff, subject to external moderation. For details, see the Department for Education and Skills website at http://www.dfes.gov.uk/index.htm

Case study 5
Waymark Holidays

Background

... we are celebrating 20 successful years as a tour operator. We have always specialised in walking holidays, and although we have expanded our operations into many different countries, we still prefer to concentrate our attention on the activity we know best – walking.

(*'Walk with Waymark', 1994 Holiday Brochure*)

We try to give our customers the best value for money, by making sure that they go on a holiday that's just right for them ... 70% of our business is from regular customers who come back.

(*Peter Chapman, Director, Waymark Holidays*)

Waymark Holidays was founded in 1974 by two people, Peggy Hounslow and Noel Vincent, who had been running the holiday side of the Ramblers' Association for several years. Peggy Hounslow was the Managing Director of Ramblers Holidays and Noel Vincent was Managing Director of 'Wings', another subsidiary of the Ramblers' Association. They both wished to have more freedom to organise holidays their own way so they left Ramblers and set up their own company, Waymark Holidays, which operated initially from a bedroom, then from a cellar, and finally from a ground floor office in Fulham, London. In 1991, the company moved to its present office on the second floor of a two-storey office block in Slough, 20 miles west of London. Waymark Holidays is a specialist direct sell tour operator offering two related types of holiday: walking holidays and cross-country skiing holidays. In 1993, they sold 2400 walking holidays based on their 'Walk with Waymark' brochure, and 1800 cross-country skiing holidays, based on their 'Cross-Country Skiing with Waymark' brochure.

Peggy Hounslow and Noel Vincent retired in 1984, and the company is now run by three director/shareholders, Peter Chapman, Martin Read and Stuart Montgomery, supported by four full-time salaried salespeople and three part-time administrative/clerical staff.

The UK tour operators industry

Between April 1990 and March 1991, the four largest UK tour operators – Thomson Holidays, ILG Travel Ltd, Owners Abroad and Airtours – accounted for 65.5 per cent of the 13 million holidays sold (Key Note Publications Ltd, 1991). The largest tour operator, Thomson Holidays, trading under the names of Thomson Holidays, Horizon Holidays, Portland Holidays and Sky Tours, accounted for 4.3 million holidays (33.2 per cent). ILG Travel Ltd went into receivership in March 1991 but the level of concentration has not changed significantly as Airtours has been the major beneficiary of ILG's collapse.

A further twenty-five operators, offering between 46 000 and 320 000 holidays per year, account for 16.3 per cent of the volume, whilst the remaining 18.2 per cent is shared between an unspecified number of small operators offering 45 000 or less holidays per year. Waymark fall into this latter group with 4000 holidays per year. For every holiday Waymark sells, Thomson sells 1000.

Polarisation of service operations of tour operators

The largest operators, such as Thomson and Airtours, are competing on price and volume. They measure their customers in millions and sell holidays primarily through the intermediary of a travel agent. They employ charter flights, and may own their own airline. For example, Thomson owns Britannia Airways, Owners Abroad owns Air 2000 and Airtours owns Airtours International. These tour operators will normally service their short-haul business through charter flights on their own airline.

They strive for efficiency in the processing of bookings by becoming highly computerised. For example, nobody, not even a travel agent, can telephone Thomson to book a holiday – a direct computer-to-computer access is required to do this. No telephone number is given on any Thomson holiday brochure. Computerised booking systems are accurate and efficient and the customer in the travel agency can have immediate feedback on availability of hotels and flights and guaranteed bookings 'on the spot'. The only personal service which customers receive is that offered by the travel agent employees.

At the other extreme, Waymark Holidays sell direct to the customer, offer a specialised service in a niche market, and make a positive effort to discuss, on the telephone, special requirements by customers for their holiday. They offer a highly personalised service, and are prepared to talk to customers at length even though it is more expensive to operate such a service in such low quantities.According to Peter Chapman, customer enquiries can range from the very general, 'What's the weather going to be like in Austria next June?', to the very specific, 'I went with you to Sardinia last year, and am considering Samos [Greece] this year. Will I like the hotel?' Other calls may request general advice, 'I would like a more strenuous holiday than last year. What do you suggest?' or 'How many people are already booked on the holiday? What are their ages?' Virtually all their customers pay by cheque. Some overseas customers may pay by credit card, for which they are charged an additional £15 per person.

As Peter Chapman's quote at the beginning of the case shows, Waymark get to know, personally, many of their customers, some of whom book Waymark Holidays two, three or four times a year, and these customers are often on first name terms with the Waymark representatives. Nearly all the holidays use seats on scheduled flights with, for example, British Airways, Swissair, Austrian Airlines, Scandinavian Airlines or Lufthansa.

At Waymark, they feel that the middle-sized tour operators, who are not big enough to compete on price and volume with Thomson, Owners Abroad and Airtours, but are too big to offer personal services and specialisation, may find it a struggle to position themselves in the future in the highly competitive market.

Waymark's main competitors are other small tour operators offering specialist walking or cross-country skiing holidays. There are 10 to 12 companies who offer walking or 'soft adventure' holidays; for example, 'Ramblers', 'Headwater', 'Inn-Travel', 'Exodus' and 'Explore'. None of them offers a precisely comparable programme to Waymark but there are some considerable overlaps. They all use direct-sell methods, believing that the ability to direct customers to the right holiday would be lost if the holiday was just being processed by a travel agent. 'The travel agent is just interested in making a booking, not if it is the right holiday for that person.' Selling direct to the customer also saves on the commission to be paid to a travel agent. On the skiing side, there are fewer competitors, with only two or three operators offering cross-country skiing holidays. Waymark deliberately keep out of the downhill skiing holidays offered by the middle- to large-size operators. They have also rejected the urge to offer what are perceived to be related specialist holidays such as cycling, canoeing or horse-riding. As Peter Chapman observes: 'We don't know anything about them. We don't want to branch out into things we don't understand. We are all enthusiastic about walking and cross-country skiing and that's all we want to do.'

Features of a Waymark Holiday

Customers who book a holiday with Waymark will be struck by two features in particular which are not present on a more conventional package holiday offered by the larger tour operators.

First, all holidays are graded according to how strenuous they are felt to be. Figure CS 5.1 shows the grading criteria specified in the 'Walk with Waymark' brochure. A similar section appears in the 'Cross-Country Ski-ing with Waymark' brochure. Waymark employees are extremely concerned to ensure that customers choose a grade of holiday that is suitable. In addition to the information given in the brochure, they take a lot of time discussing, by telephone, the suitability of a particular holiday for a customer. There have been occasions where, if the Waymark representative does not believe that a customer is physically capable of a holiday, the booking will be refused. They know from experience that if someone goes on a Grade 3 holiday, but is only capable of Grade 1 walking, that person will struggle and the experience is bad for all concerned. The Waymark philosophy is

GRADING OF HOLIDAYS

We grade our holidays from 1 to 5. Among mountains, distance is a poor guide; hours of walking and amount of ascent are better indication of how strenuous a holiday will be. Bear in mind, though, that these are rough estimates: on some days the hours of walking and amount of ascent may exceed these figures. Also remember tht hours of walking exclude stops for refreshments etc. Sometimes a combined grade is shown e.g. "Grade 3/4"; this means that some days will be at Grade 3, other Grade 4.

Choosing a grade. Bad or even hot weather can make a holiday more strenuous. Even at Grades 2 and 3, bad weater in mountains can mean walking across snow; we also emphasise that mountain paths abroad can be much steeper than in British hills, and tht there may be some degree of exposure at times on high mountain paths. Bear in mind that the walking at higher grades tends to be at a faster pace than at lower grades. So please compare theholidays with your own experience, and don't try something too tough for your first time abroad. If you are in doubt, we are always ready to help you choose a holiday within your capabilities.

Grade 1. Walking mostly on paths, sometimes rough underfoot, about four hours a day. Ascent in general each day less than 300m. Good walking shoes would do but take boots if you are used to them.

Grade 2. About five hours a day. These holidays may be in hill country, or at mountain centres, mostly on paths. In hill country there may be some longer days on modest gradients. Ascent in general each day less than 500m. On a continuous walking tour it is essential that you consider your ability to walk every day except when a rest day has been planned - a weak link spoils not only your own but everyone's holiday. boots advisable.

Δ**Indicates that most of the walking on these Grade 2 holidays is in mountainous terrain where paths are often steep; please consider this when booking. Ascent in general each day up to 1000m.**

Grade 3. About five/six hours a day walking, sometimes off paths, and occasionally scrambling*. Be prepared for steep ascents and descents. Ascent in general each day up to 1000m. Boots essential.

Grade 4. About seven hours a day walking, some scrambling*. Across the snow-line at times. Steep ascents and descents perhaps for 3–4 hours at a time. Ascent in general each day up to 1500m. Boots essential.

Grade 5. Long days of about eight hours' walking, with scrambling* in big mountains and remote terrain. Often above the snow-line and across glaciers. Ascent in general each day 1500-2000m. Boots are essential, and ice axe, crampons and climbing harness are often needed – see holiday description for details.

*****Scrambling** means that hands as well as feet are used for ascent or descent. Previous experience is not necessary for easy scrambles although a good head for heights will be required at grades 3, 4 and 5. On most of our holidays at Grade 4 and 5, the leader will carry a rope in case it is needed for security, but none of our holidays involve technical climbing.

Mountain Hut Tours. For these you have to carry a full rucksack which slows the pace and increases the grade and we have to be satisfied tht you have sufficient previous experiences such as walking in big mountains and carrying a full pack. If in doubt try our Stubai Alps holiday, which combines one week at a centre with another on a hut tour.

Sightseeing and Wildlife. Some holidays are particularly well suited for visiting places of interest and viewing wildlife. Where this is mentioned in the text, time will be allowed for sightseeing but it does not lower the grade of walking on other days.

Figure CS 5.1 Grading of Waymark Holidays

summed up by Peter Chapman: 'You've got to deliver what you promise. I'd rather turn a booking away than accept it and make a mess of it.'

For their many regular customers, who are already familiar with, and realistic about, the gradings, discussions may centre on moving up a grade, or on the weather in a completely different location. For the new customers, Waymark have to base their initial advice on information contained on the booking form, where customers are asked to give details of previous walking experience, if booking a holiday of Grade 2 or above (or of any previous skiing experience, for the cross-country skiing holidays). Sometimes, the Waymark staff must politely inform customers who have, for example, been trekking in the Himalayas, that they have Grade 2 experience, and would be ill-equipped to take a Grade 5 holiday in the Alps. The two experiences are very different physically. A more common piece of advice is to regular walkers in the UK, who frequent Scotland and the Lake District where it is generally cool, that walking on a sunny day in Switzerland can be much hotter and that, on their first visit, they should avoid a Grade 4 or Grade 5 holiday.

Secondly, customers on a Waymark holiday will be members of a party or group of walkers/skiers for the whole period of the holiday. Parties, of up to 16 people per holiday, have the services of a leader appointed by Waymark (see below). The compatibility of the group members is an important aspect of the total holiday experience, as evidenced by some of the customer telephone calls to Waymark. People will say that they are booking another holiday because they had an enjoyable group experience last year. The walking was good, but it was the people who made the holiday memorable. They will ask about ages of other group members, the gender mix and whether it is mainly singles or couples.

In the past, Waymark made some attempt to 'manage' groups, for example to balance the sexes, but now they would just rather give general group details and leave it to the customer. On occasions they may advise a potential customer that he/she is 20 years younger than the rest of the party, or that he is the only male in a group, but this is to point out a possible problem rather than dictate the group make-up. On very rare occasions, a customer may write to complain about not being warned of the structure of the group. For example, one lady commented that on a particular holiday she was the only single person, and that in the evenings most couples went to their rooms leaving her at a loose end. Such an experience is unusual as most Waymark customers, single or not, enjoy the wider group camaraderie.

Specialised services

As a small company dealing directly with customers, Waymark is sometimes in a position to offer specialised services to individuals or groups. For example, a customer may ring to say that he is on a business trip to Scandinavia and would like to add on a skiing holiday at the end of it, so he only wants the back-end of the advertised holiday. Or another may ring to say that, as her daughter lives in Switzerland, she would like to fly out three days earlier to stay with her before joining the party.

Such requests can often be accommodated. If it can be done, it secures a booking and the customers remember Waymark. Giving personal service like that, it is felt, leads to satisfaction and a high probability of a repeat buy in the following year. There are occasions when holidays may go wrong. Waymark will seek every means to recover such situations. Peter Chapman recalled a case of a party who were on a 14-day tour of Mont Blanc, staying in mountain huts. The leader of the party was not performing well and had lost confidence after some navigational errors at the beginning of the holiday. His stress was clear to the whole party and he was encouraged by the group to telephone Waymark. Waymark had to act quickly to save a potentially embarrassing situation. To solve the problem they (i) brought the leader home and asked a willing customer to take the balance of funds for the hut accommodation (almost £3,000), the maps, and to keep the group going for a day, and (ii) tracked down another leader by radio telephone who was just finishing a tour in Austria and asked him to take the train from Innsbruck, through Switzerland to Geneva and meet up with the other group. The new leader took over and the remainder of the holiday was very successful. Waymark paid each member of the party £50 compensation, and received several complimentary letters thanking them for acting so quickly and praising the professionalism of the replacement leader.

Another case where Waymark was able to act quickly was when a customer had left an airline ticket in a taxi. To save embarrassment, the customer had bought a new ticket at the airport by credit card and not told anybody. The taxi driver handed in the original ticket to Swissair who contacted Waymark.

The customer was booked on a remote holiday in Italy and the leader confirmed that he was actually there. Waymark agreed to ask Swissair if the customer could have his money back. Swissair was understanding and gave a credit card refund before the credit card bill had to be paid. So it cost the customer nothing. The problem would never have come to light but for the honest taxi-driver; but when it did Waymark was able to act.

Relationships with hotels and airlines

Waymark believe in long-term relationships with airlines and hotels, just as they nurture long-term relationships with customers. By such means 'everyone knows what they are expecting and what they can deliver. If you keep changing holidays, hotels and airlines, there's always the opportunity for things to go wrong.'

Waymark prefer to deal with small hotel-keepers in each country. They believe that the similarity in attitudes, business practice and preferences for such hoteliers far outweighs any national or cultural differences. Small hotel-keepers in France, Greece or Austria all like to be treated fairly and plan well in advance. Like Waymark, they also have many faithful customers who return every year. To build up a long-term relationship, Waymark will start small and then put in more groups per year if it is popular. Small family-run hotels are preferred by Waymark customers, many of whom stay in five-star hotels on business, because of their character and charm.

Clearly some holidays have 'product lifetime', and after a promising start begin to 'fade' after three or four years. Eventually such holidays have to be phased out. Some are a failure from the outset. Many holidays, however, have been operated successfully for 15 years or more, operating on virtually the same formula throughout.

It is also important for Waymark to build up strong relationships with airlines as nearly all their holidays use scheduled flights. Their dealings with the airlines are based on 'confidence and trust' built up over many years. A Waymark representative may need to ask British Airways, for example, for 20 seats on a high-season date next year. British Airways' positive response will be based on their experience with the company. They would not wish to reserve 20 seats a year in advance to a company who may return them, unsold, a month in advance. According to Peter Chapman, 'Having a track record of doing what you say you are going to do is extremely important if you want to get seats on a busy day. We definitely benefit from having 20 years in the business and treating people right that is, as we would like to be treated.'

Information technology

Waymark have a computerised mailing list and invoicing system. Unlike the larger operators they do not have a computerised reservation system. They have decided not to do so in order to maintain flexibility and variations in holidays as part of their service. Such flexibility would be difficult, if not impossible, to offer through a computer programme. They use a manual ledger with relevant information, for instance, 'Coming home two days later', on each customer booking, and that is easily kept and understood.

Because many airlines are moving to computerised bookings, particularly for low volume tickets, Waymark have to use a viewdata system, 'FASTRAK', to make such bookings. Without the system they could not book APEX tickets with many airlines. As the airlines become more computerised, even routine information on passenger details, for example, names and ages, will have to be input directly to their computer and Waymark's current practice of sending such details by fax will no longer be acceptable to them.

Party leaders

Each party on a Waymark holiday is in the charge of a leader. Waymark use about 200 volunteer leaders. They tend to be people in early retirement or those who take two or three weeks of their own holiday to be party leaders. The basic requirements of a leader are: (i) must be a keen walker and knowledgeable about navigation and safety in the hills (the number one priority is that a leader can take people out and bring them back safely); (ii) must speak the language of the country they are in, as most hotel managers who deal with Waymark do not speak English; (iii) must be a caring person who is doing the job because he/she wants to give people a good holiday; and (iv) must have common sense and the initiative to cope with the unexpected.

Every year, a few new leaders are appointed as replacements, or for new destinations. Waymark will interview them, take up references and check their credentials. Through the interview questions, Waymark need to know if the person takes a caring attitude and will look after customers. They wish to reject candidates whose first priority is to have a free holiday. A disappointing leader can affect the enjoyment of a holiday. A good leader will ensure that 'the personal service we give in the office is carried through into the "field"'. Whilst other companies make leaders attend extensive training programmes, not only in navigation but also in, for example, how to organise a country dancing evening, Waymark have chosen not to. Their philosophy of long-term relationships extends to leader appointments and many leaders have been with them for all 20 years.

Leaders are given quite a lot of initiative. For example, in Greece where holidays are on a 'bed and breakfast' basis, leaders have the money to buy evening meals and will choose restaurants and arrange good value deals. They will choose the itinerary of walks from notes provided by Waymark and are free to investigate other suitable walks. If there is any crisis, a leader will be expected to offer three or four possible courses of action to the Waymark office rather than saying, 'I've got a problem. What can I do?'

Peter Chapman reckons that there are about 20 real 'stars' with big fan-clubs. Piles of unsolicited mail are received about such leaders, extolling the virtues of putting in the extra ounce of effort, preparing well beforehand, keeping the party well informed and explaining what is going on. Conversely, where a leader is disappointing, Waymark has very rarely received a telephone call during the holiday from concerned customers. In some cases a replacement leader may have to be flown out.

Publicity and promotion

Of the 30 per cent of customers who are new each year, half come through responses to media advertising/public relations and the other half through personal recommendations. Regarding the latter, it is known that many walkers belong to rambling clubs and when people are rambling they talk about holidays. Waymark have benefited from such word-of-mouth, but are very aware that bad news about a holiday will also gain a wide circulation.

They pay to advertise in the national 'quality' press – *The Daily Telegraph*, *The Independent* and *The Guardian* and in specialist magazines such as *The Great Outdoors*, *Trailwalker* and *Country Walking*, and have used these publications for many years. They believe in the public relations benefit of persuading a journalist to take one of their holidays and write about it. Figure CS 5.2 contains extracts from an article in *The Daily Telegraph* on 1 January 1994, about the cross-country skiing holiday to Lapland and Murmansk. Such an article generates more telephone calls than a paid advertisement.

We met for breakfast at a five star hotel in Helsinki. The 61-year-old Wakeling twins first caught the eye. In a beaver-tailed Davy Crockett hat, and a home-made waistcoat of patched reindeer, rabbit and fox, Derrick looked every inch the backwoods trapper stepping from the pages of Jack London. Derrick is psychic and lives in Suffolk, where he makes jewellery.

Edwin (the elder, by half an hour) lives at the foot of Cairngorm and knows as much about reindeer as any Lapp, having managed a herd there for years. 'Ach, Aviemore's so polluted now,' he told me apologetically, 'I'm not sure I can stay there. But where else would I live?'

My fellow trekkers were certainly a diverse bunch, as varied in age and occupation as you could imagine. The journey may smack of macho romanticism, but attracted as many women as men. Toni, an agronomist and pillar of the West Yorks Cross-Country Ski Club, was sure the trip would be too arduous for her husband and left him to water the plants.

A DTI civil servant, Richard, accompanied by his wife Anne and student daughter, were our new-kit contingent – new skis, sleeping bags, clothes, packs … no doubt even their toothbrushes were new. Anne and Richard take turns to choose holidays. This year was Richard's turn. Fine-boned Anne looked as fragile as a teacup and slightly nervous.

A chemistry lecturer from Sheffield University came with his wife. A cancer research epidemiologist brought her boyfriend. Jackie, a teacher at a Bristol comprehensive, was the only one of us with the sense to bring a supply of alcohol.

All these people were regular Waymarkers, as they call themselves, although few had tackled cross-country ski tours in regions as remote as Lapland … Our guide, David Lane, completed the group. A cartographer, orienteer and professional group leader at an activity centre in the Highlands, he oozed competence.

By the end of that first breakfast, at least we knew we would not lack conversation while huddled around the camp fire hundreds of miles from the nearest television set … Everyone found something useful to do. The chemistry professor fetched ice and water from the lake. The psychic silversmith split logs, which the DTI man carried. The agronomist made tea. For any outdoor task we had to wear skis, or sink waist-deep in soft snow … After a two-hour pancake-making competition, the civil servant and I skied across to the sauna, stoked the stove, threw water on hot coals to get a good sweat running before the roll in the snow without which no visit to the Arctic would be complete. After a few rolls and sauna re-entries, the tingle factor was quite high enough, and we decided to forgo the Finnish sauna's traditional climax, flagellation by birch branches. Even Waymarkers recognise limits to masochism … We exchanged addresses before parting and promised to keep in touch. Holiday friendships usually prove as durable as footprints in the sand, but we felt confident that ours would last. That may be the most satisfying souvenir of our Arctic adventure.

We have kept in touch, too, discussing plans for a return visit to Lapland. Once you get a taste for adventure, there is no denying the call of the wild.

Figure CS 5.2 Extract from *The Daily Telegraph*, 1 January 1994

FLIGHTS FROM LOCAL AIRPORTS

We are always grateful when customers take the trouble to write in with suggestions and queries. One of the favourite topics is the question of why we can't make more use of local airports instead of concentrating on Heathrow and Gatwick

Sometimes the answer is simply that no direct flights exist from your local airport to the foreign destination. Often if such flights do exist they are charters–and this opens up the whole debate over whether we should use scheduled or charter services for our customers– in using scheduled services rather than charter flights. Advantages such as:
● scheduled timetables are fixed many months in advance
● scheduled services offer more convenient departure and arrival times
● scheduled services suffer from fewer delays
● scheduled services have shorter check-in-times
● there is better on-board service with scheduled flights. The only significant disadvantage is tht the vast majority of scheduled services to overseas destinations fly out of Heathrow or Gatwick, with even the fast-growing Manchester airport still some way behind.

On balance, because we know that our customers appreciate the benefits of scheduled flights, we use them wherever there is a direct service; and only use charters when destinations are not served by direct scheduled flights. This applies to our holidays to Corsica, Crete, the Pindos in Greece and southern Turkey. For these holidays there are flights from both Gatwick and various local airports.

For holidays using Munich, Zurich and Geneva airports the situation is better and we can regularly offer flights out of Manchester as well as Birmingham–and for Munich we can also offer flights from Glasgow.

One alternative–although we recognise this would add to the cost of your trip–might be to take a connecting domestic flight with British Midland or British Airways, which we can organise on your behalf.

Please call us if you would like further details.

LATE AVAILABILITY

If you still haven't got your summer holiday planned, don't panic. We still have places on a number of trips, many of which depart later in the season so there is plenty of time to prepare. Here is just a sample of what's on offer: (Brochure page number in brackets).

– KERRY (4) 7 nights: 31 July, 28 August, 23 October.
– WICKLOW MOUNTAINS (5) 7 nights: 24 July, 4 September.
– TOUR THROUGH SAVOY (*) 14 Nights: 29 ugust, 12 September.
– St SAVIN (9) 7 nights: 4, 11 September.
– GORGE OF THE ALLIER (10) 14 Nights: 4, 11 September.
– BRITTANY (12) 7 & 8 nights: 11, 19 September.
– SOUTHERN CEVENNES (13) 7 & 10 nights: 18, 25 September.
– MILOS (14) 14 nights: 24 September, 8 October.
– MOUNTAINS & SEA IN CYPRUS 16) 7 & 14 nights: 27 September, 11, 24 October.
– WESTERN TAURUS (17) 15 NIGHTS: 20 September.
– SENDAS (20) 7 & 10 nights: 8 August, 22 August, 26 September, 3, 24, 31 October.
– JIMENA DE L FRONTERA (20) 7 & 10 nights: 30 September, 10, 24 October.
– TOUR IN ANDALUCIA (21) 7 & 10 nights: 26 September, 17 October.
– TRINS (24) 10 & 14 nights: 10 July, 7, 21 August, 11 September.
– AROSA (26) 10 nights: 14, 27 August.
– TOUR D'OISANS (32) 14 nights: 17, 31 July, 14 August.
– PEAKS OF THE PYRENEES (33) 14 nights: 22 August.

WAYMARK HOLIDAYS: ☎

Figure CS 5.3 'Waymark News'

Regular customers are automatically on the brochure mailing list. People who ask for a brochure for the first time get two brochures, the second in 12 months' time even if they did not book a holiday. If they do not book on the second occasion they are taken off the mailing list. Regular summer customers receive a newsletter in May/June (see Figure CS 5.3), and this always produces another 'mini-surge' of bookings for about a month.

Service quality and customer expectations

Peter Chapman believes that service quality is about trying to understand what a customer wants from his holiday and then delivering it. He does not believe that Waymark will have a satisfied customer if they have not understood at the beginning what he/she wants. To emphasise this point, he can recount a case when three ladies were very dissatisfied with a holiday on a Greek island at Easter. They had booked late and taken an available holiday. It became clear that they had expected a fortnight in the sunshine in a standard hotel, and had never been to Greece before or on a walking holiday. The weather was poor and wet and the hotel owner forgot to heat the water some days. The ladies complained about the basic hotel and sought compensation for the holiday. The other members of the group felt that such compensation was not necessary, as the weather and Greek hotel idiosyncrasies were not Waymark's fault.

Waymark, however, feel that they should have better gauged the ladies' expectations through questioning their hotel preferences. As soon as they had established that a room with modern bathroom facilities and plenty of hot water was important, they could have advised against a Greek holiday. They have a number of questions which may be used to assess customer expectations; for example, 'Do you want a strenuous or easy walking holiday?', 'Do you want a comfortable hotel, or are you prepared to rough it?', 'Do you want guaranteed sunshine, or do you wish to go into the mountains (where it may be sunny or it may be wet)?'

Finding out what the customer wants is not enough if it is not delivered. Waymark personnel are all located in the same office and communicate regularly with each other. By this means, potential problems can be solved internally before they get to the customer stage. They process thousands of details of information and get it right at least 99 per cent of the time. This is important because getting one small detail wrong can affect delivery and ruin someone's holiday.

Like other operators, no single individual employee looks after all aspects of a customer's holiday. Different employees are responsible for different airlines and different groups of hotels. The smallness of the Waymark set-up is believed to be important in maintaining communication on hotels and airlines bookings, especially for the personalised requests.

Market research, trends and the future

Two very large box-files contain the unsolicited mail, from customers, and the responses from Waymark representatives. This is one of the reasons why

Waymark can monitor customer likes and dislikes. Many letters are motivated by customers' wishes to assist Waymark's future planning. For example, the overall holiday is highly praised apart from one small hitch that the customer wishes to draw to their attention. Many customers send photographs of their holiday. Waymark run a photograph competition and pay £20 for each photograph subsequently published in a brochure. The senders of the three best photographs are offered the opportunity of a free deposit for their next holiday.

More formal market research is carried out by sending approximately 10 per cent of customers a questionnaire. Holidays are chosen at random and all customers on that holiday will be included in the survey. Questions cover such areas as the food, the leader, the brochure, the service provided, reasons for booking the holiday, and what future holidays are being considered. One question, in particular, yielded some interesting results. When customers were asked 'In which other countries would you like to see us operating?', about 50 per cent said they would like a holiday in Ireland. This surprised the Waymark staff who felt that, with Ireland being close to Britain and easy to get to, people would not want to book through a tour operator. Nevertheless, they put Ireland in the brochure and it has been successful. They now believe that, because of the relative lack of good maps and a network of footpaths in Ireland, the services of a leader with such knowledge is the key factor in the customer choice.

Eastern Europe is the second most frequently requested destination. Waymark are reluctant to offer holidays in many eastern European destinations at this time because the standards of services and hotels are being compared unfavourably by customers with those in western Europe. They are 'soft-pedalling' in eastern Europe at the moment, hoping that in five to ten years' time the levels of service will be comparable to those in, say, Switzerland.

Customers are becoming more demanding each year, as their expectations rise. The travel industry in general has a poor reputation for delivering brochure promises, and customers are made more aware of their legal rights. Whilst Waymark's record on delivering promises is excellent, they have noticed some trends in customer expectations over the last five to ten years. For example, it is now very difficult to sell rooms without private facilities, whereas ten years ago such rooms were generally acceptable for walking holidays. Also, more and more people are demanding flights from their local airports, rather than London. People are turning down a holiday if they cannot fly from Manchester. A few years ago, customers would be delighted by a Manchester flight. Now they want a Manchester flight and are demanding that they don't have to wait two hours at their destination for the other people to arrive from London!

Over the last five years, there has been a trend for people to look to Waymark for walking holidays in the southern European destinations of Greece, Italy and Spain, as opposed to the 'heartland' of walking holidays; that is, the Swiss and Austrian Alps. Some middle/large tour operators are now offering 'lakes and mountains' brochures, and between them it is estimated that they may take 200 to 300 Alpine bookings from Waymark.

Waymark is not unduly worried, as the trend has served to flatten out their summer season. Instead of having a very large peak of bookings in July and August of each year, they now have a flatter pattern of booking extending from March to October. Holidays in the Alps are still booked mainly in July and August, but there are now significant bookings in Greece and Spain in the 'shoulder' months.

And finally...

We have always believed it is right to concentrate on what we do best, and although our activities now cover many countries, we still specialise in cross-country ski-ing. Much of our success over the past two decades has been due to the loyalty of our regular customers, many of whom travel with us every year – in some cases twice or even three times per season – and for this we extend our sincere thanks.

(From 'Cross-Country Ski-ing with Waymark')

Case study 6
An individual experience with UK National Health care

Introduction and background

The case is based on the provision of UK National Health care as experienced by an individual patient, a male in his mid-forties, over a finite period. As it represents one person's feelings and perceptions, and cannot possibly be a comprehensive overview, it is written in the first person. Nevertheless, it is felt that a view of the service from a patient's perspective is of interest and value. Whilst the account is of an actual experience, some details have been omitted, and the names of all individuals have been changed.

The patient, John Smith, had originally been referred to a hospital consultant surgeon, Mr Stuart, to examine a growth on the back of his left thigh. Mr Stuart's opinion was that the growth was a malignant melanoma. It would need to be removed by surgery, and tests on the skin tissues would determine whether it was malignant or benign. The surgery took place three weeks later, under general anaesthetic, and John Smith went home the same day. The case starts when, one week later, he returned to the hospital outpatient's department for a check-up and the test results.

The outpatient department

The appointment for the outpatient clinic was for 9.30 am. The letter emphasised that patients would be seen in order of appointment times, not by order of arrival. I arrived about 9.20 am, the receptionist retrieved my file and I was directed to take a seat in an adjacent waiting area. There were seats for about 30 people, all facing the same direction. After sitting down, I realised that there were just as many seats in another waiting area to my left, behind a partition. In front of me were two whiteboards, each with hand-written messages on them. The first said 'Welcome to Mr Stuart's Clinic' and gave the names of three nurses in attendance, including a 'named nurse'. The message also stated that there were 57 patients for the clinic, and that the nurses would be willing to answer any queries. On the other whiteboard were similar details for Dr Jones's clinic. He only had 37 patients.

I was not sure what would happen next. The procedure seemed to consist of nurses (presumably the 'named nurses') standing in front of the two waiting areas and calling out names. With the general noise and movement in and out of the waiting areas, it was very difficult to hear the names being called. For the hard of hearing it would have been impossible. By 10.00 am, having witnessed the calling of many people who had arrived after me, I began to think that I had missed my call. I had also calculated that, even at five minutes per person, it would take almost five hours to see 57 patients. By 10.30 am, I sought to ask a nurse about my appointment. As I rose, the name Joan Smith was called. I assumed that it was me (correctly) and the nurse apologised for the mistake. She was having 'one of those days'.

I was then asked to sit on one of three chairs in a separate waiting area opposite the door to the clinic. The further wait did not concern me as I now knew I was not forgotten. It only took a further five minutes before I was called in. Mr Stuart was not there and I was directed to a tall man in a white coat who did not introduce himself but politely asked me to sit down. (Weeks later, I found out that he was Mr Stuart's registrar.) I had assumed that he would know the details of my case, and so I was taken aback by his first question, 'What was the operation for?' Subsequently, when contemplating the events, I acknowledged that it would be impossible for a single person to know details of 57 patients (or the proportion of the 57 patients who were not seen directly by the nurses). At the time, I felt let down – no Mr Stuart, only a doctor unfamiliar with my case. When it was clarified that it was my leg that was to be seen, he showed me to a side room and asked me to lie on a raised bed. He would be back in a moment.

When he came back, he told me that the tests on the first operation had confirmed that it was a malignant melanoma and that I would have to undergo a further operation to remove skin tissue from the wound and replace it with a skin graft. This would take place in two or three weeks' time. I had not prepared myself for another operation so soon after the first and had been hoping that, after all, the growth was benign. I did not know what was involved with a skin graft. All I could ask was whether I would need a hospital stay and he confirmed that I would be in hospital for a few days. I felt very down after leaving the clinic, but after talking things through with my wife, family and friends I came to terms with the position very quickly and returned to work as normal.

Waiting for the operation

The registrar had said that they would write to me to let me know when I would be admitted to hospital. After informing my employers of the situation, I carried on working and waited for my letter. With no news after nearly three weeks, I decided to ring the hospital. Mr Stuart's secretary, a very helpful and efficient person, informed me that my name was not down for the next two weeks. She promised to have a word with Mr Stuart the next day and telephone me back. She rang back the next day to say that there had been some cancellations, and that I was to be admitted to Ward 3 on the following Sunday for a Monday morning operation. I asked how long I would be in hospital. After seeking advice, she rang back to say that I would not be out before the Friday following the operation. At the time, I thought that this meant that I would be out on the Friday unless there were any complications.

She explained that further details were in the post and I received them the following day. They consisted of a letter stating the admission day/time, ward number and other requirements (for example, urine sample), a form to be filled in with basic details (name, address, date of birth, medical card number) and a 'Welcome to Ward 3: Information for Patients and Visitors' pamphlet. The latter was professionally presented and provided

1.   the address and direct telephone line of the ward,

2.   further details on admission,

3.   information on Ward 3 including visiting times and practices and items which are need for a hospital stay,

4.   a description of a typical day in Ward 3,

5.   a description of the medical staff and their uniforms, and

6.   details of public transport to the hospital. Having never stayed overnight in a hospital, this pamphlet was very helpful. I also consulted it on several occasions during my stay.

The covering letter had requested that I ring the ward before making my journey, to check that there was a bed available. Although emergencies must have priorities on beds, this did concern me as I was psychologically prepared for admission on the Sunday and had made both work and domestic arrangements for it.

My previous stays in a hospital ward had been for less than a full day. However, I had formed certain views of hospital life. Three aspects, I believed, would be difficult to manage. First, I assumed that, based on previous experience, topics of conversations between patients would be dominated by hospital food and meal times and/or the various illnesses/operations. Second, I assumed that most of the patients would be 60 years of age or over, suffering from a variety of age-related complaints. Third, I had misgivings about the artificially intimate environment, where men who had never previously met would be spending days and nights together, each with little privacy. I even decided to borrow my son's 'Walkman', not just to listen to music on the radio, but because the headphones would give a visible 'do not disturb' sign to other patients.

The admission day

Having established that a bed was available, I arrived, as requested, at 10.00 am on the Sunday. In fact, only about half of the twenty beds were occupied and the staff nurse offered me a choice of beds. I chose bed 9 (see Figure

CS 6.1) in a part of the ward which was less occupied. The nurse told me that there would not be much happening on the Sunday, and that I had been admitted the day before my operation to 'reserve the bed'. This seemed odd in view of the number of unoccupied beds. Over the course of the next seven

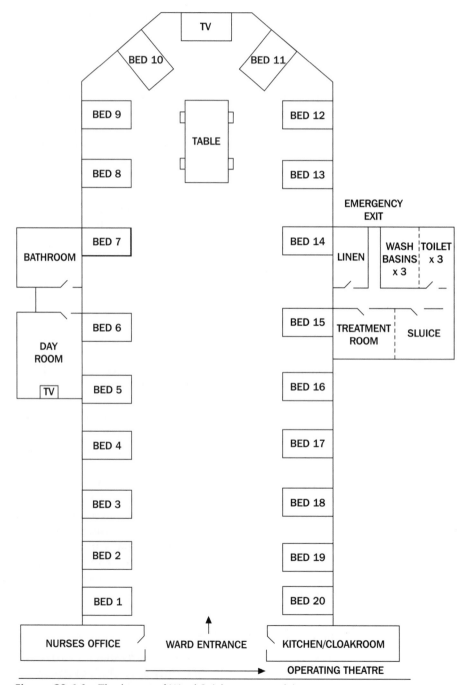

Figure CS 6.1   The layout of Ward 3 (almost to scale)

hours I had various tests – blood pressure, pulse, temperature, blood sample – and was visited by the anaesthetist and Mr Stuart. I was impressed by the fact that the consultant surgeon came in on a Sunday. He explained that the skin would be taken from the front of the right thigh for the graft. Shortly after, both legs were shaved above the knee by a male student nurse. My overall impression, however, was that what was done on the Sunday could have been carried out on Monday, as was the case for day patients. Consequently, the time passed very slowly.

By about 12 noon, I had seen all parts of the ward, including the toilets, bathroom and day room. The pamphlet had described the ward as a 'Nightingale' type ward. Florence Nightingale herself would have found no problem with orientation inside Ward 3. The building was at least 80 years old, and apart from technological advances such as oxygen supply points and radio headphones by each bed, the overall design, shown in Figure CS 6.1, has probably changed little over the period. The beds seemed very close together. Adjacent patients could easily touch hands whilst lying down! Visitors had difficulty in placing chairs beside the bed. I felt that the main design objective was to get as many beds in the available space as possible.

The ceiling was very high and the large bare walls were clean but cold-looking. There were several very large windows that gave plenty of light during the day. At night when the curtains were drawn, the flowered patterns of the curtains, at the windows and round the beds, dominated everything. Normally, however, the walls were bare, the linoleum-covered floors were bare, and there was very little colour. Each patient had a small chest of drawers, but there was only enough room to keep a bottle of water and a glass on the surface. I would have liked to display 'get-well' cards on the wall, but formed the impression that it would not be right. I had also observed my fellow patients. My prior misgivings were confirmed. They all appeared older than me and some were unable to move without assistance. Two or three were very hard of hearing. I had my first encounter with a patient with a catheter (a tube used for withdrawing urine from the bladder into a bag). The patient, carrying the bag, sat down next to me in the day room to watch television.

Lights were out at 11.00 pm and I hardly slept at all. Patients were snoring, coughing and breathing heavily. One patient was vomiting at regular intervals. The sounds of the night staff walking on the linoleum-covered wooden floorboards seemed very loud. Even whispered conversations between the nurses and patients could be clearly heard. In retrospect, the first night was probably one of the noisiest I experienced, but I did not know that at the time and was dreading the prospect of four more nights in the ward.

The operation day

I had had the 'fasting' sign over my bed since midnight on Sunday. My operation was expected to be at about 11.30 am. At 8.00 am a patient, Bruce, was admitted to bed 10, and he was due to have an operation at 10.30 am. Throughout my stay, I was never able to understand why some patients were admitted the day prior to the operation, and others on the day of the operation. I was also surprised to see two youths, Darren and Peter, both with fashion-shaved heads, admitted to beds 12 and 13. They were to have operations on Tuesday. Bruce was about my age and Darren and Peter were considerably younger. The average patient age had reduced significantly, to my relief. Darren and Peter appeared to know each other and talked in an animated fashion, each confessing their anxiety about what was to come. They soon disappeared to the day room.

At about 10.00 am, Bruce and I had to change into gowns, ready for the operating theatre. Soon after, a porter pushing a mobile stretcher came for Bruce. He was wheeled down the ward with a nurse in attendance. She was asking him his date of birth and other details. Earlier than expected, my turn came. At the entrance to the theatre there was a bit of a queue. This gave the opportunity for the various nurses in attendance to converse and their banter took my mind off the immediate environment. Eventually, I was wheeled into an ante-room next to the theatre where I knew, from previous experience, I would be given the general anaesthetic.

I was first given an injection to relax me, and when everything was ready in the theatre I was asked to breathe deeply into an oxygen mask while the anaesthetic was injected. The next thing I remember was being wheeled back into the ward. I believe that all patients are 'brought round' in a recovery room next to the theatre, but do not recall that. Both legs were hurting a bit and I noticed blood on my gown and sheets, but basically I felt well but sleepy. I vaguely remember Bruce sitting up in bed talking to Darren and Peter – reassuring them, I think. I must have slept for a while and when I awoke, Bruce told me I had got back at 12.30 pm and slept for one and a half hours.

A nurse offered me a cup of tea and I changed back into pyjamas. Just before 4.00 pm, my wife arrived and was surprised at how well I looked. I was thirsty and asked for some water. A nurse was rather reluctant to let me have a drink as it could make me sick so soon after the anaesthetic. I could not understand this as I had already drunk some tea. Eventually I did get some water. Perhaps different nurses adopted different rules. I was also informed by the nurse (subsequently confirmed by Mr Stuart) that I was not to walk for 48 hours. This was to allow the skin graft to have a better chance of being successful. Prior to that moment, I never even realised that a graft might not be successful. Some (urine) bottles were placed by my bed. The bottles were made of a grey cardboard-like material, not glass!

Throughout the rest of the day I felt fine but drowsy. I was not much of a conversationalist during visiting time. The ward television was switched on all evening, for the first time in my stay. I deliberately concentrated on watching it from 8.00 pm onwards so that I would be very tired when the lights went out. Unfortunately, my drowsiness reduced as the evening wore on and by 11.00 pm I was wide awake. Although the ward was much quieter than the previous night, I hardly slept at all again. Darren could not stand the noise and almost walked out at 5.00 am. He did not believe me when I said that it was a relatively quiet night. My main concerns at the time were what would happen if the graft did not take, and how I could manage for 48 hours confined to bed. Regarding the former, Mr Stuart's answer was that 'it would be a mess'. Apart from being ambiguous, it did not feel like a very sympathetic response. For the latter, I mastered the discreet use of bottles and realised that a nurse would wheel me to the toilets, if necessary.

Life on Ward 3

Having had my operation, and being confined to bed, I was able to observe the ward activities properly for the first time on Tuesday. The day starts with the night staff bringing round medication and cups of tea at about 7.30 am. At 7.50 am, a lady from a volunteer group brings in national morning newspapers. At 8.00 am the day nursing staff start their shift. This was a highlight of any day. They brightened up the day with cheerful 'good morning' greetings, and chatted in good humour to each other and the patients whilst changing the bedclothes. By 8.30 am, breakfast was served. During this peak period, the registrar would quickly visit all his patients, spending longer with those due to have an operation. Curtains would be closed and opened around the beds.

Between 9.00 am and 12.30 pm (lunch-time), the main activities are the routine temperature and pulse checks, the transporting of patients to and from the operating theatre, a visit to the bathroom and a mid-morning tea break. Shaving was a problem. There were no electric sockets in the bathroom or toilets and no mirror by the bed. I had to shave blind using the socket by the bed. There was barely enough space for easy chairs by beds, and although chairs were provided for some patients, they were not an automatic right. They impeded meal-serving, bed-making and temperature-taking. The ward was not designed for the convenience of easy-chairs. On occasions, the nurses would sit and talk to individual patients, particularly when dressings were changed or medication handed out. By these means, I was able to establish the ranks of the many medical staff and their levels of authority. In the background, there was the constant sound of a cleaner polishing or sweeping the floor.

The nurses had clearly been trained to communicate with patients. In fact, one of the student nurses, in response to a light-hearted reprimand from a staff nurse for sitting and looking at my newspaper, offered 'communication with the patient' as the reason. I soon realised that I would receive an empathetic response to any request for assistance from the nurses. Their approach did differ noticeably according to a patient's age. Any patient of advanced age would be spoken to in the manner of a child; for example, 'Let's just shuffle your bottom along this way' or 'Would you like some nice hot milk with your cornflakes?' I could not tell whether this approach was reassuring or not. Overall, I had great trust in the nursing staff and liked and admired them. Their handling of specific incidents (see below) served to reinforce this view.

The afternoon usually involved the consultant's rounds of the wards, and also heralded the entry of visitors. (Visiting hours were 2.00 pm to 8.00 pm, although they were relaxed for individual special cases.) Patients had either Mr Stuart or Mr Allen as their consultant surgeon. The name of the consultant was in a frame above the patient's bed. The consultant would start at bed 1 and systematically work his way to bed 20. In bed 9, I had some advanced warning. He would be accompanied by the registrar, house officer and the senior nurse on duty, usually the sister or charge nurse. Sometimes he examined my leg, sometimes he did not. He discussed my case with the other staff, issued one or two instructions and then they went on to the next bed. On the first occasion, I asked what the position was and was told to stay in bed for a further 24 hours, and that they would look at the graft on Friday. It was clear from body language and short answers that this was not the time to discuss my case in detail.

From my perspective, and given my generally anxious state, there was a serious lack of communication, and it never improved as time went on. I did notice that Mr Allen, on his rounds, always went to the head of the patient's bed and summarised the position with the patient. That was all I wanted from Mr Stuart or his registrar, but I hardly ever received it. To make matters worse, there were two occasions when, because my dressing had not been removed in advance of the rounds, I was told that it would be seen 'tomorrow'. It was as if my time was of no value, whereas their time was so important that they could not wait two minutes for a bandage to be removed. On the very few occasions when I talked individually to Mr Stuart or his registrar, I found them to be concerned and helpful, so I cannot understand why they were so uncommunicative for most of the time.

On days when I was permitted to walk, I would spend some time in the day room, reading or watching television, just to change the scenery. Time, during the day, passed very slowly, except when I had visitors. Some patients were allowed home after one or two nights in hospital, as was the case with Bruce and Peter. Each departure increased the importance to me of knowing when I would leave, and this served to make the days seem longer. Darren articulated such concerns frequently to doctors and nurses alike, always asking when he could go home. Interestingly, on the first Thursday, after we had both slept well the previous night, he described it as 'worrying' that we should be able to sleep and that 'we must be getting used to this place'.

At about 4.30 pm each day, the local evening newspapers were brought in by a confident paper boy with a very loud voice. After visitors left at 8.00 pm, and after another cup of tea, I would usually watch television. There were no arguments about which channel to watch. Normally, it stayed on the same channel all evening unless there was a special event such as a football match. Thankfully, my bed was ideally placed for the ward television. The night staff, a staff nurse and a student nurse, took over at 9.00 pm and lights were out by 11.00 pm. Each bed had an individual light for those wishing to read in private.

Certain aspects of daily life in hospital take on greater importance as days go on. An example is the language that is used by staff and patients to indicate the basic bodily functions. At first, I thought it quaint and British that there is an unwritten code not to use single, well-known words, presumably because they are impolite. Consequently, patients were asked by staff if they had 'passed water' or 'opened their bowels'. In some cases, patients were unfamiliar with an expression or couldn't hear properly. In these cases, other euphemisms would be tried. The nearest to plain speaking was an exasperated 'Do you want to wee?'. These conventions may be regarded as silly and are not adopted by other languages and cultures. (Patients even adopted the conventions with each other in the ward. I am certain that, once outside the ward, these same people would use single words.) My original fascination with such staff–patient interchanges turned to annoyance when a patient was admitted in so much pain he could hardly talk. After several minutes of frustrating non-communication, the patient finally uttered the word 'shit'. This brought immediate action by the staff and some relief to the patient's pain. I wondered how many times such scenes are repeated over the years and how much staff time and patient suffering could be saved by being explicit.

Interaction with other patients

During each day, I would chat with other patients. Quite often it was to discuss our operations and other side-effects. Sometimes it was about the food, which I thought was generally OK but bland. Sport, and in particular football, was a popular topic of conversation. The football season was reaching an interesting climax. Contrary to my prior misgivings, I was pleased to join in with most discussions with fellow patients. It was noticeable, however, that the older patients would congregate from time to time around bed 7, occupied by Jack, the longest resident. From snatches of overheard conversation, I realised that my approval of greater variety in the food – chilli con carne, for example – was not shared by others. This was an example of a discernible generation gap in viewpoints. I vowed not to talk politics. Jack was liked and respected by patients and staff alike. He never complained, even though he knew that he would be in hospital after we had all left. His bed became a natural meeting point.

Darren was a good companion. He was discharged on the second Monday. His bed was then occupied by Bill, a man in his mid-fifties. Bill was immediately 'at home' in the ward environment. Much to my surprise, he opted to stay in hospital rather than go home when his operation was delayed from Tuesday to Thursday. He was a friendly person who helped the nursing staff with meal-tray collection and instigated newspaper exchanges. He liked to lighten the conversation, announcing that he had ordered wine with the meal, and inviting the nurse to share his bed when she said she was cold. His chirpiness was not always well received. One patient, carrying a catheter, blatantly ignored Bill when asked if he had been shopping. When he was eventually discharged, Bill felt they were rushing things. I would willingly have swapped places.

During the second half of my stay, Matthew was admitted to bed 13. He was in his mid-thirties and a fellow sports enthusiast. It transpired that he lived near me. He also shared a desire to go home as soon as possible. Unfortunately his wound became infected and his departure was delayed. We shared mutual moans about the doctors and lack of information. On one occasion Matthew missed the registrar's visit by choosing to go to the toilet at the wrong moment. This meant that he had to wait several hours for an update on his progress.

I was grateful for the company of Jack, Bill and Matthew. For several days we were the main, and sometimes only, occupants of our part of the ward. They helped me through the overall tedium. I was thankful that I was not too close to Alistair, the occupant of bed 6 for several days, who voiced an opinion on everything from the food to politics and laughed loudly at his own jokes, some of which I thought were in poor taste (normally involving comparisons between the hospital and concentration camps).

Incidents in the ward

From time to time, incidents would occur which were outside the normal routine. The first was a pleasant surprise. On the Friday of my first week, all the nurses marched up the ward together. I soon realised that, in the centre of the procession, there was the charge nurse carrying a large cake. It was Jack's birthday and the nursing staff had got together to celebrate it. A chorus of 'Happy Birthday' was followed by the cutting of the cake, with a slice for all patients. Jack wanted to thank the person who had baked the cake. It was the charge nurse's daughter who worked in the hospital kitchen. They knew about Jack's birthday as, being on registered drugs, he had to recite his date of birth every time he was issued with them.

One night, an elderly patient was admitted at midnight. At 3.00 am he demanded attention in a very loud voice. 'Nurse, can I have a cup of tea?' 'When is the doctor seeing me?' 'Where am I, I can't see very well.' 'Where's the toilet?' 'I need a frame to walk with.' 'I'm confused.' The night staff were doing their best to reassure him, but with little success. He was waking all the other patients. As Darren put it, we all felt like throwing a pillow at him. The staff nurse finally persuaded him to walk to the nurse's office to have some tea and a talk. This seemed to work. No longer were the other patients affected and his confusion was gradually reduced. On the next morning I saw him for the first time. He was old and nearly blind and apologised to everyone for the noise. 'I've been told off.' I felt guilty about my previous night's thoughts towards him, and was very impressed with the nurses' handling of the whole incident. A few nights later, when a different patient kept insisting on going to the toilet, even though he was told that his bladder was empty, the nurses could not adopt the same strategy for reassurance. The patient's blood pressure was low, and it was unwise for him to stand up. The impasse – 'I want to go to the toilet', 'No we can't let you. Your blood pressure is too low' – was only resolved when a doctor was called in to reaffirm the nurse's advice.

Matthew's temperature rose after his operation because the wound was infected, and he became very lethargic. One afternoon, as his wife was visiting, he suddenly called the nurse. He was bleeding a lot. His wife was quite upset. The nurse immediately drew the curtains round his bed and found time to reassure his wife that this was not unusual. After a few minutes, she beckoned Matthew's wife to join her and explained what had happened. The bleeding had reduced the pressure built up by the infection. Almost immediately, Matthew began to recover and his temperature dropped.

The outcome was positive. The nurse's professionalism and empathy was exceptional.

There were a few occasions when patients queried their treatment or the judgement of the nursing staff. An example was when Michael, a patient in bed 14, was put on a catheter. Despite several independent nurse assessments of the equipment, he insisted that it was not working properly and that this was causing him pain. He supported his complaint by stating that he knew what he was talking about as he had previous experience of 'intensive care'. He did not accept that the catheter was working properly until later when his pain was less. The pain, the nurses said, was caused by the packing of his operation wound, not by the malfunctioning of the catheter. In all other matters, Michael was quiet and cooperative. On this issue he would not be budged and made sure that everyone knew.

For the record

The length of my stay turned out to be 16 nights and not five as I had originally convinced myself. After examination of the graft on the first Friday, it looked as though 'we have got away with it'. However, I was advised that it would be better for me to stay in hospital a few more days to ensure that the dressing did not slip and affect the graft. They would take a further look at the leg after the weekend. I was, however, allowed to walk, with care.

Mr Stuart's visit on the Monday resulted in a 'Let's leave it until Wednesday' pronouncement. On Wednesday, Mr Stuart had emergency surgery and so his registrar examined my leg. Apparently only 70 per cent of the graft had taken. 'What a shame,' he said. He thought that the remainder might take on its own. I asked when I could go home. He said, Friday. On Friday, Mr Stuart examined the leg and suggested that the remaining 30 per cent could be grafted using skin they had kept in the fridge from the operation. He was gone before I could take in this development. I did, however, ask the charge nurse if this meant another operation. He said 'Yes'. My face dropped and he promised to come back after the rounds.

Whilst I was working out how I could go home prior to any further operation, the charge nurse came back with a gown and hat for me. I was to have the second operation immediately under local anaesthetic. The registrar, not Mr Stuart, carried out this operation. He explained that I must stay in bed until Tuesday to give the graft a chance. I had got over my initial reaction. At least something was happening after days of inactivity. On the Tuesday, it was obvious that the second graft had been unsuccessful. It is likely that I will always have a small scar on my leg. This does not worry me at all. As it happened, my last five days in hospital had been unnecessary, though it had been worth a try. I was released from hospital that day, with notes to give to my local GP and district nurse, details of a check-up visiting time at the hospital and bottles of antibiotic tablets to take.

Case study 7
Waterstons, Business Analysis and Computer Consultancy[1]

Background

Waterstons was founded in 1993 by Sally Waterston as an Information Technology (IT) Service Provider, based in Durham in the north of England. The business originally focused on the provision of independent advice on computer-based accounts for small-to-medium sized enterprises (SMEs). By the year 2001, it was providing business analysis and computer consultancy services for SMEs in manufacturing, distribution, production, accounting, retail and catering and industrial services.

Waterstons service offer is summarised on the website (http://www.waterstons.co.uk) as follows:

> Waterstons aim to provide a complete and independent IT service to companies in the medium enterprise sector. With our approach you get the right people at the right time while avoiding the need to recruit, train and retain skilled IT staff.

In the early days, as the business grew, clients demanded more and more complex technical services and Waterstons recruited staff to respond to clients' needs. Mike Waterston and Ajaib Singh joined the company in 1994, forming a tripartite partnership. They now employ a further 38 staff, offering independent, expert assistance with selecting software, advice on making the best use of established legacy systems, help to get the best out of the internet, support for desktop, server, WANS and LANS, security against attack by hackers and viruses, retail, manufacturing and distribution consultancy, systems development and systems integration, website design and business-to-business applications, facilities management and disaster recovery, networks and email. Increasingly they found there was a need for supporting clients IT infrastructure on a daily basis and formulated the Facilities Management group.

Developers and facilities management staff are Microsoft certified, Novell, Lotus and Cisco specialists. Business analysts are trained in accounts and have first-hand experience in their respective industry sectors. Waterstons won the 'Fast 50 Technology' award in March 2001, as their three consecutive years of 58 per cent per annum growth put them in the top 50 fastest-growing technology companies in the north of England. Two months later, they won a national Microsoft award. Their IT solution for the National Salvage Group came top in the Enterprise Agility Category.

Waterstons was originally located in rented accommodation above a franchise garage. From using only part of the space, they eventually took over all the space, and they finally outgrew the space. In May 2001, they relocated in purpose-built offices in Belmont Business Park, just off the A1 Motorway in Durham.

The nature of the business

Waterstons place high value on independence, and on the quality of their independent advice. This is reflected in relationships that are conducted in an open and unbiased manner. Indeed, many of the company's early clients are still with them. They tended to be small enterprises whose IT spend was limited, and who did not have dedicated IT resources in-house. Many of them used a wide portfolio of services offered by Watersons. Watersons also offer 'hand-holding' support to clients who wish to upgrade their IT services. The consultants are careful to identify the 'right' IT solution, and will not sell solutions that cannot be delivered.

Waterstons' employees are highly valued, and recognised for their knowledge, experience and contribution. Before an offer of employment is made, potential recruits have to meet most of the existing staff to see how they 'fit in'. Finding staff with the right mix of skills and willing to locate in the north is challenging; many IT professionals with relevant experience tend to be based in south-east England. Senior management adopt a philosophy that is based on employee empowerment and trust. There is a flat organisational structure, split into divisions, with each division having a team leader and the other employees known as 'consultants'. Mike Waterston is a firm believer of 'management by walking around' and has instilled a company culture that drew on ideas from Tom Peters, Peter Drucker and Warren Bennis.

The business normally falls into one of three categories: consultancy, facilities management, and software development.

Consultancy

Consultancy is offered to clients who wish to assess their IT needs. Consultants at Waterstons take on clients in the role of a key account manager. They work with a client to analyse the IT systems and strategies to identify the current adequacy and effectiveness. Normally the consultants would identify the specific needs and opportunities within clients' businesses, and facilitate the development of either a new 'off-the-shelf' software package or a customised solution. Comprehensive project management services are provided to ensure implementation of the solutions, and other factors connected with project completion. Where a company has already made substantial investments in IT, consultants can help businesses to get more out of them.

Facilities management

The facilities management service is offered to clients that do not have the resources to provide total in-house IT expertise. Waterstons provide day-to-day tactical network support with up-to-date IT knowledge and capabilities. Flexible contracts allow clients to use the consultants when needed. Waterstons support the University of Durham Business School (UDBS) in this capacity; for example, Ray Knox, the IT Manager at UDBS, values the technical competence of the Waterstons staff, their flexible approach to the different cultures within UDBS and their very high work ethic.

Software development

The development team can provide solutions where bespoke software is required rather than 'off-the-shelf' packages. The software may range from simple databases to company-wide management systems, and include email and internet. The team can also provide support services to systems implementation in the form of data transfers and other bespoke work.

Growth and development of the business

Accommodation and communication

Waterstons has achieved tremendous growth since its inception. When the business started, it only occupied one room of the three available above the franchise garage, and so communication between staff was relatively easy. As the business grew, and more people were recruited, they expanded into the other two rooms. At this stage, staff were divided physically, and communication became more difficult. Indeed, when the Development Section was formed in 1998, it was separated from the Facilities Management and Consultancy Sections by a wall. The 'management by walking around' policy was adopted in recognition of the physical division of the sections. As a further response to the need for clear communications, Waterstons set up an intranet that contained newsworthy items and monthly financial information.

Nevertheless, staff in the development section were often referred to as the 'back-room boys' or 'the techies'. Despite their own perceptions of working in the back room, direct client contact has always been essential on all projects and contact was occasionally carried out by email or presumed not necessary. Indeed, some clients had written to Waterstons to ask why they had not heard from them on certain projects, and Mike Waterston has had to ask the development section to visit clients on a regular basis.

The original office led to serious overcrowding and, as the number of employees grew, a 'hot desk' policy became necessary within the facilities management section. With the move to new offices in 2001, Waterstons hoped to alleviate many of the growth-related accommodation problems, but are aware that as the new offices are on two floors, there may still be problems with internal communications.

The client base

The clients that Waterstons served in the early days of the business were typically small enterprises with a limited budget for IT and no in-house experience. Clients with no IT knowledge were heavily dependent on Waterstons to provide IT skills in all areas from help with Microsoft Office to the design of complex databases. The time required to service 'small' clients properly and the amount that they are able to pay means that the margins from small clients are small and often negative. Highly-skilled and expensive people were often required to sort out jobs which only require very basic skills (mainly due to the nature of the relationships between staff and clients). The nature of relationships with clients means that also the opportunity of earning higher rates elsewhere is lost. Margins are better for medium-sized businesses.

The dilemma for Waterstons is that they have ongoing relationships with many small clients from the early period and yet they need to increase the annual spend of clients to maintain profitable growth. One way of maintaining growth would be to devise a strategy for moving the focus of Watersons' activities from small to medium-sized enterprises. Such a strategy would have to be managed extremely carefully – the opportunity of increasing earnings must be weighed against potential lost business from long-standing small business clients.

Client contact and handovers

During the period up until the move Waterstons used key account managers as points of contact between major clients and the organisation. The majority of key account managers worked in the consultancy section, with a few from the facilities mangement section. The largest, and most important clients were handled by one of the three partners. For major consultancy projects, Sally Waterston was normally the key account manager. Key account managers have to ensure that they are in close contact with major clients on a regular basis, especially during a consultancy project, or through project management of an installation. There were, however, no set procedures that provide guidelines for the key account managers as to the regularity of client contact, neither was there a formal review. It was left to the discretion of the individual.

Clients viewed the service offered through contact with the partners very highly. They described Sally Waterston's service as excellent, and it is un-likely that all members of the consultancy team can provide the same service experience for clients as Sally. Differences in client service experiences could arise from the lack of formal procedures to follow during a consultancy project, or from a lack of contact by members of the consultancy section with the more important clients. It may have required the key account manager to bring in other staff to work with the client as the project develops. Sally Waterston managed the Suncrest account, for example, but once the project moved from consultancy to facilities management, staff in the facilities management section deal directly with the client. Such a hand-over means that clients obtain a different 'Waterstons relationship' depending on the individuals involved. The management of clients' expectations during handover is known to be very important.

Developing the company culture and awareness

At Waterstons, principles of excellent service are transmitted through the company via its culture; that is, influenced by the values held by the partners. For example, staff in the development section speak of 'going the extra mile' for the client. In 1998, a 'customer perception' survey, carried out by Waterstons, confirmed that clients were generally satisfied with the service received. Such surveys have been repeated in a less concentrated manner each year, with similar findings. Waterstons has established a reputation for the quality of its service, but getting an initial meeting with a potential client is still a challenge. Proposals have been submitted, but then rejected because the honest evaluations of resources and costs required for a project (based on an assessment of value for the client) had not matched clients' price expectations.

At Waterstons, only a few people hold knowledge pertaining to some of the key aspects of the company's operation. The partners acknowledge that the absence of a middle management layer within the company impacts on the manner in which critical decisions are made regarding its operation. Employees are generally keen to take on challenging assignments that allow them to develop their competencies and feel rewarded for their achievements, but the gap in the management structure is a hindrance. There is a perceived gap in the transference of service delivery knowledge that could ultimately lead to employee disillusionment. Mike Waterson is aware of this issue and has a plan to resolve the situation within the next year.

Watersons has many informal relationships with other service providers and retailers in the north of England, whose referrals can often lead to additional business. However, in some cases, where the relationship is only, as yet, weak, Waterstons may simply be one of a number of IT consultants that are given the opportunity to submit a quotation for the work. This happened recently when a graphic design company, known to Waterstons, had won a contract to provide a consumer e-commerce website design for a well-known jewellery retailer. The graphic designers approached Waterstons, as well as other software developers, to quote for the IT work to support the e-commerce site – mainly bespoke software to be created by the development section. Watersons did not win the contract in this particular case.

The company intranet reflects their openness with clients. There is a customer feedback page which includes comments from customers good or bad. Clients can also access any employee via the telephone, and calls will always be handled and dealt with within three rings and it is often by one of the three partners.

Company philosophy and values

At Waterstons, we place high value on our independence and on the quality of our independent advice. Our people are valued and recognised for the breadth and depth of their knowledge and experience, their ability to establish good working relationships, and their total commitment to customer satisfaction.

The company statement above is endorsed by the National Salvage Group (NSG), a client of Waterstons. NSG needed seamless and efficient communications with a complex network of members and customers. Waterstons used the latest internet technology to link together all the different systems used by the national network of salvage agents and the insurance and fleet management companies with whom NSG do business, thus enabling NSG to increase their business significantly.

According to NSG's General Manager, 'The system is truly groundbreaking, and is already making a significant impact on police forces, insurance companies and NSG members across the country. Waterstons did a fantastic job developing NSGenius for us.'

Note

1. This case study was written by Norman Gordon, Yves Hausammann, John Robinson and Chris Storey, and adapted by the authors.

Case study 8
Søren Madsen, Village Mechanic

Background

Søren Madsen founded his own business as a car mechanic in 1968, after working as an apprentice for Volvo for five years in the mid-size provincial town of Aalborg in northern Denmark. Aalborg is situated on the Limfjord in North Jutland, 385 km north-west of Copenhagen and 228 km north-north-east of Esbjerg. It has a population of 155 000 inhabitants and is a cultural centre with a theatre, museums, a university (founded in 1973) and a large number of educational establishments. He bought a small house in the village of Uggerby, 10 km north of Aalborg, for his home and business premises.

Uggerby has a population of 3000 inhabitants and is situated on the main E3/A10 road from Aalborg to Frederickshavn, from where the car ferry can be taken to Gøteborg in Sweden. Consequently, many tourists will drive by Uggerby, particularly in the summer months of July and August. When Søren bought his house, the village was seen as having possibilities as a residential area and several private houses were being built.

The village community

Søren believed strongly that he should settle into the local community and meet as many of the people as he could. He joined the sports association, the local professional business society, the 'Lions' and volunteered to be a sponsor for the scouts. He became known to village people of many backgrounds and professions. There are a high proportion of social workers and teachers living in Uggerby and a number of people are employed as sales staff in Aalborg. Most families need a car to travel to Aalborg for work or shopping or both.

Once Søren's business was established and his name was known in the village, he came to recognise and accept that local word-of-mouth and visibility – his house/garage is situated on a corner at the entrance to the village – were going to generate most of his business. Only very occasionally would he pick up business from the passing tourists, accounting for less than one per cent of his turnover. The village represents his market and his reputation within the village community is all important.

The service offer

Søren offers villagers an alternative, for car repairs and 'checkups', to the big authorised dealers located in Aalborg. In Denmark, the big dealers have to make a profit from repairs. Dealer profits from car sales are limited, as taxation makes cars very expensive for the purchaser – approximately 2.5 times as expensive as in the UK! Consequently, although the dealers have state-of-the-art equipment and well-qualified mechanics, the pressure on making profits from repairs makes their repair and check-up prices seem very high for car owners whose vehicles are no longer under factory guarantee.

Søren decided to keep his prices as low as possible. On average they are 30 per cent lower than the dealers', and he feels he can justify this pricing policy because of lower overheads and less rental for his business premises. Whilst the lower price is important in attracting business, Søren is aware that his reputation also depends on other features of his service that address the specific needs of the villagers. One particular customer complaint is that when a car is being repaired, not only is there a repair bill to pay, but also there is an additional expense of finding other transportation for the day's work. Søren, therefore, will attempt to attend to some customers' cars on Saturdays or late afternoons in order that the disruption to work travel, and associated expense, is minimised.

He has also built up trust and a stream of regular customers (many of whom have been with him for more than five years and who come back once or twice a year) through never doing more repairs than have been requested, and never encouraging big, expensive 20 000 km check-ups. The customers are totally confident, however, that he will keep their cars safe and within the limits of the law. He will also offer an extra service, for a small sum, to regulars whereby he will look underneath their cars and make minor adjustments on Saturdays. This may often lead to extra business in the following week for Søren if faults are detected.

His regular customers are given special treatment over what is normally a routine climax to any service – the payment. Payment is usually by cash, except for very large jobs, and locals enjoy being invited to Søren's den in the basement for a cigar and a brandy when they come round with the cash – usually a week or so after the invoice date.

For some larger jobs for regular customers, Søren may agree to a credit payment over a six-month period. Such an agreement will be made orally and he will not charge any interest on the credit. Søren's local area knowledge, and relationships built up with the village residents, allow him to operate in this less formal manner. When asked what happens if customers contest the bill, he simply replies, 'They do not.' Understandings and trust govern the relationships with his customers. Similarly, he does not have problems with non-payment of bills as he knows his 'customer circle'. By dealing with customers he knows on a regular basis, he is able, to some extent, to choose his customers and declares that he 'has not got the time' to undertake repairs on cars belonging to people who could or would not pay.

As a side-line, Søren will occasionally restore second-hand cars (usually Volvos) bought at the local auction and advertise them for sale in the local *Aalborg Stiftstidende* newspaper (circulation 75 000 readers), or drive them for his own private or domestic pleasure. He is well known in Uggerby for driving 'an endless stream of restored second-hand Volvos'.

Locals will flock to Søren for car repairs and check-ups and the average repair bill for a family car is 2500 kroner (approximately £250) per year. Despite this enthusiasm for his repair work, few of them would contemplate buying a second-hand car from him.

Operations

Søren operates from a workshop and basement den attached to his house, from Monday to Saturday. Normally he has an apprentice working for him. Currently this is his 17-year-old son, Michael. There will never be more than two mechanics and there are no other staff working for the business. The accounts are kept by Søren in the den in the basement, in a manner which customers find 'charmingly old-fashioned' and which tends to reinforce trust. As one customer put it: 'We never receive computer-based bills with funny additions and obscure percentages from Søren.' He simply writes the price for the work, the spare parts and the VAT and nothing more.

The spare parts can be delivered on the same day if Søren rings the distributor by 10.30 am. By this means Søren can keep stock levels at a minimum. The one distributor carries all kinds of spare parts and has a fleet of forty vans covering North Jutland. Such logistics enable Søren to repair his customers' cars in one or two days only.

He operates from the workshop, which is largely DIY-built by himself. Customers comment on how tidy the workshop is. Søren and Michael are always in overalls in working hours, and will only be seen in leisure-wear on Sundays. On rare occasions when work carried out by the apprentice is less than satisfactory, Søren is always willing to discuss extra work on his customers' cars free of charge. Within the family-type business he runs, however, any potentially unsatisfactory work can be spotted, discussed and rectified before a car is returned to the customer.

Service quality

Søren is very adamant that the customer should only get the work done which is requested and that the temptation to do, and charge for, more work is resisted. He says that good service quality is 'to provide the work that is necessary only, and within a reasonable time'.

Running his own business

Financially, Søren seems content with his annual turnover of 1.5 million kroner. He has a disposable income that is quite limited but he is his own master and would rather live the way he does than earn twice as much as a salaried foreman at one of the dealerships in Aalborg. 'Just think of my commuter's cost if I worked for a firm in Aalborg – 1000 kroner per month. That's like having to earn an extra 3000 kroner per month before tax!' He spends most of his short holidays in the garden behind the garage, or goes for a camping expedition with his family in one of the restored Volvos. He has no desire to live any other lifestyle.

Case study 9
NorthWest Design Associates Ltd[1]

Background

NorthWest Design Associates Ltd (NWDA) is an Architectural and Interior Design Practice that was founded in 1971 by Martin Rocke. It is a totally independent business, located, since 1986, in Kelsall, 8 miles from Chester in north-west England. Martin Rocke outlines their service offer as follows:

> We provide expertise and knowledge in design and space management: producing drawings and specifications, obtaining statutory approvals and tenders, and supervising the construction phase to completion.

The structure of the business is divided between commercial (interior) and architectural (exterior) work.

Interior work:

This is interior design work on shops, public houses, offices and restaurants, carried out entirely for commercial clients. The regular client list is small, but includes Laura Ashley, Elvi (a ladies' outsize retailer), and Pets at Home. These clients provide continuous work and regular instalments of revenue (NWDA have long-established relationships with the clients, and standardised budgets). NWDA work within the clients' corporate designs to make appropriate changes to the interiors of new stores/outlets.

Work includes furniture design, space planning, new building and refurbishment, specifications, measured building and site surveys, statutory approvals, planning appeals, obtaining tenders and on-site supervision and project management.

Architectural (exterior) work

This is work on the design of industrial units and offices for commercial clients, and also on individual designs of houses and renovations for a range of domestic clients. There are a comparatively large number of clients, each requiring individual and very different services from NWDA. New relationships have to be built on many occasions, and methods of payment for work are variable. There is an extensive range of potential designs, dependent on a range of available client budgets.

Work includes design plans, obtaining planning permission, advice on and appointment of contractor, and supervision of work relating to private housing developments, house renovations, and individually designed houses, offices and industrial units. The architectural department particularly like working on listed and historic buildings, but such opportunities are rare.

The length of a particular design project could be from one week to six months. In turn, on-site supervision can last from as little as two weeks to completion of the job, to as much as 18 months for large projects. NWDA can have 30–40 jobs 'live' at any one time. A job is 'live' until the payment is made.

Employees and resources

In 1974, Martin Rocke was joined by John Law, who became a partner in the business, with responsibility for expanding the 'interior' work. By the year 2000, NWDA was employing four designers for 'interior' work, two designers for 'architectural work', two CAD technicians and three further people to oversee administration and accounts. Only the designers and technicians are fee-earning.

Martin Rocke had studied civil engineering and worked as an engineer for a water authority, a local authority and for a national firm of building contractors before starting NWDA. John Law studied at the London School of Furniture, before working at the Design Centre in London, and as a partner in a furniture/exhibition design company in Hull in north-east England. The other designers have all obtained degrees in architecture or interior design.

The offices in Kelsall are in a converted church hall, with plenty of interior space, and easy access and adequate parking space. There has been a major investment in equipment since 1984, when the first computer aided design (CAD) system was installed. All drawing is now done on CAD on two screen computers – a big change from the hand drawings which had been used prior to 1984. The drawing process is much faster by CAD, but CAD is expensive. Each program costs up to £4500 per workstation, and there is an accompanying investment in digital copying to allow printing direct to the copier, and in training on new developments in CAD. NWDA chose the CAD system MicroStation® offered by Bentley Systems. Bentley Systems, in turn, publicise the use by NWDA of MicroStation's 3D capabilities to meet the needs of a major client in their own case study of Laura Ashley (see http://www.bentley.com/success/casestudies/ashley2.htm).

NWDA's records are 100 per cent electronic, but they still use paper-based job files to take to sites for discussion with clients. Printing and photo-copying of large plans is very expensive. The offices also have the normal fax and telephone resources, and there is also a large product library.

The business and competitive environment

Throughout their history, NWDA have found that demand for their work can vary with the economic climate. For example, in periods of recession, there may be fewer purchases of new houses, but relatively more require-ments for renovations. While NWDA have experienced 'quiet periods' between 1979 and 1981, and 1988 and 1992, it is felt that the offer of both 'interior' and 'architectural' design services does provide a potentially consistent base of clients in that the respective demands for the two types of service are unlikely to fall concurrently.

There are around 25 other architectural practices in the Chester area, whose sizes vary. Some work with only one or two designers, while others employ up to 30 people. They do not all provide the same range of services. Few provide the same 'interior' and 'architectural' services as NWDA. However, NWDA do not offer *domestic interior design*, as they perceive it to be 'too much hassle', whereas a few of the regional competitors do offer this service.

NWDA have observed that the private clients, in particular, have become more demanding over the years. Some may even look for opportunities to delay payment by identifying very minor additions to the contractor's price or by misunderstanding (probably deliberately) NWDA's conditions. Typical examples of this may be when a client sees an addition of, say, £500 to a £50 000 project – 'a mere 1 per cent' – and tries to claim it back off NWDA's fees, maintaining that NWDA should have thought of it before the con-tractor was asked to tender. Another common example is when the client has not properly read NWDA's terms and conditions that say that client amendments to the project are chargeable on an hourly basis on top of the agreed fees. In these cases, clients maintain that NWDA should have thought of it before, and so 'they're not paying'. NWDA adopt a policy of being totally committed to their clients, but it is not always possible to foresee client revisions, and they also feel that it is not necessary to spell out the content of the 'terms and conditions' to grown-up, intelligent people. Sometimes, however, they now have to take their client to the Small Claims Court to obtain payment, and very occasionally and reluctantly have to adjust their invoice.

In order to meet client needs, NWDA need to work together with many other organisations, businesses and professionals. They include:

- electricity, gas, water and telephone service providers in the area
- local authorities on planning and building regulations
- Other professionals, such as quantity surveyors, structural and service engineers

- main contractors and specialist sub-contractors
- solicitors and agents.

To work effectively with such a network of business and professional contacts requires good 'people skills', which is a particular strength of Martin Rocke. The really crucial relationships on the architectural side of the business are those with the contractors and quantity surveyors, who work on specific client projects with NWDA as the 'design team' (see below), and those with local authority planners and building inspectors. While NWDA may know well, and have good relationships with contractors in the Chester area, when a job is in a different part of the country, they have to work with unfamiliar contractors that requires careful research to avoid problems on site.

NWDA feel that it is extremely important to stress to clients that they are a completely independent company, not tied to any firm of contractors. They can then acquire a range of competitive tenders that often can result in cheaper and more clearly specified construction work for their clients. On rare occasions, NWDA will work for a contractor on a 'design and build' basis. In NWDA's experience this tends to happen with commercial work where, say, a client has a plot for a new industrial unit, and has used and trusted a contractor before. The client therefore asks the contractor for a 'turnkey operation', and the contractor includes all necessary design fees in their price. Usually the contractor stipulates the specification and supervises their own work, requiring NWDA solely to carry out the basic design and to obtain the necessary statutory approvals.

The interior services

With a relatively small *number* of clients for their interior services, the loss of any of these clients would affect the balance of NWDA's portfolio of work.

They have made steps to enhance their services to these clients. For example, in acknowledgement of the small lead times involved with work in Laura Ashley stores, NWDA has installed a PC in the office of Laura Ashley's shop development manager, in order to speed up the flow of information. This enables John Law to take control of the PC in Laura Ashley's office using a modem link. This, in turn, means that NWDA can load up a drawing on the Laura Ashley PC, so that the Laura Ashley team can make alterations if they wish, that then go back to NWDA's reference file. The client (Laura Ashley) can be assured that their views are acted upon, but that they would not be making drastic alterations to the whole scheme. So far, Laura Ashley are the only company with whom NWDA have such a 'live link', but more such remote stations are likely to happen in the future where the volume of work and the speed of response dictates.

The architectural (exterior) services

The range of existing and potential clients for these services is wide. NWDA currently gets business largely through client satisfaction resulting in repeat business (60-70 per cent) and word-of-mouth (30-40 per cent).

For example, NWDA were introduced in 1980 to a potential client who had a nationwide glazing business specialising in replacing glass in construction vehicles and machinery, with headquarters in Chester. The company wanted a glass store on a tight site, and NWDA were commissioned to design, obtain approvals and tenders and supervise. The client had strong opinions, and despite not always seeing eye-to-eye, a good mutual respect was built, and soon after the company branched out into the building of a small industrial estate, again commissioning NWDA. In the ensuing 20 years NWDA have designed a further five industrial estate developments, two business centres, several house renovations/alterations for directors as well as many more minor works. There has also been a 'word-of-mouth' spin off, in that this client has recommended NWDA to many others who have produced projects ranging from small domestic to a £1m (1990) office block.

Word-of-mouth may originate from satisfied clients, or through referral from other professional practices or contractors with which NWDA have worked on other projects. New business can arise through client contact with *any member* of the 'design team', consisting of architect, engineers, quantity surveyor and contractor. The architectural input on a project is normally the lead input, and engineers of different disciplines, quantity surveyors and professional advisors join the pyramid below the lead practice as necessary, usually working under the control of the architectural practice, but employed directly by the client. However, this is not always the case, and NWDA are not infrequently called in by one of the other disciplines to provide the architectural input, when the initial approach from a client has been to, say, a structural engineer. This would usually happen when the project was heavily structural, and the architectural input was somewhat secondary in terms of importance. At the time of compiling the case study just such a circumstance was taking place where NWDA were working for a company of process engineers designing a multi-million pound waste incineration scheme. In this case, NWDA's architectural input was limited to designing a few simple (but big) 'sheds' to keep the rain off sensitive areas of the plant. A great asset on this project was NWDA's ability to produce three-dimensional drawings of this complicated project – a great tool in illustrating the scheme to the client, and also to planners and other interested parties.

NWDA do not often advertise in general. Occasional box advertisements in trade publications, and advertisements in the *Yellow Pages* have not resulted in any discernible increase in trade. Attendance at local business functions is thought to be more effective, but the company employees do not relish these events. A company brochure, produced in-house, and which can be tailored to the perceived needs of the client, is sent to those who make contact with NWDA. Designers keep in touch with good clients, usually over lunches.

The process of dealing with the many and varied clients who require the architectural services is quite complex, starting with the initial meeting (usually at NWDA's offices) up to the final payment for the job, and £000's of work can have been carried out before the client is billed. In addition, the client is often unaware just how much work has been done 'backstage' in dealing with statutory legislation (planning and building applications), indicative plans and elevations, specifications, liaising with other consultants and drawing up the 3D schemes.

In general, the stages of the design process are:

1. *Client meets architect in the NWDA offices*. Here the client will also see the offices (the converted church hall), and be able to view the display of qualifications of the designers and photographs of previous jobs, and look at company brochures. The previous experience of the designers will be demonstrated.

2. *Project brief established*. A brief for the project is agreed with the client, and then confirmed in writing, together with proposals for charging fees. This is accompanied by a standard NWDA 'terms and conditions'.

3. *Basic outline proposals prepared*. The basic scheme is drawn up with the client, including a budget for the project (calculated in conjunction with a quantity surveyor).

4. *Assignment agreed or not*. The client, at this stage, may not wish to proceed with the project. If agreement is reached then . . .

5. *Scheme drawings and statutory approvals*. NWDA prepare detailed final proposals to enable planning and building regulations applications to be made to the local authority. At this stage they will also interact with any other consultants on the project, consult with fire officers, highways departments, parish councils and any other body deemed necessary to successfully progress the scheme.

6. *Specification and contract documents*. This stage involves the putting together of all the necessary contract documents to enable tenders to be sought. It will include detailed specifications of all the products to be used, contractors' 'prelims' which basically are the 'rules' under which the contract will be carried out, and all special detail drawings not required at the earlier stages.

7. *NWDA will advise on the contractor to use*. Having received tenders from the contractors on the tender list, NWDA will then make a recommendation to the client as to which one to choose, that is not always the cheapest. If the client is in agreement, NWDA and the quantity surveyor will then check the tender to ensure that nothing has been omitted or misunderstood, and then a contract will be signed by the contractor and client.

8. *NWDA monitor the on-site activity*. This includes facilitating the relationship between the quantity surveyor and the contractor, checking whether the work is meeting specifications, and maintaining the ongoing relationship with the client.

9. *Gathering photographic evidence of the job*. This is mainly for potential inclusion in NWDA's portfolio of completed jobs.

10. *Receiving payment*. Usually, clients are billed in four stages: After planning applications (5 above); after building regulations application

(also 5 above); when the job is sent to tender (6 above), and at completion of the project.

Clearly, there is a risk at stage 4 that an assignment will not go ahead (after substantial amounts of time and money have been spent on stages 1,2 and 3) and that NWDA would like to minimise the likelihood of this happening for all their clients. NWDA's terms and conditions do now try to make it abundantly clear to their clients that they will charge for this initial work, after having 'caught a few colds' in the past where clients have maintained that they thought that the initial outline proposals were at NWDA's risk.

Very occasionally, there is dispute as to whether NWDA have put together proposals which are in accordance with the client's brief or not, and therefore whether the client should pay. Unless this is a deliberate attempt by the client to get out of paying, NWDA would normally be prepared to re-present proposals at no extra cost if they considered that the client had a genuine case. Also very occasionally, a design detail may just not work for some reason or other, and it may then cost the client to put it right. NWDA would normally come to an agreement with the client over some consideration for such rare occurrences. In the worst scenario, where a serious error could be made, NWDA maintains a professional indemnity insurance policy to cover any such eventuality.

And finally...

Martin Rocke states positively that

> *NorthWest Design Associates is committed to providing a comprehensive design service to suit the needs of each individual client . . . Our philosophy is simple:*
>
> *1. We listen to our client*
> *2. We evaluate the options*
> *3. We provide the design solution.*

Note

1. This case study was written by Neha Gudka, Charlotte Fairhurst, Lindsay Rocke and Sara Simmonds, and adapted by the authors

Case study 10
G. A. & R. E. Noar & Associates, Dental Practitioners

Background

In November 1960, Geoffrey Noar started a dental practice in Whitefield, seven miles north of Manchester in the north-west of England. He purchased a large, early-twentieth-century house at the end of a quiet cul-de-sac, just off the wide main road connecting Manchester with the small town of Bury. He and his wife lived in a comfortable flat upstairs and the ground floor was converted into two dental surgeries – an active surgery and a spare surgery in case the equipment broke down, which it quite often did in the 1960s. He chose the location because it was 'off the beaten track' and he deliberately wanted to avoid passing trade. In those days there were 'far too few dentists and far too many patients' and an out-of-the-way location ensured that, to some extent, the patients who came to him did so because they wanted especially to see him.

There were two reasons for his reluctance to be too visible. First, he was trained to carry out the (at the time) more specialised work such as crown and bridge dentistry, and was not trained, nor particularly interested, in the routine extractions and dentures which made up most of the work in many practices. Second, prior to setting up in Whitefield, he had had one year working in a 'swish' practice in Rodney Street, in Liverpool, where his patients included Lord Cohen, Lord Leverhulme, the Marquis of Salisbury and the Bishop of Liverpool. Such patients expected very high-quality dentistry and, according to Geoffrey Noar, 'once I'd got myself involved in that scene, I wasn't prepared to reduce any standards'. Despite his own preference for a specialised offering, he has made it a rule of the practice that anyone who rings up in pain is always seen on the day they phone.

The patient groups

From the outset, Geoffrey Noar has always taken on private patients, that is, those outside the 'health service'. In the early days, this was considered 'crazy' for a practice not located in a recognised 'private area' in a city centre. The balance, in numbers, of different categories of patients has always been an issue with the practice. Currently, there are three main types of patients:

1. private,
2. national health,
3. independent.

The distinctions between the three categories of patients are mainly related to the fees charged, and how they are paid.

Private patients tend to consist of those patients who request private treatment. By so doing, they pay considerably higher fees than patients in the other two categories. They will expect a greater range of available treatments, particularly those of a cosmetic type, more time with the dentist on each visit, and a more leisurely experience without any 'hustle and bustle'. They may also tend to contact the dentist directly out of surgery hours.

The National Health (Service) patients pay fees on a scale set by the health service. Some health service patients, for example, children, students, pregnant women and senior citizens, are exempt from payment of fees. The government will pay all their fees to the practice. Other health service patients will pay an 80 per cent contribution to the gross fees, with the remaining 20 per cent being subsidised by the government. Where dentists are not taking on any new National Health Service patients, they may offer to take on independent patients. The fees charged to such patients will be comparable to health service fees, but the 20 per cent subsidy is not available. Thus, independent patients pay higher fees than Health Service patients, and pay them all directly to the practice.

Geoffrey Noar has always been convinced that within the health service alone he could not make the business pay. His feelings were reinforced when, five years ago, his son Richard did a detailed financial analysis of the practice and calculated that they had lost nearly £20 000 on the National Health side of the practice in one year. Subsequently, Geoffrey Noar has taken on no new National Health patients (although he has still kept on those existing National Health patients who wish to stay with him). Richard Noar is following in the same pattern. They have, however, always offered a facility to Health Service patients, and there has always been at least one dentist in the practice who will take them on.

Geoffrey Noar believes that the practice provides the highest standards of treatment to Health Service patients, although it is recognised that this is difficult and involves a commitment to long hours. Any reduction in time spent with patients – a temptation for some practices in a striving towards profitability – will reduce standards, and 'cutting standards is a thing we've never done in the practice and are not prepared to do'.

The personnel and surgery hours

By November 1993 the practice had grown to its present size; there are now five dentists (although Geoffrey Noar himself only works half the time on the Whitefield surgery and spends the remaining half at a surgery in Hale, 12 miles away), and three hygienists. They are supported by seven full-time dental nurses (one of whom works half the time at Hale with Geoffrey Noar), two full-time receptionists, and one part-time receptionist and two part-time secretaries, including the ex-practice manageress. They cope with approximately 8000 patients.

Geoffrey Noar is a Licentiate in Dental Surgery, a member of the Royal College of Surgeons and holds a Diploma in Orthodontics. The other dentists have a Bachelor in Dental Surgery (BDS) qualification. Apart from the Noars, two other dentists are classified as self-employed (as are the hygienists) and one is an assistant and paid a salary by the Health Service. She is on a recently introduced scheme of vocational training for newly qualified dentists; four days are spent in practice, with Richard Noar as her trainer, and one day spent attending a postgraduate course. The scheme is now compulsory for newly qualified dentists. Most dental nurses take a Dental Surgery Assistants (DSA) Course, paid for by the practice, after an initial training period provided by the practice. The DSA is studied and examined through evening classes at a local college.

The receptionists are trained for the particular practice because, according to Geoffrey Noar, 'it can sometimes be a disadvantage that they have been somewhere else. I'd rather have an intelligent girl who will come to us and train in *our* ways'.

The surgery is open from 9.00 am to 5.00 pm on Monday, Wednesday and Friday, from 9.00 am to 6.00 pm on Tuesday, from 9.00 am to 7.00 pm on Thursday, and from 9.30 am to 11.30 am on Saturday. There is an out-of-hours emergency service for patients provided by a pool of local dentists working on a rota basis. Details are provided on the answerphone.

The physical surroundings

Viewed from outside, the surgery looks like the old, well-built family house that it is. It is clearly not purpose-built but is very like many doctor's and dentist's surgeries in the region. Because it is a house, patients approach the main door through a well-kept front and side garden. There are spaces for four or five cars outside the house, and another seven or eight spaces further down the street. The street is quite narrow and parking and manoeuvring is not easy, particularly at busy times.

Although many of the competing dentists have even fewer convenient parking spaces, Geoffrey Noar recognised that their own parking facilities may be perceived as inadequate. He has considered knocking the garden wall through and paving over the front garden to allow more parking space. This would not be appreciated by the local residents.

Inside the house there are surgeries, waiting rooms (one of which doubles as the reception area) and patient toilets. Less visible are the office, staff toilets, stockroom, kitchen and a darkroom for X-rays. The whole building has been subjected to a major refurbishment over the past five years, largely at the initiative of Richard Noar. 'We gave the change in decor a lot of thought, and there was a big increase in the number of patients who came after it.'

Some of the changes were to increase the comfort and others to create a more pleasing ambience. Richard Noar engaged the services of his sister, an architect, to design many of the structural changes and advise on the furnishings. He gave great attention to detail and all stages were carefully planned. 'I believe that there are all sorts of buttons you can press to put people at ease. For example, the pink on the walls is a soothing colour. All these little things help. Geoffrey Noar endorses this and adds that a comfortably warm environment is important. Authentic plants adorn waiting rooms and surgeries and small cuddly toys and novelty clocks are clearly visible in Richard Noar's surgery.

There is piped 'middle of the road' music in the largest of the waiting rooms. Each waiting room has some reading material, which seems to reflect the outside interests of the employees. Copies of *Car Mechanic* and *Cumbria* are available in one waiting room, whilst *Readers Digest* and *Photography* are in another. Colour supplements of various Sunday papers are the most widely read. The practice leaflet (see Figure CS 10.1) is displayed in racks in each waiting room. Each practice must, by a law passed in October 1990, produce such a leaflet. Richard Noar made a considerable effort to produce

---

WELCOME

Whether you are a longstanding patient or if it is your first visit, we would like to welcome you to the practice. We hope you will find the information in this booklet useful.

PREVENTIVE DENTAL CARE

The practice has a preventive philosophy. We employ two dental hygienists who are trained in all aspects of dental care including scaling and polishing teeth, treatment of gum disease and in giving advice on promotion of oral health. In addition we have a Preventive Dental Unit where further advice can be given on the latest oral hygiene techniques and diet.

CHILDREN

We always regard children as special patients and encourage them to come from an early age. This allows us to get to know one another and make visits to the dentist fun. We can then help them to form good dental habits which will prevent problems with their teeth later in life.

NERVOUS PATIENTS

We especially welcome nervous patients to the practice and have a special interest in helping people overcome any fears they may have of dental treatment. Over the years we have had tremendous success in this respect.

NEW PATIENTS

We are always pleased to welcome new patients to the practice.

EMERGENCIES

It is our policy to see emergencies promptly and on the same day. If you need urgent treatment telephone the practice and we will please arrange for you to be seen quickly.

COSMETIC DENTISTRY

We are able to carry out a wide range of cosmetic dentistry including crowns, bridges, porcelain veneers and white fillings on posterior teeth. With modern techniques, everyone should be able to enjoy the confidence of having attractive teeth.

IMPLANTS

Another new advance enables us to replace teeth which have been lost due to disease with dental implants.

HOME VISITS

Home visits are available for the housebound, primarily to provide dentures for patients who are unable to attend the surgery). Please ask the receptionist if you would like more information.

FACILITIES FOR THE DISABLED

If you need to be seen in a ground floor surgery our receptionist will be please to arrange this.

MEDICAL INFORMATION

Please keep us informed about any changes to your general health as this may occasionally have a bearing upon your dental treatment.

SURGERY HOURS

Monday	9.00 a.m.	5.00 p.m.
Tuesday	9.00 a.m.	6.00 p.m.
Wednesday	9.00 a.m.	5.00 p.m.
Thursday	9.00 a.m.	6.00/7.00 p.m.
Friday	9.00 a.m.	5.00 p.m.
Saturday	9.30 a.m.	11.30 a.m.

(EXCEPT BANK HOLIDAY WEEKENDS)

OUT OF HOURS EMERGENCIES

If an emergency arises outside normal surgery hours we will do our best to arrange treatment within 24 hours. During Bank Holidays and Weekends dentists of this and other practices provide cover on a rota basis. For up to date details please telephone our Answer phone on . . .

Figure CS 10.1 The practice leaflet

an informative and attractive leaflet printed in pale blue and white, whereas it was felt that some other dentists had made only a token effort. 'There is no point in knocking up a rubbishy leaflet. It may distract from people's perceptions.' He would rather patients read the leaflet than the other reading material in the waiting room. Over 2000 leaflets had already been taken by November 1993.

Many patients will spend as much, if not more, time in the waiting room as in the surgery. Quite often the waiting rooms are well occupied. Patients can have a positive or negative influence on each other. Both Geoffrey and Richard Noar were able to recall positive interactions between patients. Geoffrey Noar told of a recent occasion where a private patient who wanted a bridge was quoted a substantial fee. She was not put off by the amount, but what convinced him that she would agree to the treatment was the observation of a chance encounter in the waiting room. The patient in question met and talked to another patient who had already received the treatment. The tone of the conversation, together with visible evidence of the effect of the treatment ('lovely smile') had removed any lingering doubts in the mind of the first patient.

Richard Noar recalled an instance of a new patient seeing him for a filling. The patient was initially extremely agitated and administering the injections was difficult. The patient returned to the waiting room for the injection to take effect and was seen to be reassured by a regular patient of Mr Noar's. On returning for the filling, the former patient was far more relaxed having been told of Richard Noar's manner and style by the other patient in the waiting room. On the negative side, Richard Noar described a situation where two friends, who always come together, appear mutually to reinforce each other's anxieties.

Waiting room noise and activity varies according to the time of the day. At about 4.00 pm to 4.30 pm, when patients with children arrive, there is much more activity and greater patient interaction. When it is really busy, with people packed together, the dentists sometimes have to steel themselves to go out and face the crowd.

Payment of fees

Private and independent patients pay all their fees directly to the practice. Health Service patients who are not exempt pay 80 per cent of the scaled fee to the practice. Payments are normally by cash or cheque. In exceptional circumstances a form of direct debit agreement may be reached. Credit cards are not accepted, although as Geoffrey Noar observes, 'Sometimes patients take credit anyway – they'll take two or three months to pay.' There have been cases when the practice has had to take legal action to recover individual fees.

For private patients, a written quotation has to be given for the more expensive treatments. For new private patients, the normal arrangement is to ask for a third of the fee up front, a third on completion of the treatment, and the final third a month afterwards. The first two elements pay for the appliance – the cost to the dentist is calculated at two-thirds of the fee charged. The final third is the 'dentist's fee', and it is felt to be fair that the patients can hold that part back for a month in order to ensure that they are fully satisfied with the treatment.

Richard Noar has spent many Sundays filling in, and checking, the paperwork associated with the 20 per cent government subsidy for Health Service patients. If it is not completed on time there will be a month's delay of payments. He believes that a disproportionately high percentage of time is spent by the practice on recovering the 20 per cent subsidy. 'It is a nightmare. Nurses, receptionists and dentists are spending more time than they should on administration – rather than dealing with patients – the aim has to be to cut down the amount of administration.'

Business efficiency

Geoffrey Noar, whilst understanding business methods, has not given them first priority. The practice has prospered despite, on his own admission, 'my lack of organisational interests'. If the practice was a bit short on staff, he took on another employee. When materials were needed, he would buy them. He is the first to acknowledge that since Richard joined the practice, it is better organised. Monthly cash flow figures are available, staffing levels are carefully calculated, and the buying procedures have been reviewed. The practice now breaks even, or a little better, on the Health Service side, compared with the substantial losses of five years ago.

Richard Noar has introduced IT systems into the practice. To date, the benefits are seen on two fronts. First, the cost and management accounting systems for the practice are fully computerised. This has resulted in more complete management information, a means for applying cost control, and a clarification of the relative contributions of different aspects of the business. Second, the patient recall system is now computerised. Patients receive an automatic timely written reminder for their next six-monthly check-up. Previously, patients had been given a card before leaving the surgery reception, with a date for an appointment in six months' time. It was known that many patients would forget to turn up or lose the appointment card. The more timely reminders have increased the reliability of recall.

While there is scope for increased IT support for the paperwork involved with the government subsidy, it may not be an appropriate investment at a time when the practice is reducing the number of new National Health Service patients. Another potential use of IT is for keeping and updating patients' record cards, as is already done at other practices. Geoffrey Noar does not believe that this would be advantageous. 'I will never face that. Records have to be typed in by the dentist.' He does not believe that such a task can be undertaken by a confidential secretary because of the technical terms used and possible illegibility of handwriting. 'I've got patients who go back 20 years. It might take five hours work each day to type records in. I'd rather just write it by hand.'

Changing perceptions of dental practices

In the 1960s the public was generally uninformed about dental treatment and practices, and deferred to the dentist. Crowns and bridges were relatively unknown. Nowadays patients will discuss with the dentist the merits of a particular type of treatment. They go to other dentists for opinions, and quotations, and have a greater knowledge of price ranges.

Over the same period, dentists in general have been taking a more customer-focused look at the overall operation of their practices. As Richard Noar observed, 'Whilst everyone was quite personable, there always seemed to be a barrier between the receptionist and the patients. As the reception is the first point of contact, we try to ensure better public relations as far as reception staff are concerned.'

Geoffrey Noar adds, 'I know of a doctor's surgery where patients appear to be an encumbrance when you go in there. The patients' interests, for us, are first and foremost the most important thing.'

They train the receptionists to be polite and always to answer the phone with 'How can I help you?' This is known to be repetitive but is believed to create the right impression. Early patient feedback confirms this view.

The extended surgery hours, including evening and Saturday surgeries, are responses to patient needs and changing patterns of work. Interestingly, there is evidence that patients are now considering add-on services. In particular, a dental insurance scheme, 'Denplan', is being offered at some of the competing practices, and Geoffrey Noar believes that he may have lost three or four patients to those practices. The scheme, which requires that patients are declared 'dentally fit' initially, allows patients to pay up to £20 monthly as an insurance. Whilst, on average, a patient may only spend about £60 a year on treatment (without insurance), some patients appear to want an insurance scheme, and Geoffrey Noar is seriously considering the introduction of their own dental plan and insurance scheme to meet the demand.

Quality and standards

Quality is not just craftsmanship. There are dentists who do perfect fillings but whose patients hate them. Quality includes the reassurance and talking as well as the technical skills. (Geoffrey Noar)

Quality of care encompasses everything from the actual clinical dentistry carried out, to how patients are treated by the staff, to being quoted for treatment, to the decor of the practice, and includes dealing with problems and complaints. (Richard Noar)

Clearly, both agree that quality is more than the ability to carry out the technical dental treatment. Indeed, it can be argued that, as far as the technical treatment is concerned, patients are often not in a position to know what is good treatment or not.

Geoffrey Noar points out that the National Health Service does not require practitioners to reach a high standard, but states that they have to achieve a reasonable standard. A practitioner may use discretion regarding, for example, polishing of fillings or choice of amalgam. If a patient goes away in agony it would not be reasonable, nor if the treatment looked strange. If, however, a patient goes away and the treatment lasts a few years, that can be said to be reasonable. More generally, if the patient is satisfied it may be deemed reasonable. Geoffrey Noar feels that the criteria for satisfaction can vary from person to person and from area to area. What may be deemed satisfactory in a very crowded surgery in a semi-deprived area may not achieve the same rating in a more prosperous location.

To achieve quality of care on purely Health Service work is seen by Richard Noar to be a real battle. The work is very intense with a lot of extra hours spent on the paperwork and it is felt to be getting harder and harder. Under those circumstances, dentists have to put in very long hours to make a living. Geoffrey Noar's interest is in 'high-quality, conservative dentistry'. People come to him who have 'had their mouths condemned, or who are very nervous and want somebody to spend time'. He believes that dentists basically sell time. Expertise is sold at the same time. He will set aside half an hour for a filling for a private patient and that allows him to talk to the patient and outline the stages of the treatment. It is physically possible to do four fillings in half an hour, but he feels that this would require exceptional skills, and any talking or reassurance would have to be forsaken.

Richard Noar also considers quality of life for the employees as important, and one of his aims is to allow people to earn a little bit more and work a little bit less. The staff are working flat out and to be under stress all the time is not healthy. He would like to improve quality of care for patients and the quality of life for employees.

Advertising

Everyone in the practice believes that word-of-mouth recommendation is the most effective way of generating new patients. They are confident that they will retain the majority of existing patients through providing a high standard of service. As mentioned earlier, the practice leaflet has been a popular piece of literature in the surgery. Richard Noar noted that after the leaflet was made available, people began to realise that the practice did see new patients and was prepared to take them on. Many people apparently assumed until then that the patient list was full. The section of the leaflet saying 'new patients are welcome' is particularly important.

The practice puts advertisements in the *Yellow Pages* where, under the heading 'National Health and Private Treatment', there are the four bullet points:

- Children and Nervous Patients Welcome
- Evening and Weekend Appointments
- Emergency Service
- Cosmetic Dentistry

Neither Geoffrey nor Richard Noar is sure how effective this advertisement is. They both, however, after one or two expensive trials, feel that newspaper advertising is simply not effective. An advertisement in a local council brochure 'brought us in nothing'. Richard Noar is particularly interested in attracting nervous patients to the practice (see below) and is considering how to get the appropriate message across to this particular group (which, according to a recent survey, may include up to 50 per cent of the population).

A marketing tool exists in the form of a patient mailing list. The mailings at the moment consist of patient recall letters, and occasionally factual details of Health Service changes when they occur. No promotional material has ever been included in case patients thought they were being conned.

An informal arrangement with a local GP (General Practitioner) means that the Noars' practice leaflet is on display in the doctor's waiting room. A number of doctors are treated by the practice and their personal recommendations are believed to be particularly effective.

The future

Richard Noar would like the practice to expand, but not too quickly. He would like them to be able to hold surgeries seven days a week – 'That, I think, would be the ultimate service.' There could be problems in fulfilling this aim. Local residents may object. The limited fee scales recommended by the National Health Service would make it difficult to pay staff 'double time' on Sundays. He feels that to offer such a service they would have to increase the non-Health Service side of the practice, so that they can take control of the fee scales and cut down the paperwork.

Another aim, dear to his heart, is to attract nervous patients to the practice. He feels it is good for the practice because they enjoy working with nervous patients and derive much satisfaction from successfully overcoming their fears. It is also beneficial to the patients, who are mostly very grateful, and often require quite extensive treatment to make up for that missed over the years. The patients' gratitude may, in turn, lead to word-of-mouth recommendations to others, and a feeling of comfort with the practice and loyalty to the particular dentist.

An issue is how to get the message to nervous patients – not an easily targeted group. One idea is to introduce a Nervous Patients Clinic. This can be advertised in regional publications, with the information also displayed in the waiting rooms. Essentially, the message would be that in addition to their normal services the practice has a nervous patients clinic, where patients can, on an individual basis, discuss their fears and anxieties with a dentist.

Richard Noar is very concerned that the message is seen positively. He is deliberately proceeding slowly on this development and is carefully examining issues of social acceptability and internal communication within the practice in order to increase the probabilities of success.

Index